Investigating Crime and Deviance

Stephen Moore

Collins Educational

An Imprint of HarperCollinsPublishers

Published by Collins Educational
An imprint of HarperCollins*Publishers*
77–85 Fulham Palace Road
Hammersmith, London W6 8JB

First edition published in 1988
Second edition published in 1996
Reprinted 1997

ISBN 0–00–322439–2

Stephen Moore asserts the moral right to be identified as the author of this work.
A catalogue record for this book is available from the British Library.

Illustration Acknowledgements

J. R. Docherty (p. 1)
Shaun Williams (pp. 13, 52)
The Bridgeman Art Library Ltd (p. 19)
P.A. News Photo Library (pp. 23, 73, 80, 81, 115, 143, 171)
BBC (p. 25)
Photofusion (pp. 45, 68, 127, 247)
Nathan Betts (pp. 53, 108, 139)
Rex Features Ltd (pp. 56, 131, 161, 199)
Magnum Photos Ltd (pp. 98, 156, 178, 233, 239)
Hulton Getty Picture Collection Ltd (pp. 123)
Tony Husband (pp. 150)
Paramount (p. 183)

Commissioned by Emma Dunlop
Edited by Victoria Ingham
Production by Delphina Kitson-Mills-Jones
Cover artwork and design by Derek Lee
Illustrations by Chi Leung
Typeset by Harper Phototypesetters Ltd, Northampton
Printed and bound by Scotprint Ltd, Musselburgh

Contents

Introduction to the perspectives

This book explores the contributions sociologists have made to the study of crime and deviance. Most of the chapters in the book are devoted to specific theoretical approaches to crime, with each chapter providing an exposition of a particular theory, and then illustrating this with the problems of most interest to that theoretical perspective. The major sociological approaches or 'traditions' that have their own chapters in this book are:

- functionalism
- environmental approaches and subcultural theories
- Marxist or left idealist approaches
- left realism
- social constructionism or labelling theory
- the New Right.

Each of these perspectives asks different questions and focuses on different issues within the broad area of crime and deviance. Consequently each provides a distinctive analysis of the causes and nature of crime.

However, there are other areas of debate among sociologists of crime and deviance that are not concerned with theoretical approaches as such, but instead are focused on particular groups of people or issues. These too have chapters devoted to them.

There are thus chapters on:

● **Women and crime**. Women are most likely to encounter crime as victims – usually victims of crimes committed by men. Some women do commit crimes, but the theories that we explore in this book do not really seem to explain female crime. In fact, for feminist sociologists the paucity of theorising about women and crime is less a result of the different rates of offending by males and females than it is about the bias inherent in sociology. Chapter 8 explores the male bias in the sociology of crime, and then examines the relatively few sociological explanations of female crime offered by sociologists.

● **Victims**. In Chapter 9 we explore the experience of being a victim of crime and the fact that, contrary to common sense, being a victim of crime may not be as 'random' as first appears. This chapter includes discussions of domestic violence and rape.

● **Criminal statistics and methodology**. In this book, the reader will find a range of debates concerning the causes and extent of crime . The different approaches are often based on beliefs about the extent of crime, who commits crime and who the victims are. These beliefs are in turn based on the statistics uncovered by researchers and official agencies. Unfortunately, different methods of collecting statistics produce quite different results, so before we can accept the arguments put forward by the various theorists who claim to explain criminal behaviour we need to be aware of and understand the weaknesses of the different methods of collecting statistics. These issues are explored in Chapter 10.

● **Control, policing and race**. Crime and crime control are part of a much wider picture in which groups of people are perceived as threats to the established order. In Chapter 11 there is a wide-ranging discussion on the nature of social control in contemporary society, illustrated with a discussion on the perceived relationship between criminality and race. This is a very controversial area, and for some commentators merely discussing the issue is tantamount to racism.

Figure 1.1 Guidelines: theoretical traditions in sociology

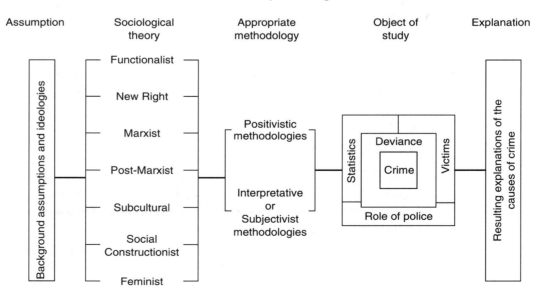

Nevertheless, using race as an illustration of social control allows us to examine the role of the police and the criminal justice system, and to explore the complex relationship between social deprivation, discrimination, the media and criminality.

Theories and methods in criminology

What is 'theory'?

A simple way of understanding 'what is theory' is to compare theory with a kaleidoscope, the child's toy consisting of a tube, a number of lenses and fragments of translucent, coloured glass or plastic. When you turn the tube and look down the lens of the kaleidoscope the shapes and colours, visible at the bottom, change. In a similar way we will see social theory as a sort of kaleidoscope – by shifting theoretical perspective, the world under investigation also changes shape. The components of the world being investigated combine and recombine into new patterns as they are viewed through different theoretical perspectives.

Of course, there is much more to sociological theory than this. The purpose in making this comparison between theory and the kaleidoscope is simply to provide an image of why theory is important in sociological research. The role of theory is precisely to make things that were hidden visible, to define some patterns and give some meanings to the sorts of observations that social researchers continually make when investigating society. Seeing the world in different ways is the essential and fundamental role of social research and the ability to see these differences and to make sense of the different points of view that a researcher can take, is the basic contribution that theory makes to the research process.

Source: O'Brien (1993)

1. Can we ever construct one theory which will explain all the reasons for crime?

2. What is the advantage of having more than one theory?

3. What, according to the extract, is the 'role of theory'?

Before we examine the various theoretical approaches to crime and deviance discussed in this book, it will be useful to outline a framework within which we can locate the theories, and to relate them to the methodology they are most likely to use. This will help you to distinguish between them and will strengthen your awareness of the differences and similarities between the different approaches.

Theories

Sociological theories tend to stress one of three 'levels of analysis' when explaining social phenomena. Their starting point for understanding crime can be to focus on:

- the *structure* of society
- the *perceptions* and ideas of people in that society – that is, the *culture*
- the *individual motivation* of criminals.

Structure

Sociologists who follow a structuralist approach maintain that the actions of individuals are ultimately determined by the nature of the social and economic forces that shape society. Both culture and individual action are dominated, and can only be understood by reference to, the economic and social structure of the society. Only by gaining a full understanding of how the broader structure forms and moulds the activities and perceptions of people can crime be understood.

Marxist-based and functionalist writings tend to be heavily influenced by this argument, although the explanations for criminal behaviour that they provide are rather different.

Culture

Approaches based on culture tend to stress the way that people's beliefs determine they way they act. Cultural or action-based theories do not necessarily deny the importance of structure, but see it as a mere background to beliefs and perceptions about the world. In order to understand why a person may commit a crime, or indeed to explain why an action is viewed as a crime, it is necessary to examine the meanings that this action has for the people concerned. Culturally based approaches argue that, if a structure exists at all, it is literally meaningless except for the interpretations people put upon their actions.

The theoretical approaches covered in this book that enter the debate at the level of culture are the subcultural and social constructionist approaches. Environmental theories also partially belong in this category.

Individual motivation

Theories based on individual explanations tend to start from the viewpoint that 'society' is a term used to describe the totality of the actions of individuals who make their own choices. To understand why people act the way they do, it is necessary to start by studying individuals, not the wider society. Culture is not ignored in this approach – indeed it is seen as very important – but it is assumed to be shared without paying much attention to the ways people actively create it. Individual motivation is seen as emerging from psychological conditioning as a child, or from the biology of the person.

As this is a book on sociology, there is no detailed discussion of the psychology of criminal behaviour, which is the approach most commonly linked to the level of the individual. But New Right theory draws heavily on this sort of explanation, and we examine this in some detail.

Methods

Theories that seek to explain society are distinguished not just by their levels of analysis, but also by their assumptions about the best way to study their subject.

There are two extremes: at one pole are the positivistic approaches, which stress the scientific nature of sociology and the objectivity of social occurrences, and at the other are the *subjectivist* approaches, which stress that understanding people's beliefs and values is crucial to explaining their actions.

Positivistic approaches

These derive from the belief that sociology is a science like any other, and that it should as far as possible adopt objective and statistical techniques to explain social phenomena. Typical *positivistic* methods include surveys, experiments and comparative statistical analyses. In effect, this approach seeks to demonstrate its findings by presenting objective and irrefutable evidence.

A good example of this approach has been the work undertaken to relate unemployment statistics to levels of burglary. Statistics are collated on burglary over a period of, say, thirty years, and then compared with the statistics on unemployment over the same period. Clear statistical relationships are then demonstrated, purporting to show that increases in burglary are a result of increases in unemployment. The argument in support of this methodological approach is that the evidence is available for all to examine, test and replicate.

Subjectivist approaches

These approaches stress that there is no objective world that can be said to exist outside the consciousness of people. The reason that people act in a particular way is the result of their perception of reality. Gathering statistics never uncovers the meanings that people give to their actions. Explaining burglary by correlation with unemployment statistics does not explain *why* some unemployed people are motivated to commit crime and others are not. For example, most burglary is committed by young males; why don't young females engage in it to the same extent? Clearly, according to proponents of this approach, citing statistics is not an adequate explanation. Instead, it is important to explore the cultural meanings of gender and unemployment.

Approaches which are subjectivist–based tend to favour observational or ethnographic studies.

Two approaches to understanding crime

Bauman draws our attention to a major split in sociological analysis. A split between what we might want to call, on the one hand, a 'positive' tradition, begun at the very inception of sociology by August Comte, and, on the other, an 'interpretative' tradition, largely associated with the work of Max Weber.

I do not wish to give the impression that sociology is an 'either/or' enterprise; sociology is not a coin with two faces which shows either head of tails. In fact, there are incessant and interminable – and potentially insoluble – disputes about where the boundaries of these versions of sociology lie: about which bits of sociology can be called 'scientific' in some sense, and which bits are more properly 'interpretative'. Many of these debates revolve around seemingly tangential issues such as the role of social institutions in society, around the description of social structure, around the nature of cause and effects, and so on, and if you decide to pursue sociology further you will encounter many of these debates in your journey through different sociological perspectives. Thus sociologists are not looking for the one ultimate answer that solves all questions. Sociology, properly conducted, involves the continual generation of new questions about social life so that our ability to explain and understand what is happening in society improves.

Adapted from: O'Brien (1993)

Using the above extract and referring back to your reading in this chapter, answer the following questions.

1 *What are the two parts of the split in sociological analysis identified by the author?*

2 *How is 'positivistic' defined?*

3 *What do positivists seek to do?*

4 *What does the 'interpretative' or 'subjectivist' tradition seek to do?*

5 *How do these two traditions relate to theory?*

6 *Would it be better to describe the division between the perspectives as a 'split' or a 'continuum'?*

7 *According to the extract, what does sociology 'properly conducted' involve?*

The relationship between theories and methods

Sociological theories of crime and delinquency can all be located along two axes, as shown in Figure 1.2. One axis indicates the extent to which the theory stresses structural or individual explanations for crime, and the other shows the type of research methods used, varying from the positivistic through to the subjective.

This diagram is only a guide, but it may give you to a mental map of the differences between the various theories that we describe in the book.

Figure 1.2 The relationship of theories and methods in criminology

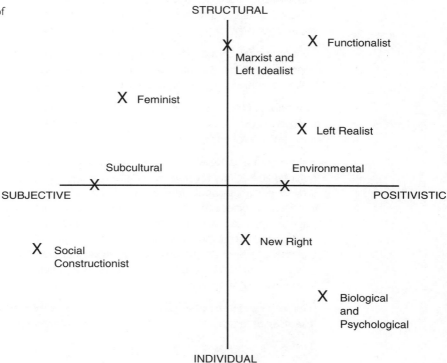

Using the three headings *structure, culture* and *individual motivation, suggest an explanation:*

1 *for organised violence at football matches*
2 *for individuals injecting heroin on a regular basis.*

You should do this individually at first and then compare your different explanations.

How do you think you could best prove your explanation? Suggest methods of research for both of your explanations.

A framework of theories

We will now quickly look at the main theoretical perspectives, asking each one similar questions and providing simple, clear answers that can be developed further in the chapters that follow.

We have noted that the theories start at different levels of analysis, and they also tend to make rather different assumptions about the nature of society. The explanations they give for criminal and deviant behaviour vary considerably, as do their favoured research methodologies. They also differ over where they draw the line between criminal and deviant acts.

There are two common-sense approaches which most non-sociologists would adopt to the subject of deviance. The first suggests that deviant acts are statistically speaking uncommon or rare behaviours, good or bad, that deviate from the normal pattern of life; according to the second, a deviant act is something that offends the morals of society, but is generally not so serious as to be criminal.

It is commonly agreed that criminal behaviour, on the other hand, generally does harm to someone. Criminal acts are regarded as bad enough to warrant decision makers passing laws that forbid their committal.

Not only can the acts committed by people be distinguished in this way, but people themselves can be categorised into deviants, criminals and normal people, based on their patterns of habitual action.

Functionalist and New Right thinkers generally accept the common-sense definitions outlined above. However, most other sociological approaches are more circumspect; they suggest that popular definitions of deviance and crime tend to reflect differences in power in society. Thus labelling the behaviour of one group as 'deviant' is one stage in a process by which other, more powerful groups attempt to stigmatise and degrade them; branding their behaviour as 'criminal' is a further stage, applied to groups that present a challenge to the existing power structure. Thus for Marxists, social constructionists and feminists, the categories of crime and deviance tend to be manifestations of power.

The key questions underlying theories of crime	**The key factors affecting choices of methodology**
1. What is the nature of social cohesion?	1. Quantitative methods (e.g. statistics) or qualitative methods (e.g. participant observation)?
2. How do we define deviant behaviour?	
3. Are people who commit crime different in some way from those who are law-abiding?	2. What is the aim of the study?
	3. How complex is the study (e.g. how many people are involved)?
4. Is there a clear distinction between an illegal, criminal act and a deviant, non-conformist act?	4. Are there constraints on the researcher (e.g. time or resources available)?
5. What are the causes of crime?	5. Are there other constraints (e.g. will criminals, police, etc., cooperate)?

Functionalist approaches

The nature of social cohesion

Functionalist approaches make the assumption that societies exist because they are based on fundamental agreement about basic values. We all share beliefs about what constitutes good and bad behaviour, according to this view.

What is deviant behaviour?

Deviant behaviour is in some way 'abnormal'. Sometimes it may be regarded as good, and sometimes bad. Good behaviour may be deviant because very few people would have the courage to do it, as when a fire-fighter sacrifices his or her life in a blazing house in order to save the life of a child. However, mostly deviant behaviour is immoral and at worst illegal. A third form of deviance is exhibited when people behave in a bizarre way – possibly through mental illness; such people are often said to be 'not bad but mad'.

Deviants and normal people

Deriving from this definition of deviance is an important belief which most police officers, magistrates, social workers and all others who process the deviants of this world share with the functionalists: deviants are in some way different from the rest of us normal, rule-following types. A 'normal' person may commit an isolated deviant act, but the real deviant is one who consistently proves himself or herself to be different from the rest of us.

The difference between illegal and deviant

Why are some deviant acts legal – for example, 'odd' forms of sexual activity – yet others are illegal? The functionalists share the common-sense answer to this question too. The further an act deviates from a society's usual standards, particularly if it involves harm to others, the more likely it is to be made illegal. In particular, laws are passed because there is a common belief that certain actions are wrong and ought to be prevented. In a democracy, the laws will therefore reflect the views of the majority of its citizens.

The causes of crime

Generally, functionalists suggest that crime arises from a weakening of the social cohesion that binds society together. They assume that most people are naturally selfish, and that it is only through a process of socialisation that they are persuaded to act in socially responsible ways. If, for whatever reason, socialisation breaks down, then crime occurs.

Methodology

Functionalists have tended not to engage in much detailed research, preferring to concentrate on theory.

The New Right

The basis of society

Much of the academic thinking of the New Right overlaps with functionalism. The basis of society is said to be a set of generally shared values that hold society together.

What is deviant behaviour?

Deviant behaviour is best understood as actions which are beyond the boundary of these shared values.

Deviants and 'normal' people

The New Right agree with functionalists that there is a distinction between the majority of criminals and the general public. The majority of people do not commit crimes against others.

The distinction between deviant and illegal

New Right theorists agree with the proposition that deviant behaviour is usually less far removed from shared values than illegal behaviour – it is a matter of how extreme the behaviour is compared to the central shared values. However, unlike functionalism, the New Right suggests that quite a number of illegal acts – particularly those which are not harmful to others – are only illegal because of the desire of bureaucrats and certain politicians to interfere in people's lives. So the distinction between crime and deviance is not necessarily one of degree, but may be heavily influenced by the interests of powerful groups, representing their own interests.

The causes of crime and deviance

These are generally located in the poor upbringing of individuals, or even in biological or genetic defects. However, some criminal acts are seen as being created by an interfering government.

Methodology

New Right sociologists have rarely engaged in research, but tend to theorise. However, they do use statistics and research evidence gathered by others to support their views.

Environmental and subcultural theories

The basis of society

These theories tend to see society as being formed from a number of different sets of values (subcultures) which overlap with each other in some respects and clash in others. Society can best be seen as a whirlpool of changing and conflicting values.

What is deviant behaviour?

Environmental and subcultural approaches combine such a wide variety of ideas and methods that it is difficult to give a short summary.

Deviant behaviour is seen in general terms as behaviour in which only certain groups engage and which is different from the socially dominant behaviour. Most subcultural theories recognise that in any society at a given time there is a variety of different sets of values according to which people measure their behaviour; nevertheless, most such theories accept that the mainstream 'dominant' values are the 'true' values of the majority of the population and deviance is the result of following subcultural values.

Deviants and 'normal' people

Deviants are seen as different from 'normal' people in that they follow quite distinctive sets of values from the majority. There is nothing 'wrong' with deviants – they merely subscribe to different values and therefore behave differently.

The difference between illegal and deviant acts

The functionalist contention that laws reflect the views of the majority is accepted by most subcultural theorists.

The causes of crime

Crime is seen as resulting from the inevitable clashes of values between different subcultures. One group's crime is another group's normal values.

Methodology

Subcultural and ecological theories stress that we need to understand the meanings which people give to their actions within their subcultures. Thus proponents of these theories have often used participant observation, which involves joining a group of people and trying to see the world through their eyes. Most subcultural approaches are still based upon observation of unusual or deviant subcultures. However, in the UK one strand of subcultural and environmental theories which stresses the impact of housing conditions and the influence of the whole environment on an individual's actions has tended to be rather more positivistic in method, using longitudinal surveys in particular.

Social constructionism and labelling theory

The basis of society

Social constructionist theories argue that the social world is best understood, not as some sort of real objective world which imposes itself upon us, but rather as something constructed by people themselves through their beliefs and ways of acting. To put it simply, if somebody believes something to be true then they will act as if it really is true, and this will have social consequences both for the person himself or herself and for others. Crime and deviance are also constructs which have real consequences.

What is deviant behaviour?

The labelling approach stresses that what is defined as deviant varies widely according to a number of factors, including time, person and place. Deviance cannot be defined in terms of particular acts, but rather in terms of how certain acts are defined by people in particular circumstances. For example, killing another person can be deviant or heroic, legal or illegal, depending upon the circumstances.

Deviants and normal people

Deviants, according to this view, are little different from non-deviants. There is not a separate class of people who commit crimes because they are motivated by some special factor which distinguishes them from normal people. The distinction lies in the fact their behaviour is defined as deviant through the actions of other people.

The difference between deviant and illegal

Labelling theory argues that certain deviant behaviour becomes illegal as a result of pressure group activity. A group of people band together to force through a change in the law to reflect their own interests or what they perceive to be in the interest of the population in general.

The causes of crime

Deviance and crime are the result of groups imposing their definitions of crime and deviance on others. In reality, there is little difference between the normal and the deviant. The process whereby certain people manage to impose their views on others is the main area of study of social constructionists.

Methodology

Labelling theorists have overwhelmingly used fairly small-scale observational or participant observational studies in the belief that they should try to understand the beliefs and patterns of behaviour of the groups they are studying. They have also used case studies in order to find out why and how certain acts, such as drug use, have been branded deviant or illegal.

Traditional Marxist approaches

The basis of society

According to Marxist approaches, society is based upon the exploitation of the majority of people by a powerful minority, whose power is based upon their control of the economy. This power is regarded as illegitimate.

What is deviant behaviour?

Deviant behaviour is seen as activities that are disapproved of by those in power. Deviant actions usually somehow threaten the continuing power of the ruling class. If the activities of deviants become too dangerous, laws are brought in to control them. In the 1990s New Age travellers were seen as a threat because they provided young people with an alternative role model; at first they were demonised in the media as drug takers and scroungers, and eventually the government passed the 1994 Criminal Justice Act which included a number of powers specifically aimed at them.

Deviants and 'normal' people

Generally, criminals and deviants are the same as 'normal' people. They are the victims of a repressive state which picks on the poorest and least powerful. On the other hand, when the rich and powerful are caught engaging in illegal acts they are rarely branded as criminals.

The difference between deviant and illegal

The difference between an illegal act and a deviant one depends upon how threatening the act is to the ruling class. It is also true that 'theft' by the powerful and well connected is more likely to be defined as deviant than as criminal.

The causes of crime

Crime originates in the unfairness and corrupt nature of capitalist society. Most typical working-class crimes are the result of people fighting back against their oppression and exploitation. However, Marxist writers are also interested in the crimes committed by powerful organisations, which tend to be ignored by the other perspectives.

Methodology

Marxist approaches tend to be far more abstract than most other methods except for functionalism, and there is perhaps more theorising than actual research. However, as the label 'Marxist' covers a very broad range of approaches, a number of different techniques are used. In particular:

- *participant observation* has been used in the study of groups of delinquent youths

- *case studies*, mainly using secondary information drawn from newspapers, official investigations, etc., have been conducted to uncover white-collar and corporate crime.

Left realism

The basis of society

Left realism derives from Marxism and shares very similar assumptions about the nature of society. Ultimately, society is held together by oppression – but within this oppression there are shared values and a sense of shared interests among large sections of society.

Left realism differs from Marxism in that it claims to be concerned with the practical problems of people living in capitalist society. As such, it accepts the status quo and concentrates on practical solutions to crime within capitalism.

What is deviant behaviour?

Left realist models of the basis of deviance are a combination of Marxist explanations and social constructionist ones. Essentially, powerful groups construct the definitions of deviance in society, but the outcomes of these constructions are not a direct reflection of their will, but rather the result of a series of complex 'negotiations' between different groups, reflecting differences in power and perceptions of the world. Left realists emphasise that other factors besides social class are important, including race and gender.

The distinction between crime and deviance

Left realism stresses that the difference between illegal and deviant acts is very small indeed. The law is the outcome of various pressure group activities, but law enforcement and the real concerns of individuals can vary widely from the written law.

Left realists are not particularly concerned with the law as such, but more with actions that are threatening or hurtful to people, no matter what their legal status. Left realists have, for example, concentrated much of their research on 'minor street crimes' which in themselves are not particularly serious in the eyes of the law, but are very significant in terms of their effects on people's lives in the inner cities. On the other hand, sexual harassment in the street is in most circumstances not a crime, but surveys show that heterosexual women, gays and lesbians all find this a significant problem.

The causes of crime and deviance

Left realists point out that capitalist society tends to marginalise young, working-class males, and this is an important factor in explaining crime.

Methodology

Left realism has been particularly influential within the sociology of crime and deviance in the last fifteen years in terms of methodology.

In order to discover the reality of people's lives left realists have undertaken a considerable number of small-scale but very detailed surveys of inner-city areas. These have largely been both victim and attitude surveys: they have asked local people what crimes have been committed against them and what behaviour particularly concerns them. The results are then handed over to local authorities and police committees so that local policy can be adjusted to take into account the people's concerns.

Feminist theory

The basis of society

Society is based on the exploitation of women by men. Control is in the hands of males; although feminists are aware that there are major inequalities among men, nevertheless the majority of men have control over women. This is achieved through control of the dominant values of society and through economic power.

Defining deviant behaviour

According to feminist theory, the definition of deviant behaviour can be related to sexual inequality. The lives of women are controlled by man-made mores concerning how they ought to behave, so that women are not free, but rather closely controlled. It is very easy for women to be defined as deviant: they can be regarded as such if they simply do the same things as men. For example, having a number of sexual partners and drinking alone in pubs are defined differently according to the sex of the person involved.

Deviants and normal people

Feminists believe that all women are controlled by men in some way or another. Women are likely to be defined as deviant when they engage in behaviour which is regarded as a rejection of their roles in society. Feminist theorists question the very idea of what is normal and focus their analysis on the construction of 'normality' (for women) by men.

The difference between illegal and deviant behaviour

One of the interesting facts to emerge from studies of crime and gender is that relatively few women commit criminal acts. According to feminists, prostitution reflects the combination of the way sexuality is constructed in our society and the economic inequalities that exist. In a male-dominated society men are justified in seeking out sex because it is claimed that they 'need' it because of their (theoretically) greater sex drive. Women, according to feminists, are driven into prostitution through economic motives.

However, the main issue for women is not illegality; rather it is the social control imposed on them and the definition of their role in such a way as to make 'normal male' behaviour deviant for them.

A final important point is that women encounter the law more as *victims* of particular crimes (rape and marital violence, for example) than as perpetrators.

The causes of crime

There is a distinction between male and female crimes. They are products of the different forms of socialisation and styles of life. Male crimes are more likely to include violence and very often are targeted at women. Women commit fewer crime as they do not have the same opportunities as men. When women do commit crime, they usually do so from economic need; their crimes take the forms most available to them, ranging from theft from shops to prostitution.

Methodology

There is not yet a large body of feminist studies of crime and deviance, although the field is a very active one. Feminists have tended to draw from a wide range of studies to prove their points about the social control of women:

- *Secondary sources* – official studies and sociological surveys – have shown that women are discriminated against and 'repressed' in many areas of life. Feminists researching the area of female deviance have used this evidence in some detail.

- *Intensive case studies* have been used by feminist researchers, usually on groups of teenage girls in school, in order to find out more about their attitudes and behaviour.

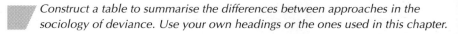 *Construct a table to summarise the differences between approaches in the sociology of deviance. Use your own headings or the ones used in this chapter.*

Summary

This chapter has given an overview of the book. We have briefly explored the main theoretical approaches, noting their similarities and differences and their implications for methodology. We have seen that sociological theories are very often dependent upon assumptions about such things as the nature of society and the meaning of crime and deviance. Once a theoretical perspective has been developed, the various competing theoretical traditions commonly adopt quite different research methods. Background assumptions, theoretical positions and methods of research are all therefore related.

Readings

A 'scientific' approach to crime

We have calculated the effect upon the crime rate of a 10% change in the explanatory variables, the most important of which are police numbers, levels of punishment and unemployment. These results are shown in Figure 1.3 and, as can be seen, all of the variables have their expected effects. Increases in (i) the number of police officers, (ii) the proportion of offenders sentenced to immediate imprisonment, and (iii) the average length of prison sentences, serve to reduce the rate of property crime. These results lend support to the 'get tough' approach to criminal justice policy.

Table 1.1 Estimated costs of reducing property crimes by 1 per cent

	Policy option	Cost (£ million)
Either	Increase number of police officers	51.2
or	Increase number of people sentenced to imprisonment	4.9
or	Increase average length of imprisonment	3.6
or	Reduce unemployment	?

Notes: (a) The cost of employing an additional police officer is estimated as £16,000 per annum.

(b) The cost of keeping someone in prison is estimated to be £15,000 per annum.

(c) As explained in the text, there are various alternative measures which could be implemented to reduce unemployment and the costs of these options vary widely, so no estimate is given here.

Figure 1.3 The effect on the rate of property crimes of a 10 per cent increase in five variables: numbers of police officers, rate of imprisonment, length of imprisonment, illegal gains and unemployment rate

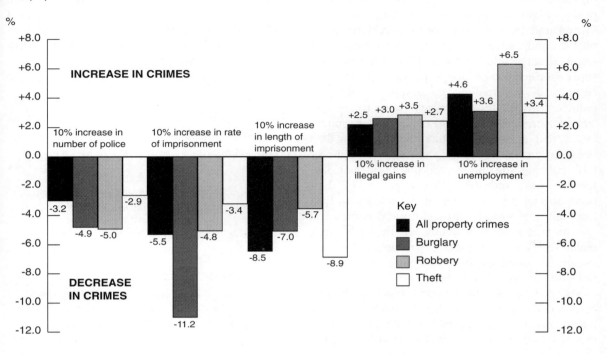

Notes: (a) The rate of imprisonment refers to the proportion of convicted offenders who are sentenced to immediate imprisonment.
(b) An increase in illegal gains, or profits from crime, is measured by the rateable value per head.

However, Figure 1.3 also shows that criminals respond to positive incentives too. An increase in potential illegal gains (measured by rateable value per head) encourages offences against property, as do increases in unemployment. It is noticeable that the effects shown in Figure 1.3 are relatively small. Rates of recorded property crime do respond to changes in deterrence and incentives variables, but the response is quite small.

Source: Pyle (1987)

In the extract above Pyle has constructed a theory which purports to relate a number of variables statistically in order to show their relative effects on crime levels.

1 *Where would you locate this approach in Figure 1.1 on p.2?*

2 *What strengths might this sort of model have?*

3 *What are its weaknesses?*

4 *Give examples of where you would consider this sort of approach (i) most useful in sociological research, (ii) least useful.*

Watching the detectives

I became interested in the relationship between the detectives who frequented *The Pump* and the rest of the pub's clientele, an interest that coincided with an approach to coach another soccer team. When I realised that one of the parents who followed the team was Simon, a detective who used *The Pump*, I willingly gave up one evening a week and my Sunday mornings to stand freezing in a damp field cajoling various Waynes, Damiens, Troys and Justins to 'close each other down' and such like. My relationship with Simon steered the course of the research during those early months. Our relationship was most enjoyable and was initially a trading relationship; I had notional coaching skills that might complement his son's outstanding athletic ability, and he had knowledge of, and contacts in, the CID. Simon emerged as my principal police informant, granting me both formal and informal interviews, access to documents, and introductions to individuals and settings that would otherwise be inaccessible. My supervisor encouraged me to pursue this emergent strategy of informal access despite a recurring panic on my behalf concerning a desire to conduct 'real' research in order that I might metamorphose into a 'real' academic. Despite my misgivings, data began to emerge concerning the unique nature of CID policing, the commercial nature of their day-to-day work, and the reflexive nature of their occupational culture; that is, its parallels with East End culture. I went to pubs, clubs and parties and the unstructured timetabling of my field-work meant that I could spend time writing up at leisure, usually 'the day after the night before', and without fail with a massive headache.

My analysis of detective work has been limited by the decision not to seek formal access to the police organisation. The degree to which detectives exposed both themselves and the nature of their work to me depended largely upon my ability to strike up a rapport with individuals.

In a similar manner and for parallel motives, other groups are missing from my analysis. I am white, male and of working-class origin, and I traded this profile with others who were dealing in the same market-place, ignoring women, Afro-Caribbeans, and Asians.

Source: Adapted from Hobbs (1988)

The extract above comes from an absorbing study of East London life, and in particular of the nature of 'thieving' and policing.

1 *Where would you locate this study in Figure 1.1 on p.2?*

2 *Specify the differences between this approach and the one described by Pyle above.*

3 *What weaknesses can you find in this approach?*

4 *What are its strengths?*

5 *Give examples of where you would consider this sort of approach (i) most useful in sociological research, (ii) least useful.*

Examination Question

'Let us be done with the arguments of participant observation versus interviewng and get on with the business of attacking our problems with the widest array of conceptual and methodological tools that we possess.' (Trow, 1957)

Give a brief account of the theoretical issues underlying the arguments to which Trow refers. Discuss how far, and with what degree of success sociologists have taken his advice. Illustrate your answer wih examples from published research.
University of London Schools Examinations Board, June 1988, Specimen Paper

Bibliography

Hobbs, D. (1988) *Doing the Business*, Oxford: Oxford University Press

O'Brien, M. (1993) *'Social research and sociology'*, in Gilbert, N. (ed.) Researching Social Life, London: Sage

Pyle, D.J. (1987) *'The fight against crime'*, Social Studies Review, January

2 The functionalist tradition: values, strain and control

How far did nineteenth century social change, brought about by industrialisation, challenge and break down the established values of the community?

Functionalist approaches in sociology derive mainly from the work of Emile Durkheim at the end of the nineteenth century. He believed that societies were held together by shared values and economic interdependence. There is always, according to Durkheim, the possibility of a collapse of society if its values are not constantly reaffirmed and passed on from one generation to another. Therefore the maintenance of values is an absolutely crucial 'function' of society.

 Collect newspapers for one week and collate as many stories as possible under the headings of:

1 promoting unity

2 social change.

How easy has the task been? Do you find the distinction useful?

There are a number of ways in which societies reaffirm their values and ensure continuing social cohesion. The most obvious are education and religion, but interestingly Durkheim also pointed to the importance of crime and deviance. We will explore this fascinating idea in this chapter. We will also see how Durkheim's work led other writers, not necessarily functionalists, to put forward a number of interesting insights into the nature of crime. Apart from Durkheim himself, two other approaches have been associated with his views – *strain theory* and *control theory*.

Strain theory was developed in the 1930s by Merton in response to the 'Great Depression', a period of enormous unemployment and social upheaval in the USA. Merton argued that crime was one possible outcome of a society which attempted to impose upon people values that were incompatible with economic reality.

Over thirty years later, Hirschi developed control theory from Durkheim's early writings. Hirschi took up Durkheim's view that crime is normal in society and explored the ways in which society controls the dangers this poses to it.

This chapter also contains a substantial discussion on the nature and causes of suicide. This discussion highlights many of the strengths and weaknesses of the functionalist approach, and demonstrates how it can be applied to a variety of social problems other than crime.

Figure 2.1 Guidelines: the Functionalist approach to crime

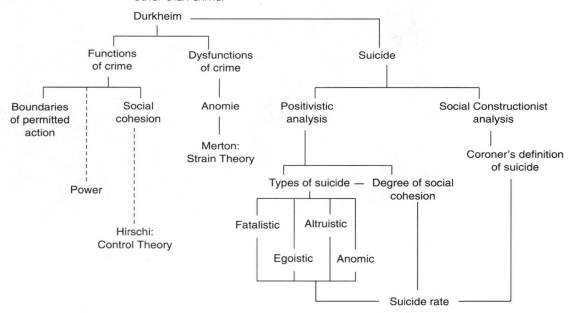

Durkheimian explanations of crime

Functions and dysfunctions of crime

According to Durkheim, there are two crucial elements in understanding crime, which at first sight appear to be contradictory. A *limited amount* of crime is necessary and beneficial to society, so much so that society could not exist without some form of deviance. On the other hand, *too much* crime is bad for society and can help to bring about its collapse.

Thus the *amount* of crime determines whether it is good or bad for society. This contrasts with the typical view that crime, by its very nature, is harmful to society.

The necessity of crime

Durkheim held that a society consists of common expectations regarding behaviour, based upon shared values and beliefs. We all agree what is right and wrong, and act accordingly. However, the boundaries of acceptable behaviour need to be defined and made known to all. This is the role of criminal law.

First, the law unambiguously marks the extremities of acceptable behaviour. Each time the police arrest a person, they are making it clear to the rest of society that that particular action is unacceptable. Second, the boundaries must be made known to everyone in society, so some form of publicity and drama needs to be generated. Erikson (1966) has pointed out, for example, the dramatic setting of the courtroom where the lawyers and judges dress in special clothes, and where there is a ceremony which condemns a person's actions in a public arena. In contemporary society newspapers also help to perform the publicity function, with their often lurid accounts of criminal acts. In effect, the courts and the media are 'broadcasting' the boundaries of acceptable behaviour, warning others not to breach the walls of the law (and, therefore, society).

Figure 2.2 The boundaries of acceptable behaviour

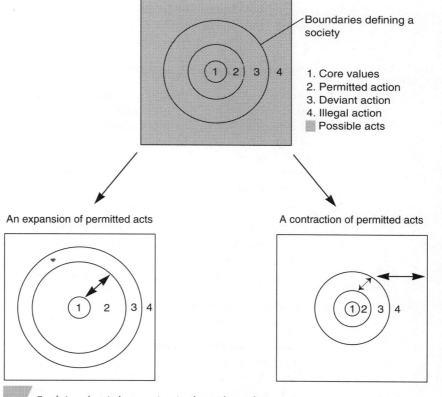

Changes in:

(i) The interpretation of the law by the courts.

(ii) Public opinion

(iii) The law itself

Can all lead to changes in the relationship between core values, deviant acts and illegal acts.

Explain what is happening in these three diagrams.

A further function performed by criminals is to provide a constant test of the boundaries of permitted action. For example, every time a person is prosecuted for a crime, attention is drawn to the commission of that act. People can express their feelings about this – in most cases they simply and unquestioning accept the illegality and evil nature of the act, but sometimes they may feel sympathy for the criminal. When the law is clearly out of step with the feelings and values of the majority, legal reform is necessary. Criminals therefore perform a crucial service in helping the law to reflect the wishes of the population and legitimising social change.

A final element of Durkheim's model follows from this 'boundary-testing' function. When particularly horrific crimes are committed, people are drawn together in feelings of mutual horror or fear (or both), so the bonds between them are strengthened.

Durkheim suggests that crime is both inevitable in society and also necessary. Even in a society of 'saints' there would have to be 'crime', for without crime society would not exist.

1 *How could there possibly be crime in a society of saints?*

2 *What common values do you think all of us share? How could you find these out in practice?*

3 *In the last ten years there has been a large growth in the number of young people who want to construct less competitive, less materialistic alternatives to our current society. Amongst the most prominent are so called 'New Age Travellers'. These people try to live in harmony with nature and with one another, sharing what they have. They try not to impose rules and regulations on others. Could this model be taken for British society as a whole?*

The effect of crime on society

Durkheim was careful to balance his arguments for the necessity of crime with an acknowledgement of its damaging effects if allowed to go unchecked. According to Durkheim and the functionalist tradition that followed him, society is based on a set of shared values which he calls the 'collective conscience'. People do not always follow this collective conscience – they are naturally self-seeking and prefer to look after their own interests at the expense of others. What stops them is the law and inculcation by the institutions of society of the collective conscience, taught to all of us through the process of socialisation.

The law is the weaker of the two socialisation agencies. Far stronger is the pervasive 'self-control' that we all learn. However, in periods of great social strain or dramatic change, the power of the collective conscience is weakened. When Durkheim was writing, for example, there was great fear that community life had been shattered by the growth of major cities and of industrialisation. As the community collapsed under the weight of the dramatic social change brought about by industrialisation and urbanisation, so the collective conscience was weakened.

The result, according to Durkheim, was the development of a state he called *anomie*. In essence this means that people regard as unimportant the social expectation to respect the rights and needs of others and prefer instead to look after their own interests, even at their neighbours' expense. They return to their 'natural' state of greed and self-interest. For society this heralds the long-term collapse of order and harmony. Anomie, then, is a harmful and dangerous state.

.. almost half the country, led by the right-wing Likud opposition party, disagreed with [Rabin's] deals to give away territory to former enemies in return for promises of peace.

Right-wing extremists, hard-line settlers in the occupied territories, and religious fundamentalists openly branded him a traitor for what they saw as a betrayal of the historic right of Jews to live in 'eretz Israel' – the biblical land of the Jews which they claim stretches from the Mediterranean to the Jordan river.

The peace process, they believed, was moving with indecent haste and the Likud party has vowed to annul Mr Rabin's pact with the PLO if it is put into power at the elections due next year.

For now Likud, embarrassed by Rabin's assassination at the hands of a right-wing extremist and stung into silence by allegations that it had whipped up hatred against the Prime Minister, has pledged to back Shimon Peres in forming a new Labour government.

Source: Martin Phillip, 'Shaken ... by the enemy within', *Today*, 6 November 1995

Early yesterday, hundreds of memorial candles and bouquets covered the murder spot.

There was a sign, in Hebrew, saying, simply: 'Why?'

The premier's flag-draped coffin lay at the parliament, the Knesset.

Here, Leah Rabin, in a black suit, sat beside the coffin, face in her hands. Weeping.

Cabinet ministers and generals hugged her, in gestures of attempted comfort. And no one made speeches: the enormity of Saturday's madness was all too obvious.

Tens of thousands of Israelis lined up to walk past the coffin. Many wept.

At sombre morning assemblies throughout the land, children wept as they, too, sang Premier Rabin's epitaph, Song for Peace.

'They feel terribly afraid,' said teacher Hani Hyperman, at a school near Jerusalem.

Pupil Gitit Raz, 12, said: 'I feel strange, in shock. Suddenly he's gone. They told us in class that the killer was crazy and thought he was doing the nation a favour.

'He thought he would stop the peace process this way. But he won't. He won't.'

Source: Grant Jones and Barry Wigmore, 'The bullet ripped through the folded hymn ... it was called Song for Peace', *Today*, 6 November 1995

1   *What appear to be the effects of the assassination of Prime Minister Rabin, according to these newspaper reports?*

2   *How do these extracts relate to the work of Durkheim?*

The contribution of Durkheim

Durkheim's writing represented a major breakthrough in understanding the nature of deviance. Most other late nineteenth-century writers on crime were trying to find out what was wrong with criminals and deviants. Durkheim argued that crime and deviance are not created by a small number of 'sick' individuals, nor is it in any way 'unnatural', rather they are an integral part of society which performs an absolutely crucial function.

However, there are a number of problems connected with Durkheim's view. The first is that he offered no real explanation as to why certain people are more likely to commit deviant acts than others. He was not really concerned with this problem; he was most interested in the nature of the relationship between deviance and order in society. However, if questioned on the individual motivations of criminals, he would probably have invoked their lack of adequate socialisation.

A second problem lies in his stress on the harmony of society and the belief that the law reflects the interests and views of the majority of the population. He seems almost wilfully to ignore the concept of power. It is generally accepted that in all societies some groups have greater ability than the bulk of the population to influence the law-making process.

So, although Durkheim led the way in relating crime and deviance to the very structure of society, he failed, first, to explain the reasons why some people commit crime, and second, to explore the element of power in law-making.

The central elements of Durkheim's writing have been extended by later sociologists. The positive aspect of deviance has been taken up in the work of Erikson, while the negative aspect of deviance has been developed by Merton.

Erikson: the positive aspect of crime

In the mid-1960s Erikson developed Durkheim's ideas on the boundary-setting and maintenance functions of crime. However, he made a particularly important alteration to Durkheim's original explanation. According to Durkheim, the collective conscience and the laws that derived from it were a reflection of the will of the people. Erikson suggested that Durkheim had omitted the differences in power that exist in society. He showed how crime sets the boundaries of permissible action, but does so in the interests of the powerful. Thereby Erikson made a bridge between the functionalist and Marxist schools of thought.

In *Wayward Puritans* (1966) Erikson explored how Puritan religious leaders imposed their rulings on their followers. In the seventeenth century the European Puritans began to emigrate to the 'New World' in order to escape persecution. This persecution was a reaction to the Puritan belief that God speaks directly to each person, without the need of any intermediary such as a church. The churches played a central role in maintaining social order in the European states. They often conveniently interpreted God's will as a reflection of the views of their governments. By preaching the irrelevance of the church, the Puritans were undermining a major prop of government.

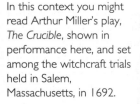
In this context you might read Arthur Miller's play, *The Crucible*, shown in performance here, and set among the witchcraft trials held in Salem, Massachusetts, in 1692.

Within the Puritan communities, the leaders derived their authority from leading the opposition to oppression. After the flight to North America this basis for authority was removed – for if God spoke directly to each person, what role did leaders have? To give themselves a role, the old leadership began to alter the previously held beliefs. Yes, they said, it was true that God spoke directly to individuals, but only a select few (the leadership) could correctly *interpret* what God said!

Many Puritans were unhappy about this and one, a certain Mrs Hutchinson, rebelled. She was brought to trial, accused of witchcraft (in other words, she was said to be listening to the Devil, not God), convicted and thrown out of the congregation. The effect of the trial was that the new social order was legitimised and the threat to the leadership was repulsed. Furthermore, the rest of the Puritan community was drawn together in horror at the idea that the Devil was at work.

Strain theory: the work of Merton

Robert Merton took up Durkheim's concept of anomie, but he regarded the idea as too vague in its original form and so altered it to mean a society where there is a 'disjunction between goals and means'. In such a society, according to Merton, there is a tremendous cultural stress on being successful (the goal), yet it is virtually impossible for the majority of the population to achieve success in a socially acceptable way (the means). Thus the burning desire to achieve the socially stressed goals actively promotes deviant behaviour.

> There is a money madness in the air which goes beyond the traditional American passion for the almighty buck. Like the steady drinker who one day slips into alcoholism, America has lost control of its greed.
>
> Greed is fashionable, and restraint is out of style. Greed is driven by a fearful sense that there may not be much time. Slow accumulation, long-term strategy and forward planning are relics from an earlier age of innocence. The sense of economic doom which hangs over the country is almost palpable.
>
> At a recent conference in Boston on 'The American Dream', not a single paper that I heard deviated from the convention that the dream has nothing to do with freedom or democracy, and everything to do with living standards. In the annual opinion poll of entering college students this academic year, 70 per cent gave as their reason for entering college 'to make more money', and more than a quarter of all students were headed for business studies. On the wall of the men's room in the University library, some young philosopher has summed up the zeitgeist: 'Whoever dies with the most toys, wins.'
>
> *Source*: Bouchier, 'The great greed of 1987', *New Statesman*, 12 June 1987

1 Explain how the extract from Bouchier's article relates to Merton's concept of anomie.

2 *Merton's argument is based on the idea that people share similar values. Devise a series of questions which will indicate whether people hold, or do not hold, a range of values which you decide may be important. For example, a question concerning future career choice could indicate whether people were interested in making money alone. Ask a small sample of people. As a result of this, would you agree with Merton that there are agreed goals that people are keen to obtain?*

Merton was not simply putting forward an abstract argument; he was describing the United States of the 1930s, as he saw it. He believed that American society had become obsessed with the desire to make money – indeed the possession of wealth had become the only measure of success in life. Yet the great majority of Americans had little or no chance of ever becoming rich legally. For blacks, the urban poor and struggling immigrants the 'American dream' was just that – a dream.

This account follows Durkheim, and is 'structural' because Merton locates the cause of deviance in the very nature of American society, not in any defect that originates in the individual.

Merton did not suggest that everyone who was denied access to the peaks of wealth entered the state of anomie, rather he argued that there were quite clear bands of expectations. Those who start at the bottom do not necessarily expect to get to the very top, but aspire to a prosperous standard of living. On the other hand, those from relatively affluent backgrounds seriously aspire to be rich.

Having laid out his general principle that being blocked from success leads to deviance, Merton then moved on to explain how people choose *different* patterns of deviance: for example, one person may steal while another may take drugs.

Table 2.1 summarises the various responses that Merton suggested may take place in a situation of anomie.

Table 2.1 Merton's responses to anomie		
Responses	*Means*	*Goals*
Conformity	+	+
Innovation	–	+
Ritualism	+	–
Retreatism	–	–
Rebellion	±	±

Notes: + acceptance of the goals or means
– rejection of the goals or means
± rejection of the goals and means, and substitution of a new one

- *Conformity* occurs when the person continues to accept the goals and the means set by society, even though 'failure' is the likely outcome. This is the response of the typical law-abiding citizen.

- *Innovation* is the response when a person accepts the goals set by society, but rejects the socially acceptable means. Here people may turn to crime for financial rewards, or may simply find a new (legal) way of making money.

- *Ritualism* is where the means to the goals are accepted and conformed to, but the person loses sight of the goals. The person therefore 'goes through the motions' but has no real interest in the outcome. An example would be the teacher who stresses the importance of neat handwriting, but ignores the content of an essay.

- *Retreatism*: is where both the goals and the means are forgotten. The person simply 'drops out of the rat race'. Typical responses of this kind are drug abuse and alcoholism.

- *Rebellion* occurs where the person rejects the current society with its stress on success and also rejects the means that society provides to obtain the goals. In terms of the model, a rejection of both means and goals takes place, and alternative goals and means are substituted. Political radicalism and terrorism are examples of this response.

This model provides us with the reason why people deviate (anomie) and the *types* of deviance they may adopt (in terms of rejection or acceptance of means and goals). Because it stresses that crime is the outcome of a strain between what people wish to achieve and what is possible, the theory is often known as *strain theory*.

Merton's explanation for deviance has been criticised by a number of sociologists. It has become a standard textbook criticism to suggest that Merton gives no explanation as to why a particular person chooses one form of deviance in preference to another. In fact this is not true: Merton argues that the different levels and types of ritualistic and innovative behaviour found in different social classes reflect the different emphases in socialisation between the classes. So a working-class person, having been socialised in a less rigid way, can violate conventional expectations of behaviour with less guilt and anxiety than a middle-class person. Socialisation channels people into various responses by limiting the choice of deviant adaptations open to them.

This is not to say that Merton is in any way sympathetic to subcultural theory. Rather, he regards normal societies as those which agree on basic values and acceptable patterns of behaviour. But he does concede that emphases on socialisation vary from one social group to another.

> Links between social deprivation and crime are also well known. One survey of Newcastle's young people found that 60 per cent of boys and 9 per cent of girls from 'multiply deprived' families eventually gained criminal records – roughly double the average. It suggests that poverty can detract from parents' ability to exert effective influence over their children.
>
> A recent British Youth Council report, *The Time of Your Life?*, paints a bleak picture of increasing deprivation among 16–25 year olds. It says that unemployment is running at 16 per cent for under-25s, compared to the national average of 9 per cent; young people represent 32 per cent of the UK's jobless population; income support for most 16 and 17 year olds has been abolished; and a government promise to provide Youth Training places for every teenager remains unfulfilled.

Long-term youth unemployment is linked to suicide, according to a 1984 study by Leslie Francis. In the past 10 years the suicide rate among the under-25s has risen by 30 per cent. Alcohol and drug abuse is also growing.

Source: 'It wasn't like that in my day', *Guardian Education*, 30 March 1993

The news about young people's morals is not all bad. A few criminally inclined young people hog the headlines, but plenty of people show great concern for others. For example, more under-24s are becoming involved in voluntary work than any other section of the population.

Last year's National Survey of Voluntary Activity, carried out by the Volunteer Centre UK, looked at how much unpaid help young people offered their communities. A total of 55 per cent of people between 18 and 24 were current volunteers, most with groups that reflected their own interests – sports, working with children or in recreation. The equivalent figure for 1981 was only 42 per cent.

Many commentators predict that after concern about HIV and AIDS, successive generations of young people will become increasingly conservative in their sexual values. Last year's Euromonitor survey of 1,000 teenagers found that the 'average teenager' believes in sexual caution, green politics and hard work.

Source: 'The good news', *Guardian Education*, 30 March 1993

1 *What support is suggested for Merton's theory by the first extract?*

2 *What light does the second extract throw on Merton's theory?*

3 *Would you say that Merton's description of the conditions leading to anomie could be applied to the UK today?*

4 *What policies would Merton suggest for limiting crime?*

5 *Merton's idea is extremely interesting and possibly useful in understanding crime – but it has been suggested that it is rather hard to 'operationalise'. Could you suggest ways of measuring the extent of anomie in society that are both practical and useful?*

6 *If you can think of a way of measuring anomie, conduct a small-scale experiment to test Merton's theory. If you cannot measure anomie, do you think a theory that cannot be tested is useful?*

Control theory

Control theory originated in the work of Hirschi and Kornhauser in the USA. Variations of the theory have been developed into the New Right approaches we will examine in Chapter 11.

As you might expect, most theories of crime set out to explain why people commit crimes. The various explanations offered vary from the claim that some people are genetically programmed to break laws to the argument that it is all the fault of the capitalist system which exploits and degrades people.

Hirschi

However, in the true spirit of Durkheim's analysis of the functions of crime for society, Hirschi asked not why people commit crime, but why *don't* people commit crime? The shift in approach has important implications. Asking *why* people commit crime assumes that law-abiding behaviour is normal, that the majority of people do not commit crime and that there has to be some predisposing factor which encourages or causes them to commit crime. The implications for research are that the causes need to be isolated, and if this search is successful some programme could be devised to tackle them. On the other hand, asking why people do not commit crime assumes that law-abiding behaviour is abnormal and that the majority of people are potential deviants, but most importantly that there is no cause, as such, of criminal behaviour. The implications for research are that attempts to seek the causes of criminal behaviour are to be largely abandoned, and that instead efforts should be made to enforce social control.

Functionalist theory basically argues that society is held together by bonds based on culture. In *The Causes of Delinquency* (1969) Hirschi argued that criminal activity occurs when the individual's attachment to society is weakened.

The 'bonds' that bind people to society are composed of four elements: attachment, commitment, involvement and belief.

- *Attachment* concerns the extent to which we care about other people's opinions and wishes. Psychopaths, for example, are characterised by their lack of concern about the welfare or views of other people; they are entirely self-centred.

- *Commitment* refers to the personal investments that each of us makes in our lives. For example, a successful middle-aged career woman with a salary, marriage, family and mortgage may have invested years of education, emotion and income in what she has. Compare this to a single young male living in rented accommodation and receiving state benefits. The person with less to lose is the one more likely to turn to crime.

- *Involvement* describes a person's level of activity or business interests. A person who is extremely busy with a wide range of legitimate activities may be too preoccupied to engage in deviant behaviour.

- *Belief* refers to a person's conviction that they should obey the rules of society. Conformists have a very high moral commitment to the standards of society and oppose rule-breaking behaviour.

Hirschi's approach to control theory is quite conservative, but a rather more radical version can be made. Below is a diagram which shows the range and extent of factors which are most important in socialising us into conformity in the first place and then maintaining us in that conformity, or at least persuading us that the society and political system is 'legitimate' and therefore it would be wrong to commit criminal acts.

Figure 2.3 An ecological model of socialization in explaining offending

Source: Martens (1993)

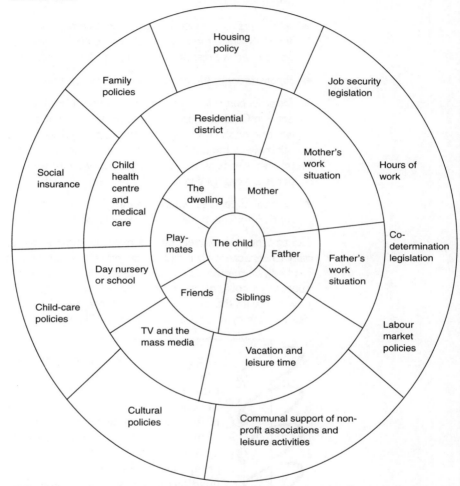

The concentric circles move out a long way from the immediate family to such issues in the outer ring as job security legislation and childcare policies. Can you suggest ways in which the factors mentioned in each of the concentric circles might influence the propensity to commit crime in a society according to (i) Hirschi, (ii) Box?

Box

A writer who would hate to be linked to Hirschi, or even to have his views included in a chapter on the functionalists, is the Marxist Steven Box. Nonetheless, from his very different political perspective Box (1983) has argued essentially the same point as Hirschi – that it is release from the agencies of control which leads to crime. The main difference is that for Box the agencies of control serve *capitalist* society.

According to him, there are five factors which weaken social bonds: secrecy, skills, supply, social support and symbolic support.

- *Secrecy* refers to the chances a person has of hiding deviant acts. This is an important point because it applies especially to white-collar crime, as those engaged in corporate or white-collar crime are more likely to be able to 'get away with it'.

- *Skills* refers to the fact that, to commit crime, one needs specialised knowledge and skills which the majority of people do not possess. We will return to this point when we discuss Cloward and Ohlin's work on pp. 51–2.

- *Supply* refers to the availability of the necessary equipment, tools and accomplices.

- *Social support* is linked to the notion of a subculture which is discussed in more detail in Chapter 3. Essentially, it means to what extent a person's peers support what he or she is doing. Very strong disapproval from peers may prevent a person otherwise attracted to deviant behaviour from engaging in it, and of course the reverse is true, as a person may be drawn into deviant activity because his or her peers are engaging in it.

- *Symbolic support* essentially means that if there is powerful tacit or symbolic support for rule breaking, it is likely to occur.

Control theory is a direct derivative of Durkheim's concept of anomie. It provides an alternative, potentially radical perspective for examining criminality which differs markedly from most of the other perspectives discussed in this book. As a theoretical approach it could of use to both the left and the right of the political spectrum; however, with the exception of Box, those most influenced by control theory have been on the right wing, as we will see in Chapter 7.

> The values of an equal or meritocratic society which capitalism inculcates into people are constantly at loggerheads with the actual material inequalities in the world. And contrary to the conservatives it is the well-socialised person who is the most liable to crime. Crime is endemic to capitalism because it produces both egalitarian ideals and material shortages.
>
> A high crime rate occurs in precise conditions: where a group has learnt through its past that is being dealt with invidiously; where it is possible for it easily to pick up the contradictions just referred to; and where there is no political channel for these feelings of discontent to be realised.
>
> *Source*: Lea and Young (1984)

1 *Explain in your own words how this is a criticism of control theory.*

2 *Lea and Young are referring in particular to crime committed by young males, both white and black. Could you explain how their arguments and those of Hirschi could both be used to explain crime?*

Suicide

Why include suicide in a book on crime and deviance?

Suicide is, in many ways, the ultimate deviant act. The basic building blocks of society are people. Without members a society cannot exist and, therefore, according to functionalists, one of the prerequisites for a society is that it contains within its values some means to persuade its members to keep going and to fulfil their social roles.

Until relatively recently in the UK suicide was illegal, and those who made unsuccessful attempts at suicide were arrested in their hospital beds. This may seem strange, but from the point of view of society, which wants to keep its members and wants them to continue fulfilling their social roles, the death of an individual as a result of suicide is little different from their loss through murder. Yet suicide is especially intriguing, for some societies have actually encouraged certain of their members to kill themselves. Suicide thus raises a range of interesting questions for sociologists who are concerned with how societies maintain social cohesion.

The analysis of suicide presented by Durkheim, and the criticisms of his work subsequently made by Atkinson and Douglas, offer us a clear insight into the methodological and theoretical rifts that have developed in sociology. Deep divisions are evident between the positivists, who believe in following the methods of the natural sciences wherever possible, and subjective or phenomenological sociologists, who prefer to explore the construction of meanings by individuals.

Figure 2.4 The suicide debate

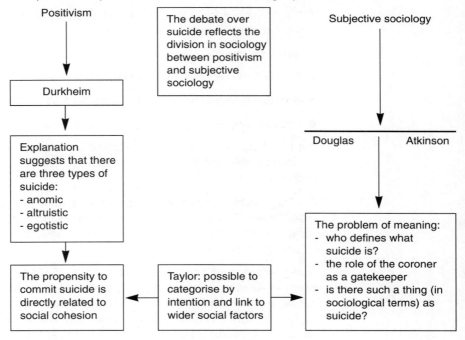

The background to Durkheim's study

Suicide had fascinated researchers throughout the nineteenth century. A great variety of explanations for the phenomenon were offered, including insanity ('organico-psychic dispositions', as Durkheim phrased it!); geographical features such as climate, temperature and length of day; and finally, that suicide was the result of people imitating each other. It is worth remembering that all three of these explanations are still offered today, with phrases like suicide 'while the balance of mind was upset', or in newspaper discussions of 'copycat suicides'.

Durkheim dismissed all of these explanations by collecting statistics from a number of countries and testing each of the causes mentioned above against them to show there was no relationship. However, he was impressed by the work of some statisticians who showed that suicide rates increased in times of social change and that they varied according to religious groups. These ideas fitted in with his theories about social integration.

Durkheim had chosen suicide to prove the usefulness of sociology in explaining social phenomena at a time when the subject was not taken seriously as an academic discipline. If he could prove that one of the most *individual* acts any human being could perform, that is, killing himself or herself, could be explained through social factors, then surely *any* action could be examined in such a way. Durkheim's chosen method, now called 'multivariate analysis', consisted of comparing the incidence of various social factors with the known incidence of a particular event, in this case suicide. Durkheim did this work so well that seventy years later his study was still being cited in textbooks as an excellent example of research methodology. We shall see later just how mistaken the writers of these textbooks were.

The theory

The starting-point for Durkheim was a close analysis of the available official statistics, which showed that rates of suicide varied:

- from one country to another

- between different regions within countries

- between different social groups (e.g. the married and unmarried)

- between different religious groups (Jews, Protestants, Catholics)

and that these rates were relatively stable over time for each group, that is, they retained the different levels of suicide relative to each other over a twenty-year period.

If suicide was an entirely individual matter, untouched by the influence of social factors, it would be an astonishing coincidence if these statistical patterns remained so constant over a long period of time. Entirely individual decisions should lead to a random pattern.

Durkheim's explanation centred on his concept of *social integration* and cohesion, which, as we saw earlier, underpins his analysis of crime. For Durkheim, people are not naturally social animals; humankind has to be constrained and 'bonded' to the values of society, otherwise individual greed and self-interest will take over. Societies are social organisations based upon common values that allow people to co-operate with each other in harmony, as long as they feel a common bond.

According to Durkheim, people are 'bonded' to society in a variety of ways, but the main means of social integration are the family and religion. Durkheim suggested that the individuals who feel most closely tied to society have close family relationships, in which there is a strong commitment to others which becomes generalised to society.

It follows that those without close family (or similar) ties are the least bonded to society.

Religion operates on a broader level, influencing the whole ethos of society by providing people with a moral underpinning for social rules. However, Durkheim noted that different religions place different levels of stress on the relative importance of achieving individual satisfaction and pursuing personal interests. At one extreme, Protestant religions give considerable importance to individual fulfilment, while at the other, religions such as Hinduism and Catholicism stress the importance of the group and consider the search for personal happiness relatively unimportant.

It should be remembered that religion was a far more powerful influence on social life in the last century than it is now, and directly affected the way individuals behaved. In any event, Durkheim held that as a result of the interaction of various influences, societies could be placed on a scale depending on the extent to which they stressed individual or group interests.

Durkheim defined suicide as 'death resulting directly or indirectly from a positive or negative act performed by the victim himself which he knows will produce this result'. An example of a positive act would be taking an overdose; there would be a negative act when a Hindu wife allowed herself to be burned to death according to the traditional (but now illegal) Indian custom of *suttee*.

Recently, Befrienders International, the world-wide Samaritans organisation, called for the European Union to establish its own suicide prevention policy. Nearly 44,000 suicides are adjudged to have occurred yearly in the 12 member states of the EU in the early 1990s – almost as many deaths as those caused by traffic accidents. It has been suggested that Catholicism and strong family networks in southern Europe may account for the lower rates in countries from those areas (see Fig. 2.5) and that countries experiencing 'social disintegration' – from the old Soviet bloc, for example – were also now showing booming rates of suicide.

In the UK, Michael Rutter and David Smith (1995) in *Psycho-social Disorders in Young People* have argued that work uncertainties, rising expectations and family problems combine with lengthening adolescence to produce an insecure status and uncertain personal identity, especially for young males.

Source: Adapted from Williams (1996)

Figure 2.5 Suicides in EU
countries

Source: Befrienders
International quoted
by John Williams

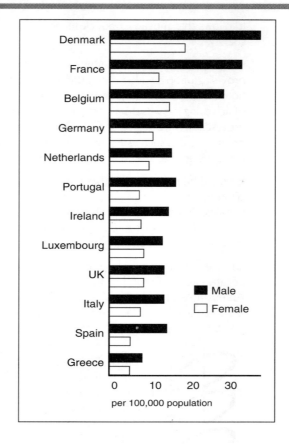

Figures 2.6a and 2.6b
Death rates in the UK
from suicide, by gender
and age

Source: Office of
Population Censuses
and Surveys, quoted
by John Williams
(1996)

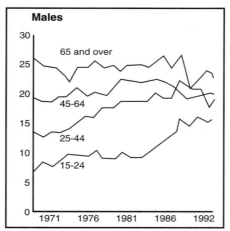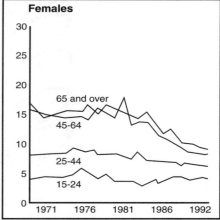

1 In what ways can the text be seen to support Durkheim's arguments?

2 Does Figure 2.5 fully support the claims in the text about the different levels of suicide in different countries?

3 Can you suggest any problems there may be in comparing levels of suicide across different countries?

4 *Look at Figures 2.6a and b. What statements can you make about:*

(i) male and female suicide rates over the period of the diagrams?

(ii) the different rates by age group?

What explanations could you offer?

It was Durkheim's hypothesis that suicide is directly related to the levels of social integration in a society or group within it. Durkheim identified four types of social structures which he placed at different points along the line of social integration:

● egoistic

● altruistic

● anomic

● fatalistic.

We will examine each of these structures in turn.

Egoistic

In egoistic social structures individual rights, interests and welfare are heavily stressed, and allegiance to the wider group is weak. People are encouraged to look after themselves and those particularly close to them at the expense of the wider society. As a result, social bonds are weak and there is a low level of social integration.

This form of social structure is typical of modern Western industrial societies, where the competitive pursuit of individual happiness is promoted as a central value. According to Durkheim, the Protestant religion was a strong influence on the development of this form of social structure, mainly because Protestant values stress individual decisions and responsibilities. Furthermore, success and happiness on earth were taken to be a sign that God was looking favourably upon a person. In this sort of environment, individual failure or unhappiness are adequate grounds for people to take their own lives.

Within the wider egoistic society, however, there are social institutions that provide people with strong social bonds and partly counteract the wider egoistic values of society:

● *The family* stresses the importance of mutual obligations between members, and in particular the role of husband/father and wife/mother.

● *Other religions*, such as Catholicism, place far greater stress on the importance of an individual's responsibility to the wider church. They also insist on the observance of clear-cut religious rules, which give the individual a strong sense of belonging. In the case of Jews, Durkheim pointed out the extremely strong community feeling and the way this was maintained through the experience of persecution.

● *Times of external oppression*, when a society or group (like the Jews) is threatened from outside, draw people together, strengthening social integration.

Durkheim concluded, that there are likely to be relatively high rates of suicide in societies with low levels of social integration, but that, within those societies, individuals in institutions that provide greater levels of social integration are less likely to take their own lives. For example, married people are less likely to commit suicide than are single people.

Altruistic

At the other extreme from egoistic societies stand altruistic ones. Here the individual is completely subsumed into the group and views its existence as far more important than his or her own. Altruistic social structures exert an extremely powerful influence over the actions of individuals, so that what the social structure dictates, the person will do. Durkheim described this form of society as having insufficient individuation.

In these societies suicide rarely occurs for individual reasons of unhappiness. Suicides that do happen tend to be demanded by the culture of the social structure, and the individual accepts death as the only possible action (as in *suttee*). Soldiers, and in particular officers, are more likely to sacrifice their lives for the good of the army than an ordinary individual would. Durkheim explains this by claiming that a soldier 'must be drilled to set little value on his person'.

Anomic

The third social structure related to the level of suicide was termed by Durkheim 'anomic'. We discussed the concept of anomie earlier, so you will recall that Durkheim believed people were naturally greedy and self-interested, and only if they were restricted in their desires by social controls could they live in harmony together. Durkheim further argued that people learn to measure their wants and desires against norms or guidelines given them by society. If social constraints are removed, people feel lost and bewildered, as they have no standards against which to measure their behaviour. In periods of rapid economic improvement people may never be satisfied, and the resultant disillusionment may lead to suicide. On the other hand, in periods of rapid economic decline people may not be able to reconcile themselves to a lower standard of living.

Fatalistic

In extremely oppressive societies people may lose the will to live and prefer to die rather than continue in misery. Durkheim considered this form of suicide 'of little contemporary importance', but it could be seen among the inmates of concentration camps during the Second World War.

Each week the homeless persons' magazine The Big Issue *carries a page with photographs and details of 'missing people'. Let us apply to the phenomenon of missing people the sort of analysis that Durkheim developed to explain suicide.*

1 *The concept of 'missing person' has no specific legal status. What possible meaning can the term have? Define the term. Could there be a number of types of missing person, as Durkheim suggested for suicide? Give reasons for your definitions.*

2 *What could cause someone to go missing? You should look at individual factors, family factors, social factors and structural factors. Can you develop a framework or advance some hypotheses?*

MISSING
can you help?

WHAT'S WORSE than having a phone call at 3am?... Not having a phone call at 3am! Imagine your child is missing. It's been four days since you last saw him or her. The police are doing everything they can. All you can do is wait. Who can you turn to? The Missing Persons Bureau Helpline offers 24 hour support for those left behind when someone goes missing. It provides practical support such as bureau street workers looking for vulnerable missing persons, posters, a computer register and literature. We also feature a missing person on Carlton TV four times a week just before the 5.40pm news. The Helpline now receives over 500 calls a week, but urgently needs more funds to keep the lines open. If you can help please send a donation to: The Missing Persons Bureau, Parkway House, Sheen Lane, London SW14 8LS.

The Missing Persons Helpline

Featured in
The Big Issue

Sian Davies
Sian Davies, 40 years old, from Wales has been missing for eight years. She stopped contacting her mother after she became involved with the Bala Krishnan sect.
Sian read Politics and Economics at Aberystwyth University. After she graduated she travelled with her boyfriend to India. and was moved by the suffering she was there. When she returned to England she seemed a changed person. Sian and her boyfriend moved to London and joined the Bala Krishnas; she last visited her mother in 1985 and she has not contacted her since then. "Not a day goes by when I don't pray for my daughter," says Mrs Davies. "I want her to know that her home is still her home."
It is known that Sian lived in Brixton for a while and that she attended London University around 1987 where she completed a Law degree.
If you have any more information please phone the Helpline.

Patrick Pollard
Patrick Pollard from Maidstone, Kent has not contacted his mother for almost two years. He had been working as a cook in a pub in Kingston, Surrey. Mrs Pollard found out only recently that he left his job in November 1992. He then stayed with a friend called Nigel for about three weeks before moving on, saying he was going to look for work. He left all his belongings at a friends house and has not been back to collect them. His mother is very concerned because it appears that he hasn't contacted anyone since November "All I want to know is that he is alright," says Mrs Pollard.
Patrick is 38, 5' 11" tall, medium build, with fair short hair and blue eyes. When he was last seen he had a moustache. Patrick usually does kitchen or bar work. He smokes and drinks heavily.
If you have any idea as to Patrick's present whereabouts please phone the Helpline.

Phillip Donovan
Does anyone know the whereabouts of 37 year old Phillip Donovan? When he last contacted his father three years ago Phillip said he was working with a friend as a builder in the Southall area of London. None of his family have heard from him since May 1990.
Phillip had been living with a friend in Ealing. According to this friend, Phillip did not take even a change of clothing with him when he left. Phillip's father feels he may have had financial problems. Phillip worked for MACA for eight years untill 1990, he was a warden in a halfway house for people recovering from mental illness.
Phillip is 5' 8" tall, of heavy build with brown hair, thinning on top. He sometimes has a beard and may be wearing glasses. Phillip's father, Peter and his brother Martin are concerned for Phillip's well being, and would very much like him to contact them to assure them that he is alright.

Dennis George Gunnell
Dennis Gunnell, 60 years old, has been missing for over eight months. Dennis had been living rough in London for the last seven years. He separated from his wife Pamela in 1972 but they have remained friends since. Pamela concerned about his whereabouts. "We used to meet each other occasionally and I would often see him on my way to work. But for the last 10 months there has been no sign of him," says Pamela Gunnell.
Dennis, who used to work for the *Daily Express*, regularly collected his pension from a bank in Baker Street. He has not been seen since February 18, 1993. Dennis is a heavy drinker and suffers from epilepsy. He usually slept in the Paddington Station area, though he has also slept in other central London stations including Charing Cross.
Dennis is 5' 7" tall, of medium build with short neat brown hair. He has blue eyes and a long scar on his forehead.

081-392 2000

3 How would you go about researching your hypotheses? Describe the methods you think would be the most effective in exploring the subject.

Criticisms of Durkheim

The internal criticisms

There have been various criticisms of Durkheim's methodology:

● His concept of social integration was too vague: he simply relied on intuitive ideas of what integration was.

- His variables of religion and the family were not as clear-cut as he suggested. How can these be 'isolated' as distinct influences on behaviour?

- The official statistics on which he based his research left much to be desired. For example, in Catholic countries, where suicide is regarded as a sin, family doctors are reluctant to classify deaths as suicide.

However, until the late 1960s no one seriously questioned Durkheim's general approach and conclusions.

Phenomenological criticisms

Durkheim has been strongly criticised by two writers, Douglas and Atkinson, who have accused him of assuming that his 'interpretation' of suicide is correct, and ignoring the meaning the concept may have for others.

Douglas (1967) pointed out that although one can define the *physical act* of a person taking his or her own life as suicide, this ignores the fact that suicide also has different meanings to those who take their own lives. Douglas suggested that those who commit suicide may define their action in at least four ways:

- *as a means of transforming the self*. This is where a person commits suicide as a means of gaining release from the cares of the world and entering paradise. There have been also been examples of mass suicides by religious groups.

- *as a means of transforming oneself for others*. In this case suicide is a means of telling others how profound one's feelings are on a particular issue. For instance, a person who had caused a death through dangerous driving may commit suicide as a means of expressing repentance.

- *as a means of achieving fellow feeling*. This is where the person is asking for help or sympathy; it includes 'suicide' attempts in which the person hopes to be found.

- *as a means of gaining revenge*. The person places the blame for his or her death on others. Usually there is a note accusing others of failing the person in some way.

Thus there is no single act which can be termed 'suicide'. Since the meanings that individuals place upon their acts are so different, is it possible to lump them all together in one category? If there is no such category, Durkheim's statistical comparisons are worthless.

Atkinson (1971) further developed the criticism that Durkheim failed to understand that categories such as 'suicide' are really socially constructed. Before a death can be classified as suicide in Britain, a coroner must investigate the death at an inquest. The coroner's decision on whether the death was natural, accidental or suicide effectively determines, as far as the official statistics are concerned, what *really* is a suicide. Atkinson argues that the official statistics therefore reflect coroners' decisions and little else.

Obviously, only those who have killed themselves know exactly the motives and circumstances for their suicide. In order to determine if a death was deliberate or not, the coroner must piece together a series of 'clues' and then decide whether or not these point to suicide. Atkinson suggests that the following clues are particularly important:

- *suicide notes*. In only 30 per cent of suicides is a note found, although more may have been written but the family destroys them because of the accusations often contained in them (see above).

- *mode of death*. Some types of death are seen as clear indications of suicide, for example hanging, whereas others such as drowning are more problematic.

- *location and circumstances of death*. Coroners believe that suicides are committed in places and circumstances where they will not be discovered and where the person is sure the outcome will be successful.

- *life history and mental condition*. Coroners believe that suicide is related to depression caused by particular events (financial or emotional). Evidence to support this is therefore sought, together with information on the person's medical history.

> If the evidence does not fit the commonsense model embraced by the coroner, suicide verdicts are not recorded. The verdict therefore reflects the assumptions made by the coroner and his or her interpretations of the clues, rather than any 'reality'.
>
> A brilliant young musician, Marcus Batchelor, was found hanged at his public school after an experiment that went tragically wrong. Marcus, aged 13, had been told by his trumpet teacher that he should imagine himself as a corpse in a coffin in order to understand a sombre piece of music.
>
> The next day he was found hanging from a scarf tied to the ceiling and with his legs chained together.
>
> Mr Roger Stokes, coroner, told an inquest at Yeovil, Somerset yesterday: 'All the evidence suggests that he was trying to rehearse in his mind what it might feel like to be near death.'
>
> The coroner said Marcus was trying to gain an insight into a state of mind which would enable him to interpret music he was studying. He was absolutely sure that Marcus – 'a happy, balanced young man' – did not take his own life. He recorded a verdict of accidental death.
>
> Marcus of Bessacarr, South Yorkshire, was in his second term as a music student at Wells Cathedral School, Somerset. He played trumpet, piano and cello.
>
> The school's head of brass, Mr Ruari Wilson, said Marcus was an exceptionally talented pupil whose ambition was to be a professional composer and musician.
>
> *Source*: 'Sombre 'rehearsal' led to boy's death', *Guardian*, 15 March 1983

1 What alternative explanations could you offer if you were a different coroner 'reading between the lines'?

2 Prepare a 'content analysis' of your local newspapers over the last year. You can find microfiches or back copies in the main public libraries and in the offices of the newspapers. Take a sample of suicide reports, and then see if you can work out feasible alternative interpretations. How does your research

support the arguments of Atkinson and Douglas? What does their work tell us about statistics in general?

The criticisms voiced by Douglas and Atkinson illustrate a wider debate in sociology between those who believe in using the methods of the natural sciences and those who accept that there is a real, objective social world ready to be studied and measured (positivism), and those who believe that the social world is an insubstantial social creation which derives from the meanings that people create in their daily lives (phenomenological or subjective sociology).

Suicide and parasuicide: linking the two approaches

Durkheim suggested that one of the key factors in understanding suicide was the level of social integration. But the concept 'social integration' is vague. How, if at all, did Durkheim suggest levels of integration could be measured?

The criticisms made by writers such as Douglas and Atkinson have generally been accepted by sociologists as a useful corrective to the more positivistic approach of Durkheim.

Taylor (1990), however, has suggested that both Durkheim and his critics have missed the point that suicides, however defined are only part of the picture. Taylor points out that death as a result of self-action is only one possible outcome. In fact, in the majority of cases, individuals do not actually die. Furthermore, when questioned as to what they wanted to achieve, it seems that the majority of people have simply 'gambled' with their lives, not being sure of the final outcome of their attempt at suicide. This is not the same as people who do not want to die and are making a plea for help. Taylor calls the situation between 'plea for help' and absolute certainty of death as '*parasuicide*'.

He suggests that the majority of suicide acts are therefore something like a 'medieval ordeal' in which the person throws his or her fate to the winds, putting themselves into the hand of fate. If they survive then they were not meant to die, and if they die then that was what fate or God intended.

If it is true that the majority of people who perform acts of self harm that could lead to death are actually unclear if they really mean to die or not, then this adds an extra dimension to the complexity of explaining suicide, as it is also necessary to explain these parasuicides. Durkheim's approach does not allow for the level of individual purpose, but nor does Douglas' set of categories cover these situations.

Taylor suggests that parasuicide allows us to widen the discussion of suicide into one of 'risk-taking'. Developing the analysis of Durkheim further, he suggests that successful suicides could be categorised into 'ordeal' suicides, which can be related to a profound sense of uncertainty (anomie), and the more purposive suicides, which can be categorised under the heading of 'fatalism'. Taylor then accepts Durkheim's belief that suicide is more likely in individuals too detached from others in society (egoistic suicides) and those over-attached (altruistic suicide).

The point of Taylor's argument is that it is possible to pull together the wider social factors which Durkheim emphasized with the sense of meaning which Douglas stressed. The two approaches are not necessarily exclusive.

The debate reminds us that the sorts of questions sociologists ask are generally based on theoretical and methodological assumptions. The answers to their questions are in turn in part a reflection of these assumptions and methods, so whenever we read an explanation for a crime we should ask ourselves what assumptions underlie the explanation, and whether they make sense.

 Refer back to the activity on missing people (pp. 38–9). Now that you have read the section on phenomenological approaches to suicide, would you change any of your definitions, hypotheses and methods? If so, how? What does this tell us (if anything) about the relationship between theorising and methodology?

Summary

In this chapter we have explored a range of approaches that claim there is a consensus of beliefs and values around which society coheres. Crimes are generally viewed as activities that break this consensus and consequently threaten the continuing stability and existence of society. However, there is a twist in the tail: Durkheim argued that there is such a thing as an acceptable level of crime – indeed, some level of crime is actually good for society.

Functionalists explain individuals' motivations to commit crime in terms of their commitment to society, although very different explanations have been put forward within this framework. One approach, associated with Merton, is that people commit crime because they are unable to achieve the goals of society legally. On the other hand, Hirschi claims that people perform criminal acts because they are simply not committed to society.

We also examined explanations for suicide – partially because suicide is an interesting and complex form of deviance which functionalists have made a special study of, but also because the sociological debates surrounding suicide illustrate some of the deep methodological and theoretical divisions within the sociology of crime.

Readings

Could it happen to you?

Last week Julia Somerville, the television news-reader, was questioned by police along with her boyfriend, Jeremy Dixon, the eminent architect, about allegedly pornographic pictures of her seven-year-old daughter, reportedly taking a bath. Ms Somerville and her partner have strenuously denied any wrongdoing, but the case has left every parent casting an eye over their own family album. If the pictures they contain are taken out of context, just how far might they be misunderstood? Where does decency end and indecency start in a society that is so anxious about the protection of its children, and who, ultimately, is the moral arbiter of taste? To a healthy family, the image of a child bathing or frolicking naked, or taking a bath with a parent, is a happy memento of growing up. But to the shop assistant in Boots the Chemist, where Mr Dixon picked up his photographs, or a policeman, or anyone outside the family, it may assume an entirely new meaning.

Two years ago, the photographer Corrine Day was vilified for a *Vogue* underwear fashion shoot featuring superwaif model Kate Moss looking childishly vulnerable. And last season's 'baby-doll' catwalk look again raised fears about the blurring of boundaries between good and bad taste.

If the world's fashion and art worlds cannot decide what constitutes an appropriate image of a youngster, we should perhaps not be surprised when a film processor at Boots finds himself in a dilemma. And it is an issue that the law has still to resolve satisfactorily. In 1988 the Home Office amended the law to make possession of photographs of child pornography a crime which carried a fine, in the belief that 'the shame of conviction for this new offence could be a greater punishment,' according to John Patten, then Home Office Minister.

Source: Rebecca Fowler and Decca Aitkenhead, 'Julia's pictures: could it happen to you?', *Independent*, 6 November 1995

The issue of sexuality and children has emerged as a very topical subject in the 1990s.

Investigations have revealed that child sexual abuse is much more common than had been believed. Behaviour once considered harmless may now be seen as more sinister. Social change is undoubtedly occurring, but no clear standards have yet emerged on the correct treatment of children.

1 Explain the significance of the above article according to the Durkheimian approach.

2 Does a clear message emerge from the article?

3 What implications, if any, does this have for the relationship between parents and children?

Examination Question

Critically examine the contribution of studies of suicide to a sociological understanding of deviance in society.

AEB, Summer 1994

Bibliography

Atkinson, J.M. (1971) 'Social reactions to suicide: the role of coroners' definitions' in Cohen, S. (ed.) *Images of Deviance*, Harmondsworth: Penguin

Box, S. (1983) *Power, Crime and Mystification*, London: Tavistock

Douglas, J.D. (1967) *The Social Meaning of Suicide*, Princeton, NJ: Princeton University Press

Durkheim, E. (1952/1897) *Suicide: A Study in Sociology*, London: Routledge

Erikson, K.J. (1966) *Wayward Puritans*, New York: Wiley

Hirschi, T. (1969) *The Causes of Delinquency*, Berkeley, CA: University of California Press

Kornhauser, W. (1959) *The Politics of Mass Society*, New York: Free Press

Lea, J. and Young, J. (1984) *What Is to Be Done about Law and Order?* Harmondsworth: Penguin

Martens, P.L. (1993) 'An Ecological model of socialization in explaining offending' reproduced in Bottoms, A.E. (1994) 'Environmental Criminology' in Maguire, M., Morgan, R., Reiner, R. *The Oxford Handbook of Criminology*, Oxford: Oxford University Press

Merton, R. (1938) 'Social structure and anomie', *American Sociological Review*, Vol 3, 672–682

Taylor, S. (1990) 'Beyond Durkheim: sociology and suicide', *Social Studies Review*

Williams, J. (1996) 'Suicide is killing us', *Sociology Review*, Vol 5, No 4

3 Subcultures, places and values

In this chapter several sociological explanations for criminal behaviour will be explored. These have had considerable importance in sociology. The actual explanations may appear to vary quite significantly, apparently having little in common. However, they are grouped together because they all stress the way that *groups of people create values* which both reflect their circumstances and influence their own behaviour. The sets of values or subcultures thus created are seen as the major influence in causing people to commit crime.

First, we will look at the original *ecological theories*. These stress the importance of studying particular areas of cities to uncover the values generated in those neighbourhoods which motivate people to commit crime.

Next, we will move on to *subcultural theories*, which lay greater stress on the idea that distinctive values justify crime, but these need not necessarily be generated in particular neighbourhoods. These theories are American in origin, so first we will need to examine the theories and then see how they have been applied in Britain.

This will lead us into a discussion of later *positivistic* versions of subcultural theory.

Finally we will look at contemporary accounts of crime and deviance which derive directly from these earlier studies. In particular we will examine recent attempts to blend subcultural and ecological approaches into what are often termed *environmental* theories of crime.

Figure 3.1 Guidelines: subcultural and ecological approaches

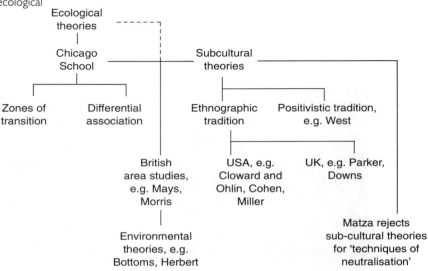

Ecological theories of crime

An enduring theme in sociological writing about crime has been the corrupting effect of city life. This view had developed particularly strongly in Europe during the nineteenth century, when cities were expanding rapidly. Writers such as Durkheim and Tönnies had stressed the breakdown of the community, as this form of social interaction was altered under the twin pressures of urbanisation and industrialisation. People felt less 'bonded' to others and were more likely to look after their own selfish interests at the expense of others.

The Chicago School

In the USA, urbanisation occurred later than in Europe and also took a different form in that cities developed as a result of massive waves of immigrants from Europe. Chicago had one of the biggest immigrant populations, rising from 10,000 in 1860 to 2,000,000 only fifty years later. It is not surprising, therefore, that the original urban studies were carried out by sociologists at the University of Chicago between 1914 and 1940. The work at Chicago University changed considerably over time, and one can distinguish a number of stages:

- the biological analogy
- social disorganisation
- cultural transmission
- differential association.

The biological analogy

Initially, sociologists such as Robert Park were strongly influenced by ideas of 'natural selection' and the 'struggle for space' – biologically based concepts drawn from versions of the Darwinian theory of evolution. Park (1936) argued that cities were characterised by a 'biotic balance' in which existing communities were disturbed by new waves of immigration, creating conflict out of which a new form of community emerged to replace the original one. The struggle for space was linked to this process. Individuals compete for the best habitats and those who lose out have to move into (or remain in) the 'area of minimum choice', that is, the city slums.

Alongside this biologically based approach the Chicago School was influenced by 'symbolic interactionism', a sociological perspective which stressed the importance of examining social phenomena through the perspective of those involved. Rather than explaining behaviour totally from 'outside', the Chicago sociologists believed it was necessary to try to get into the minds of the people under study, to understand exactly why they were motivated to behave in the ways they did. Therefore they conducted detailed studies of life in the slums, endeavouring to portray how the individuals themselves saw life.

Thus Chicago sociology was characterised by two quite distinct elements:

- the *biological* approach, stressing 'natural' processes of struggle and domination

- the *sociological* approach, stressing the generation of meaning and culture by individuals through their interaction.

Social disorganisation

Park's work gave rise to the writing of Shaw and McKay, who claimed that Chicago (like other large cities) was divided into distinctive 'zones':

- *Zone 1*: the central business district. This had very few occupants but was the hub of commerce and banking during the day.

- *Zone 2*: 'the interstitial zone' (or 'zone of transition'). This was once an area of some considerable affluence, but had decayed and was characterised by multi-occupation use. This was the cheapest zone for housing, so new immigrants settled here first.

- *Zone 3*: the respectable working-class district. This was where the 'solid' working class lived.

- *Zone 4*: suburbia. Here were the pleasanter middle-class districts further out of town.

- *Zone 5*: the outer areas on the fringe of the city where the well-off lived.

Shaw and McKay suggested that as each successive wave of immigrants arrived in the city they were forced into the cheapest and least desirable zone – that is, the zone of transition. As they settled and some were successful, they moved outwards, while the less successful remained. The places of those who had moved on were taken by new waves of immigrants, and so the process started again.

Figure 3.2 Delinquency
rates in relation to city
zones in Chicago

Source: Shaw and
McKay (1942)

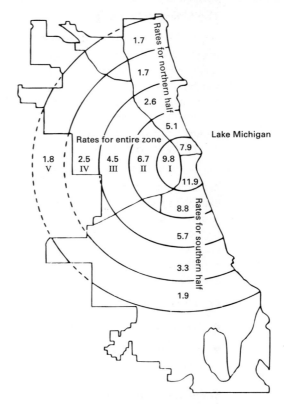

When they examined the official crime rates for the city, Shaw and McKay noted that there were quite distinct patterns of crime, with Zone 2 showing far higher rates than other residential parts of the city. This was not particularly surprising; the interesting thing was that the relative crime rates remained similar over a long period time, even though the immigrant groups inhabiting Zone 2 had changed. Each group which successively moved into the zone – Poles, Irish, etc. – had similarly high rates of crime. Therefore the crime rate could not be explained in terms of the supposedly natural criminal instincts of, for example, Italians.

Shaw and McKay's explanation was that the high population turnover produced a state of 'social disorganisation', defined by two other writers of the Chicago School (Thomas and Znaniecki) as 'the decrease of the influence of existing social rules of behavior upon individual members of the group'. By this they seem to have meant that the informal mechanisms of social control that normally hold people back from deviant behaviour were weak or absent, and this 'released' people to commit criminal acts. These informal, restraining mechanisms include such things as public opinion, gossip and neighbourhood organisations.

The result of social disorganisation was that such behaviours as prostitution, alcoholism and crime flourished. This analysis has some definite echoes of Durkheim's ideas.

However, there was a degree of circularity in Shaw and McKay's analysis in that crime and violence, for example, were seen both as *consequences* of social disorganisation and as *evidence* of it.

Cultural transmission

The next shift in the Chicago approach came in the later writings of Shaw and McKay, further developed by Sutherland (see Sutherland and Cressey 1954). Shaw and McKay radically altered the meaning of 'social disorganisation' to denote a distinctive (but coherent) set of values which provided alternative values to those of the mainstream society. This is quite distinct from earlier versions of social disorganisation which stressed the lack of coherent values. This new version of social disorganisation became known as the *cultural transmission* theory of delinquency, and was clearly the starting point for subcultural theory.

According to cultural transmission theory, in the most socially disorganised and poorest zones of the city certain forms of crime have become the cultural norm, transmitted from one generation to the next as part of the normal socialisation pattern. Successful criminals provide role models for the young, demonstrating both the normality of criminal behaviour and the possibility that crime may pay.

Differential association

Although the theories of the Chicago School had considerable influence, they were criticised at the time for being too vague. In an effort to tighten up the reasoning, Sutherland introduced the concept of *differential association*. This states that a person is likely to become criminal if he or she receives an 'excess of definitions favorable to violation of law over definitions unfavorable to violation of law'. Furthermore, such definitions may vary in 'frequency, duration, priority, and intensity'. Sutherland meant that if people are surrounded by others who support law-breaking they are likely to do the same themselves.

The significant variables in the model are the following:

- *frequency*: the number of times the definitions occur

- *duration*: over what period of time

- *priority*: e.g. at what stage in life – the assumption being that childhood socialisation is more important than later experience

- *intensity*: notably the prestige of the person making the definition.

Sutherland seems to be suggesting that some formula could be arrived at to work out exactly the combination of variables that would make a person commit a crime, yet this is clearly untestable. All the model shows is that those who commit crime have received the appropriate combination of variables, and those who do not have not. No predictions can be made.

 Can the Chicago-style ecological model be applied to your local town or city? Is it true to say there are distinctive zones? Does a 'zone of transition' exist?
   Contact your local police authority and ask them if there are any problem areas in town. They will keep statistics breaking down crimes by area. What do these indicate? Can you find any patterns?
   What explanations can these statistics offer for patterns of crime?

British area studies

Chicago sociology has been immensely influential in a host of ways. One of these was to stimulate British 'area' studies. However, apart from the very early studies such as J.B. Mays's work in Liverpool, the theoretical orientation of the British studies moved steadily away from the concerns of the Chicago School.

Cultural transmission

Mays (1954) found strong evidence to support many of Shaw and McKay's findings. After interviewing boys (note, no females) from the Liverpool University Settlement Project, he concluded that the area possessed a particular culture in which shoplifting, theft and vandalism were accepted as normal by the local people. Mays also found the answer to a riddle that had puzzled sociologists for some time: Why did only some of the people brought up in 'criminal neighbourhoods' turn to crime? Mays discovered that virtually all the local boys committed some kind of petty crime, but only some were caught.

Local authority housing policies

T.P. Morris (1957) conducted a study of Croydon from which he drew rather different conclusions. He also found that there were small 'pockets' of high delinquency rates, but there was no evidence that the people in areas of high delinquency held a coherent set of values which was any different from that of mainstream society. Morris suggested that a key factor in the concentration of delinquents in certain areas was the local council's policy of housing 'problem families' together. These council estates also had the lowest rents, so the poorest tended to choose them. The outcome was that those most likely to become delinquent anyway were collected together.

Housing classes

Other researchers influenced by Morris's study rejected the idea propounded by the Chicago sociologists that bad housing partially caused delinquency. Instead British researchers focused their attention on the fact that there were housing classes in British cities: those at the top used their greater power and economic muscle to obtain the best housing stock in the most pleasant areas, while the least powerful and the poorest ended up with the worst housing. It was therefore predictable that crime rates would be higher in the worst areas of the cities. The best example of this sort of research – though not directly in the field of criminology – was that of Rex and Moore (1967), who showed how immigrants were trapped in the poorest inner-city areas because they lost out in the competition between housing classes.

Subcultural theories

Chicago sociologists directed attention towards the *motivations* of delinquents. They put forward the novel idea, still rejected by many, that there is nothing 'wrong' with delinquents – they simply perceive the world in a different way and act accordingly. Delinquents have a distinct set of values which guide their behaviour in the same way that you and I are guided by our more conventional ideas. A distinctive set of values within the main culture of society is known as a subculture.

Status frustration

The first explicit use of the concept of subculture is found in the work of Albert Cohen (1955). Cohen was puzzled by the fact that most delinquent acts were not motivated by economic ends. Vandalism or graffiti spraying, for example, bring no economic benefit to the perpetrator. His answer was that most delinquents are motivated by *status deprivation*, meaning that they feel they are looked down upon by the rest of society and denied any status. They therefore develop a distinct set of values which provides them with alternative ways of gaining status, and may lead them into delinquency.

Those who are most likely to commit deviant acts are generally found in the lower streams of schools, living in deprived areas and having the worst chances in the job market. The effects of school are the most profound influence on delinquents, according to Cohen, because for adolescents the primary agency awarding (and denying) status is school. Those in the top streams are rewarded and feel important, while those in the lowest streams are aware that they are looked upon as the most stupid and the least interesting, with little to offer teachers or society. Aware that they are branded failures by society in general, lower stream boys (note that Cohen did not even discuss girls!) develop their own subculture with its own values. The subculture is based on a deliberate reversal of accepted forms of behaviour, so actions such as stealing, rudeness and violence that are condemned in the wider society are elevated to a central position in the boys' subculture. The subculture, it should be noted, is a *collective* response to status denial.

For the lower stream boys, the subculture has two uses. First, it creates an alternative set of values against which they can measure their behaviour and thus compete for status among their peers. Second, it provides a means of striking back at society – in Cohen's words, 'there is a kind of malice apparent, an enjoyment of the discomfiture of others'. Petty theft and vandalism, for example, provide delinquents with a measure of revenge.

Cohen therefore argued that delinquents are no different from other adolescents in seeking status; they are in fact resolving the need to gain status through their delinquent acts.

 Research Cohen's argument by questioning lower and higher stream school students about their attitudes to school and their feelings about teachers and other pupils. Stephen Ball's Beachside Comprehensive *(1981) is an example of this form of research.*

Illegitimate opportunity structure

An attempt to link Merton's concept of anomie with subcultural theory was made by Cloward and Ohlin (1961). Merton had suggested that individuals turn to crime, drug addiction and violence when society provides too few opportunities to attain socially approved goals by legal means. However, Cloward and Ohlin felt that Merton had ignored the existence of an *illegitimate opportunity structure*, running parallel to the legal one and operating on three levels:

● criminal subculture

● conflict subculture

● retreatist subculture.

The *criminal opportunity structure* exists when the following conditions hold. First, there is a stable, cohesive working-class community with contacts in both the mainstream legal community and the illegal one. This enables stolen goods to be sold through the wider community, for example. Second, there are successful role models – people from the local community who have done well from crime, achieving a high standard of living from their illegal activities. There needs to be a career structure for aspiring criminals, allowing movement by age group through the various career grades. For example, a youth may start at about ten by stealing car aerials, then move on to stealing radios at fourteen and entire cars at seventeen, before entering the world of organised crime in his early twenties. This form of subculture thus provides working-class males with an alternative to the legitimate job market.

In the *conflict subculture*, if the conditions just mentioned are absent and there is no career in crime available to young males, they may express their frustration at certain failure in both the legitimate and illegitimate opportunity structures by turning to violence. This is the cause of the gang warfare which appears in the slum areas of cities like New York and Los Angeles.

The *retreatist subculture* is the final level of the illegal opportunity structure. Here can be found the double failures, who cannot make it through crime or violence. They 'retreat' into drugs and alcoholism, paying for their addictions through petty theft, shoplifting and prostitution.

This approach has been criticised for making the same assumption as Merton – that everyone seeks the same goal of financial success. Instead, it is argued that people have a wide variety of goals, so failure cannot simply be explained in terms of lack of financial success. A second major problem with the illegitimate opportunity argument is that there is no evidence to support the idea of subcultures as described by

Cloward and Ohlin. As we shall see later (p. 64), coherent subcultures like these do not appear to exist in Britain.

Delinquency as the consequence of normal working-class values

Unlike Cohen, Cloward and Ohlin, who suggested that crime is the result of distinctive subcultures which provide alternative guidelines to action from the mainstream culture, Walter B. Miller (1962) proposed that there are six focal concerns of working-class culture which can lead working-class males into crime. According to this view, crime is an extension of normal working-class values, not a distinctive set of alternative values The six focal concerns are as follows:

- *Trouble*: Young working-class men accept that life involves violence, and they will not run away from fights.

- *Toughness*: It is believed that males ought to demonstrate the qualities of 'manliness' – being able to drink, womanise, play sport, etc.

- *Smartness*: This involves 'looking good' and being 'sharp'.

- *Excitement*: Young working-class men are always on the look-out for 'fun' and enjoyment.

- *Fate*: They believe there is little that can be done about their lives – whatever will be, will be.

- *Autonomy*: Although they can do little about the general conditions of their lives, they do not want anybody to 'push them around', so they resent authority as embodied in the form of the police or a boss.

Howard Parker's study of a group of Liverpool adolescents (*View from the Boys*, 1974) illustrates these ideas. The 'boys' (as they call themselves) go out for a night out. They are not looking for trouble (fights), but should anyone hint that they are not tough or they cannot take their drinks 'like men', a fight ensues. On these nights out, the boys' ability to pick up girls often depends on how they look, and their wit and repartee (smartness). The essence of a good night out is to have 'a laff' (excitement); when they go out they have no idea what is going to happen (fate), but they do not want to be pushed around by 'bouncers' or policemen (autonomy).

One of the problems with this analysis of crime is that it stresses these are *working-class values*, but a moment's reflection shows that these values are distributed throughout society and are as likely to be found among the middle-class members of a rugby team as among the working-class 'boys'.

 Do these focal concerns exist and, if so, who holds them (class, ethnic, gender, age differences)? In particular, do females have these focal concerns?
Devise a set of questions which will provide 'indicators' to measure them.
Is there any way of comparing behaviour against the answers you obtain? Is this important?

Delinquency and ordinary behaviour

Most subcultural approaches to deviance had two clear characteristics: they emphasised the idea of subcultures as sets of values distinct from those held by the majority of the population; and they maintained that delinquents were propelled into their actions by subcultural forces stronger than themselves, a view known as *determinism*. Yet research in Britain has rarely found any of the elusive ingredients of the distinctive subculture – indeed, it has merely shown how *ordinary* delinquents are.

David Matza (1964) rejected both these underlying assumptions. He claimed that delinquents are similar to everyone else in their values and voice similar feelings of outrage about crime in general as the majority of society. When they are caught, they express feelings of remorse and offer justifications for their acts.

Subterranean values

The first point Matza made is that we all hold two levels of values. The values that guide us most of the time are the respectable, conventional ones, in which we play the good roles of father, daughter, teacher, etc.; however, there are occasions when underlying (subterranean) values of sexuality, greed and aggressiveness emerge. The most obvious example is the Christmas party, when the hidden lusts in the office (or college) emerge for one drunken afternoon – and then life returns to normal on the next working day! These subterranean values are generally controlled, but all of us hold them and occasionally we give vent to them. Matza suggested that delinquents are simply more likely than most of us to behave according to subterranean values in 'inappropriate' situations.

 Matza is rather vague about the content of these subterranean values. Can you suggest what they may consist of?

Techniques of neutralisation

If delinquents are as much committed to conventional values as anyone else and, furthermore, express condemnation of crimes similar to the ones they themselves commit, why do they commit them at all? Matza suggested that delinquents justify their own crimes as exceptions to the general rule. 'Yes, what I did is wrong, but ...' Matza identified five such justifications or techniques of *neutralisation*:

- *Denial of responsibility*: It is not the culprit's fault — something made him or her do it; for example, 'I was drunk.'

- *Denial of victim*: The crime in general is wrong, but the victim in this case deserved it; for example, 'I hate Pakis.'

- *Denial of injury*: The victim is supposed not to be harmed by the crime; for example, 'They can afford it.'

- *Condemnation of condemners*: This is where delinquents argue that their accusers are no different than themselves; for example, 'Yeah, I was driving when drunk, but so does everybody else — even you.'

- *Appeal to higher loyalties*: The delinquent claims that he or she had to do it because of some general 'moral' standard; for example, 'I couldn't leave my mates (during a fight).'

Techniques of neutralisation provide justifications for why the general rules can be broken.

Do people really use techniques of neutralisation? Ask a sample of students in your institution whether they have done anything in the last month that was perhaps illegal or immoral. Alternatively you can ask them if they have done anything that really embarrasses them. Assure them that you do not want to know what it was, but ask them why they did it. Do their answers fit any of the five techniques suggested by Matza?

Drift

The final element in Matza's explanation for delinquency is *drift*. If we all hold subterranean values, and we could all justify our actions if necessary, why is it that only some young people commit crime? Matza suggests that youth is a period in 'no man's land', not yet adult but no longer a child. Youths feel that they lack any control over their own lives, and they long to gain some power over their destiny. This period of drift loosens the adolescent from the constraining bonds of society (note that the bonds are *loosened*, no more), so he or she is more susceptible to suggestions of deviant acts by the peer group. Finally, in an effort to show that they have control over their lives, youths may commit a delinquent act. However, there is no deviant career; the youth is not committed in any way to a life of crime, and he or she tends to drift out of crime again, for instance when a decent job opportunity presents itself.

The concept of drift is unsatisfactory in at least one respect. If a youth wishes to gain control over his or her destiny, why commit a delinquent act? Surely any act would do.

A second problem with Matza's theory is that there is no attempt to place delinquency within a wider framework (or *structural location*) of economic and social circumstances that drive male working-class youth into greater levels of delinquency than anyone else.

Is it possible to 'operationalise' Matza's concept of 'drift'? If so, how would you do it? If you think it is not possible, explain your reasons and then discuss whether the theory is of any use if it is untestable. Is his theory applicable to females?

British subcultural studies

Attempts to uncover subcultures were made in Britain as well as the USA, although here the perspective always remained entangled with the concept of area studies. The earlier work of J.B. Mays, in particular, could well be seen as the study of subcultures, since he stressed the power of the family and peer group in socialising young people into deviant attitudes. However, few studies supported Mays's conviction that there existed distinctive subcultures predisposing certain working-class children to commit crime.

Looking for fun?

D. Willmott (1966) studied adolescent males in a working-class district of London and could find little evidence of a delinquent subculture. He suggested instead that there were two explanations for the delinquency of working-class youths.

First, the youths in his study had generally boring lives, with uninteresting, dead-end jobs. In order to compensate for this, they would be on the look-out for fun and excitement. This sometimes led them into law-breaking activities – but these were rarely planned, nor were they motivated by economic reward.

Hanging around

Second, working-class youths were far more visible than middle-class youth. Their small homes and lack of private space meant that 'hanging around' on street corners or in cafés was the only possibility if they wanted to meet together. This brought their 'horseplay' to the attention of passers-by and, more importantly, the police. Minor infractions of the law were more likely to be punished, simply because they were under police observation.

Dissociation

David Downes (1966) conducted a thorough study of East London adolescents, and tested the American subcultural theories. There was no evidence to support the existence of status frustration, or of the 'illegitimate opportunity structure' of Cloward and Ohlin. Downes did find strong evidence to support the insights of Matza, however.

The lives of the working-class adolescents whom Downes studied were characterised by dissociation from work and aspirations for a career. Employment was merely a means of obtaining money; these young people neither hoped for, nor received, satisfaction from their employment. However, Downes found that they showed no resentment about their low school status (as Cohen would have predicted) or their lack of employment opportunities (contrary to Cloward and Ohlin). The lack of satisfaction at work and school led the youths to stress what Downes termed 'leisure values', which were very similar to Matza's 'subterranean values', and indeed to the search for a 'good time' which is current throughout British culture. The youths in Downes's study placed much greater stress on leisure values than middle-class youths tended to do precisely because of their relative lack of satisfaction at school and work. Thus they were more disposed to commit petty acts of crime in the process of enjoying themselves; however they had no commitment to deviant values.

The end of conventional subcultural theory

Downes's study sounded the death knell for the conventional subcultural/ecological approach. Two subsequent studies – by James Patrick and Howard Parker – could be said to follow the subcultural approach, but they had already moved a long way from its starting point and in fact can be taken to indicate how subcultural studies split into positivistic and Marxist strands.

In an exciting study of street gangs in Glasgow, Patrick (1973) concluded that there were indeed quite tightly organised gangs, formed around a particularly strong psychotic leader who maintained discipline. However, this was such a different picture from the one presented in other subcultural studies that it seems this form of gang was peculiar to Glasgow.

The second study was Parker's excellent *View from the Boys*, mentioned above. The group of delinquent youths whom Parker studied made their living by stealing 'catseyes' (car radios). He found little evidence to support any of the conventional theories and instead suggested that a structural Marxist analysis was needed to understand the situation and the views expressed by the 'boys' in his study.

Marxist approaches have themselves split into two groupings – what Jock Young refers to as 'left realism' and 'left idealism'. We examine these very important divisions in Chapters 4 and 5.

Positivist approaches

Positivism is the theoretical method which copies, in a modified form, the methodology of the natural sciences. In criminology the method involves comparing the deviant with the normal person and searching for the differences between them. These differences are then assumed to have caused the delinquency.

It could be argued that much of the subcultural theory we have looked at so far implicitly follows this methodology. However, one strand of British sociology from the late 1950s onwards *explicitly* followed this path. The studies which adopted this approach found that no single variable could be isolated to explain crime, but that there was a host of shifting variables which seemed to differ with each youth or group of youths, as noted by Mays (1972):

'It may be that they were brought up without proper control and supervision, that they were allowed to mix with street corner groups and conformed to the partially delinquent norms of their associates. It may be that they found themselves depressed by continued experiences of failure at school and elsewhere and developed chip-on-shoulder attitudes which made them resentful of authority and ... ready to indulge in hooliganism against the respectable law-abiding society ... It could also arise from a combination of these processes.'

This therefore came to be known as the *multi-causal approach*. Probably the best-known work in this tradition was undertaken by West and Farrington (1973) of the Cambridge School of Criminology. In a large-scale study of 411 working-class boys from the ages of eight to nineteen they isolated the following five factors as being particularly associated with delinquency:

- low family income
- large family size
- comparatively low intelligence
- having a parent with a criminal record
- having parents considered to be unsatisfactory in rearing children.

As the boys moved through their teens, the authors also noted that males with the backgrounds identified above were more likely to show evidence of 'aggression, unstable work records, anti-establishment attitudes, driving after heavy drinking, heavy gambling, drug use, involvement in anti-social groups, sexual activity, immoderate smoking, hanging about and being tattooed'.

This form of research, which seeks to establish statistical links between social status and crime, was subsequently elaborated to look more closely at causes, as we will see in the next section.

In order to prove that delinquents really are different from their fellows, two things must be studied from an early age to show that the characteristics of the delinquent minority are present before they appear in the courts, and so cannot be due to the baleful effects of police and court labelling ...

The study was based on 411 boys. They represented an unselected sample of local schoolboys living in a traditional working-class area of London. They were intensively studied from eight to ten years old, and have been monitored up to the age of nineteen. The early information about the boys and their backgrounds has been used to find out the

distinguishing characteristics of those who later became juvenile delinquents. A boy was counted an official delinquent if he acquired an entry into the Criminal Record Office.

In effect one-fifth of the boys became juvenile delinquents … The delinquents were always the least favoured group. For example, those more likely to become delinquents were the unpopular boys rather than the popular ones: those with high 'neuroticism' scores, rather than low; those from broken homes rather than those from intact homes; those with nervous mothers rather than those with healthy mothers; and those born illegitimate rather than those born to married parents. This confirmed that delinquents do, in fact, differ from, and are in many ways inferior to or less fortunate than, their non-delinquent schoolfellows.

… we judged five factors to have special importance: low family income, large family, comparatively low intelligence, having a parent with a criminal record, and having parents considered to be unsatisfactory in rearing children … the chances of a boy having more than one conviction as a juvenile were more than six times greater if three or more of those adverse factors were present …

In order to produce a measure of delinquent behaviour independent of official records, the boys were given a questionnaire about their own behaviour … As far as could be judged boys tended to respond surprisingly frankly and truthfully to this test ... the overlap between the boys identified as delinquent by self-report and the official delinquents was very great: forty-one out of the eighty self-reported delinquents were among the eighty-four official delinquents. The thirty-nine boys with high self-report scores but no juvenile convictions were separately examined. A disproportionately large number of these had had contacts with the police as juveniles or had got an official conviction record as young adults …

However, they did not share to any great extent many of the characteristics of official delinquents. For instance, they did not come from low-income families or tend to have low intelligence. In their case it seemed probably that official prosecutions were avoided or delayed because of their background characteristics.

Source: West (1977)

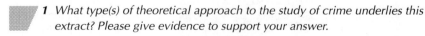

1 What type(s) of theoretical approach to the study of crime underlies this extract? Please give evidence to support your answer.

2 What approach is West arguing against?

3 *What sort of methodology was used in the survey?*

4 *What is a self-report test? In what circumstances are such tests generally used?*

5 *Briefly summarise West's key arguments.*

6 *On reading this extract, it seemed to me there was a contradiction, or at least a weakness, in the central argument that emerges in the last paragraph. Do you see a problem? If so, explain what it is.*

Environmental theories

Traditional subcultural theories and ecological approaches were overtaken in the 1970s by interactionist theories and by varieties of Marxism. For most sociologists the older theories were interesting, but part of the history of sociology rather than relevant to contemporary problems. However, during the 1980s and 1990s the traditional approaches clawed themselves back into business. Indeed there is a very good case for saying that they have been more influential on recent government thinking than any other approach.

There has recently been a concerted effort by some criminologists to bring back issues of *place* into our understanding of crime, which in turn reflects increasing attempts to make sociological theorising more relevant to policy. In the case of criminology the Home Office has been particularly interested in devising strategies to combat street crime and burglaries.

Space is important because the sorts of crimes that worry most 'ordinary' people – theft and assaults outside the home, and burglary within it – do not occur equally throughout Britain, but show much greater frequency in some places than others. Sociologists have therefore begun again to ask about two main factors:

● the dynamics of the communities from which offenders come

● why they are more likely to commit crime in certain places rather than others, and choose certain targets.

These two concerns, taken together, are often seen as a re-emergence of a form of ecological approach, renamed the *environmental approach*.

The dynamics of communities

There is no doubt that there are very great differences in the levels of crime committed in different parts of cities. The obvious explanation is that different crime levels are correlated with differences in social class – with lower-class areas more likely to have high crime rates because of social problems.

Yet studies of Sheffield by A.E. Bottoms (1976, 1989) and of Stockholm by Wikstrom (1991) appeared to demonstrate that there were distinctive differences in rates of offending according to different types of housing areas, even where the areas had identical social class compositions. This implies that social class could not be the only key factor.

Wikstrom distinguished between areas characterised by owner-occupied properties, private rented properties and not-for-profit rented properties (such as 'council' housing or housing association properties). The areas compared were similar in social class terms (income, job types, educational levels, etc.), but demonstrated quite different levels of offending.

Tipping

Bottoms's studies went even further and compared similar housing developments (two low-rise local authority estates) which demonstrated very different levels of offending. The worse of the two estates, Gardenia, showed a 300 per cent higher number of offenders and a 350 per cent higher level of crimes than Stonewall. Bottoms pointed out that both housing areas were built at the same time, were only separated by a bypass and were originally regarded as being 'good', crime-free areas. He explained the differences by arguing that, for various reasons, Gardenia came to be seen as less desirable, which in turn had a series of negative consequences. The term he used for this process was 'tipping'.

Once Gardenia had been 'tipped', those who were attracted to living there or who were housed there tended to be in severe housing need and often already had relatives there. In particular, Bottoms suggested that if there are already 'problem' families living in a 'tipped' area, their relatives are more likely to be 'problems' too.

Further factors involved in 'tipping' which widened the differences between the two areas were the existence of a 'mild' criminal subculture; different secondary schools; and increasingly different 'parental and peer socialisation processes". Here the debt to earlier ecological and subcultural criminology becomes evident, as does a close affinity with the positivistic approaches described in the previous section.

In further studies, Bottoms examined other low socio-economic areas of Sheffield, including an area of high-rise developments and another of privately rented accommodation. Both areas were characterised by high levels of crime, but interestingly they appeared to have different sorts of crime and the people exhibited different attitudes. So *types* of crime as well as the *extent* of crime can be related to area.

Figure 3.3 The process of tipping

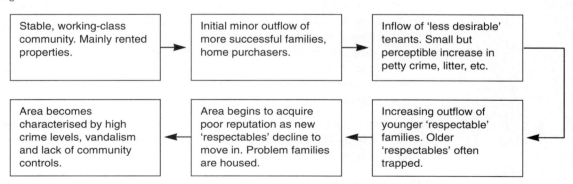

W.G. Skogan (1986) also explored the concept of tipping. He suggested that in any neighbourhood the social fabric is held together by informal social control: people do not litter the streets because they are aware of the disapproval of others, and similar concerns curb vandalism and petty crime, so it is not necessarily the law that prevents crime. However, if the informal social control processes break down, 'disorder' grows.

Disorder consists of two elements, according to Skogan – physical deterioration, such as litter, abandoned buildings and poorly kept parks, and *social* disorder, such as public drinking or drug usage, abusive language and low standards of behaviour. Disorder has three consequences:

● It undermines the mechanisms by which communities exercise control, so people keep more to themselves, they are less likely to be concerned about their neighbours, and they feel fewer bonds to other people.

● Disorder leads to concerns over neighbourhood safety and might even lead to crime itself. People start to believe there is a great deal of crime and that it is dangerous to go out. If people avoid going out at night it may become easier to commit street crime.

● Disorder undermines the stability of the housing market, erodes residential satisfaction and leads people to fear for the safety of their children. 'Respectable' people move out of the area if they can, and property values fall. Vacant properties may then be bought by professional landlords for rent – often to those on housing benefit This speeds up the process of change.

The process of tipping is not automatic, and a strong neighbourhood organisation can help prevent the breakdown of an area. An example can be found in Chicago itself. The area of Hyde Park-Kenwood around the University of Chicago began to tip, and there was an increase in crime levels. The university encouraged its staff to move there by providing cheap loans, introducing private policing, and pressurising government to provide urban renewal funding and invest in good public transport. The result has been an area in which people express high levels of satisfaction and feel safe. It should be noted, however, that even though residents subjectively feel safe, the actual levels of crime have remained higher than average for the city.

In most towns or cities there is an area with a 'reputation'. It may be where you live!

● *Approach the local community centre, if there is one (run by either the local authority or the church). Interview a selection of older people about the changes that have taken place.*
● *Approach two local schools and ask if you can interview older students about their views on their local community and whether they think 'their' area has an undeserved reputation.*
● *Approach the local councillors and ask them their views.*

When you have completed these surveys, what conclusions do you draw about the concept of tipping? In particular, is it the people who have changed, or the circumstances they live in?

Where are crimes committed?

The early Chicago theorists had stressed that crimes were committed in the central business districts by people coming in from the surrounding zones. The geographical proximity of the disorganised zone to the business district made this connection seem obvious. However, research in Britain and other US cities showed very limited support for the notion of zones or concentric circles. The major reason for this was the importance of public housing projects which created large developments outside city centres.

The large number of local and national crime surveys (such as the British Crime Survey discussed in Chapter 10) also showed that patterns of crime were complex:

> While there is indeed still something of a clustering of high offender rate areas around the central business district, the data overall show 'no tidy zonal model ... [but] areas with high and low offender residence rates were distributed throughout the city in apparently haphazard fashion' (Hope and Hough 1988).

It seems that two overlapping factors must be taken into account in understanding where crime occurs: *routine activity* and *opportunity*.

Routine activities

Sociologists who stress routine activity take issue with the original argument of Chicago theorists that crime is more likely to occur in certain *zones* than in others. They reject the notion of zones, but do acknowledge the importance of *space*. In essence their contention is quite simple: crime is committed in places through which potential criminals are most likely to move. The key is to examine the routine movements of those (usually young men) most likely to commit crime.

One example of this approach is the work of P.J. and P.L. Brantingham (1991), who have suggested that we all carry in our heads 'cognitive maps' of the towns and cities in which we live. Some parts of the city are extremely well known, while others are only vaguely familiar. For example, most of us know the areas where we live, where we study or work, and where we go for entertainment. We also know the roads which link these areas. We probably do not know residential areas where we have no acquaintances. The Brantinghams suggested that crimes are most likely to be committed where criminal opportunities intersect with cognitively known areas.

Figure 3.4 The Brantinghams' hypothetical model of the intersection of criminal opportunities with an offender's cognitive awareness space

Source: Brantingham and Brantingham (1991)

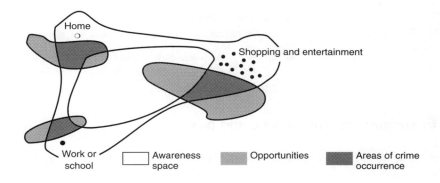

Figure 3.4 illustrates the work of Brantingham and Brantingham, who have related patterns of crime to criminals' patterns of movement. Construct a diagram of your own routine movements on a map of your town or city.

The conclusion we can draw from this is that crime occurs in areas which are familiar to criminals, not necessarily those which are the most lucrative for them. Within familiar areas, criminals choose (i) targets which are potentially lucrative, (ii) places where the perceived risk is low, and (iii) types of crime which they have the means to commit.

A US study by Rengert and Wasilchick (1985) confirmed the importance of routine activities, and succeeded in locating a high proportion of crimes committed by convicted burglars to within a short distance of their route from home to leisure activity, or home to workplace, and finally at or between home and 'known crime locations' (since it would appear that high levels of crime attract criminals). The exceptions to the rule were when burglaries occurred because an informant had told the burglar where to commit the crime.

Most interestingly, this study and earlier research conducted by Carter and Hill (1979) found that burglars tended to avoid particularly rich areas. It seems that social distance rather than geographical distance tends to protect the more affluent.

Opportunities

We can trace the origins of the concept of opportunities, in part at least, back to Cloward and Ohlin's three 'opportunity structures'. However, modern versions are more interested in physical opportunity than cultural ideas. Opportunity in the contemporary sense stresses such things as the opportunity for violent conflict between groups of young males in city centres on weekend evenings when the pubs and clubs close, or the failure to light city streets adequately, thereby providing a greater chance for street crime to take place unobserved.

Routine activities and opportunities combined

Returning to the point that crime can be less likely in affluent areas than in poorer areas, Carter and Hill (1979) have shown how opportunity and routine activities combine. They asked convicted burglars why they chose certain targets rather than others. Their results suggest that criminals make a distinction between 'tactical' and 'strategic' decisions:

- Tactical decisions concern specific opportunity factors such as the simplicity of the crime, perceived chances of success, the extent of the proceeds, and so on.

- Strategic decisions draw upon the cognitive map of an area that we referred to earlier. The important factors here are familiarity with the place, how at ease the criminal feels in the area, and so on.

Environment, subculture and power

In this chapter we have looked at detailed examinations of subculture and environment, but these have been considered as independent, isolated factors. David Herbert, a geographer, has suggested that these approaches could be incorporated in a more dynamic model, which could be linked to wider processes of power and the activities of the judicial system and the police.

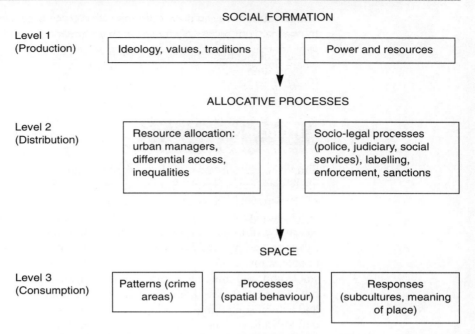

Figure 3.5 Herbert's model (1982)

Herbert's model, illustrated in Figure 3.5, suggests that both subculture and housing patterns are actually the final stage in a process which denies power to certain groups such as the working class and ethnic minorities. Herbert identifies three stages: (i) the production of values and beliefs which are (ii) directly related to differences in access to wealth and power, and below this (iii) the way in which groups obtain different resources. This stage in turn influences the patterns of crime.

 Arrange interviews with your local authority officials. Ask them about housing policy in the town when it comes to allocating new tenants to houses.
What happens if the tenants are involved in crime or cause problems locally? Do estates differ in the levels of social problems? What explanations can they offer?

Summary

In this chapter we have been examining two approaches to understanding and explaining crime which have developed from a shared background and continue to overlap even today.

Subcultural theories tend to stress the importance of the shared values and beliefs of groups of people (almost always males) who are able to justify their criminal activities. They generally live in similar areas or go to the same schools. The stress of subcultural approaches is almost always upon beliefs and values. One variation has been the rather rigid, positivist school of thought which tried to find personal and family factors statistically related to engagement in criminal activities.

The other main approach we explored in this chapter is ecological theory. Here the emphasis is more on the significance of 'space' or place. The arguments vary, but they all agree that without understanding the significance to people of living or travelling through certain places it is impossible to understand patterns of crime.

Subcultural theories, which were once the most popular among sociological theories and appeared to overshadow ecological theories, have in the last decade begun to be overtaken by newer, revamped theories of space.

Readings

Simplistic descriptions of high crime areas are not helpful. Large estates of low-income housing can combat crime, display little evidence of vandalism and graffiti, have a low population turnover, and generally be places where people want to live. Some estates are stable and well-integrated communities but are nevertheless high-crime areas and exhibit something like a local criminal subculture. The vulnerability of a particular neighbourhood to crime can therefore be difficult to predict.

The most important source of information about rates of victimisation is the British Crime Survey (BCS). The BCS groups neighbourhoods according to their demographic, employment, and housing characteristics in order to classify them in terms of crime-risk areas. The BCS identifies as high-risk areas mixed inner metropolitan or multi-racial areas with a mixture of poor, private rental housing and owner occupation: high-status, non-family areas with a mix of affluent houses and privately rented buildings in multiple occupation; and the poorest social housing estates, located either in inner cities or in the outer ring of conurbations.

Households in these areas run over twice the national average risk for burglary. Those in less well off council estates (including low-rise estates in industrial towns or inter-war estates housing older people and other social housing) are at medium risk in terms of overall crime rates, but similarly run higher than average risks of attempted burglary. According to Mayhew, crime patterns 'underline the great vulnerability of households in more urban and poorer areas – those where offenders are more likely to be more active. However, they may also reflect differences in target vulnerability. Properties in better off areas may be better secured, for instance – even though they may contain richer pickings' (Mayhew, 1993).

Although a number of factors are associated with the risk of burglary, Mayhew showed that the characteristics of the area are most relevant. Mayhew identified the proximity to offenders in particular, although Bottoms warns the people other than juveniles do not necessarily offend near home. Brantingham and Brantingham and Rengert and Wasilchick suggest instead that people are more apt to commit crimes in areas that they know – not necessarily where they live, but also areas between their home and work or city centre.

Source: Bottoms (1994)

1 *Which sorts of areas have the highest crime rates?*

2 *These areas seem to have quite a range of different social characteristics. Summarise and explain the different explanations for patterns of crime offered in the extract.*

Examination Question

Some areas appear to be more 'crime-prone' than others. Outline these geographical patterns and assess different sociological explanations of them.

AEB, Summer 1994

Bibliography

Baldwin, J. and Bottoms, A.E. (1976) *The Urban Criminal*, London: Tavistock

Ball, S. (1981) *Beachside Comprehensive*, Cambridge: Cambridge University Press

Bottoms, A.E., Mawby, R.E. and Zanthos, P. (1989) 'A Tale of Two Estates' in Downes, D. (ed) *Crime and the City*, London: Macmillan

Bottoms, A.E. (1994) 'Environmental criminology', in Maguire, M., Morgan, R, and Reiner, R. (eds) *The Oxford Handbook of Criminology*, Oxford: Oxford University Press

Brantingham, P.J. and Brantingham, P.L. (1991) *Environmental Criminology*, 2nd edn, Prospect Heights, IL: Waveland

Carter, R.L. and Hill, K.Q. (1979) *The Criminal's Image of the City*, New York: Pergamon

Cloward, R.A. and Ohlin, L.E. (1961) *Delinquency and Opportunity*, Glencoe, IL: Free Press

Cohen, A. (1955) *Delinquent Boys: The Culture of the Gang*, New York: Free Press

Downes, D. (1966) *The Delinquent Solution*, London: Routledge

Herbert, D. (1982) *The Geography of Urban Crime*, London: Longman

Hope, T. and Hough, M. (1988) 'Area, crime and incivity: a profile from the British Crime Survey', in Hope, T. and Shaw, M. (eds) *Communities and Crime Reduction*, London: HMSO

Matza, D. (1964) *Delinquency and Drift*: New York: Wiley

Mays, J.B. (1954) *Growing Up in the City*, Liverpool: Liverpool University Press

— (1972) *Juvenile Delinquency*, The Family and the Social Group, London: Longman

Miller, W.B. (1962) 'Lower class culture as a generating milieu of gang delinquency', in Wolfgang, M.E., Savitz, L. and Johnston, N. (eds) *The Sociology of Crime and Delinquency*, New York: Wiley

Morris, T.P. (1957) *The Criminal Area: A Study in Social Ecology*, London: Routledge

Park, R.E. (1936) '*Human ecology*', American Journal of Ecology, July

Parker, H. (1974) *View from the Boys*, Newton Abbott: David & Charles

Patrick, J. (1973) *A Glasgow Gang Observed*, London: Eyre-Methuen

Rengert, G. and Wasilchick, J. (1985) *Suburban Burglary*, Springfield, IL: Charles C. Thomas

Rex, J. and Moore, R. (1967) *Race, Community and Conflict*, Oxford: Oxford University Press

Shaw, C.R. and McKay, H.D. (1942) *Juvenile Delinquency and Urban Areas*, Chicago, IL: University of Chicago Press

Skogan, W.G. (1986) 'Fear of crime and neighborhood change', in Reiss, A.J. and Tonry, M. (eds) *Communities and Crime*, Chicago, IL: University of Chicago Press

Sutherland, E.H. and Cressey, D.R. (1954) *Principles of Criminology*, Chicago, IL: Lippincott

West, D.J. (1977) *Are Delinquents Different?*, London: Heinemann

West, D.J. and Farrington, D.P. (1973) Who Becomes Delinquent? London: Heinemann

Wikstrom, P.H. (1991) Urban Crime, Criminals and Victims: The Swedish Experience in an Anglo-American Comparative Perspective, New York

Willmott, D. (1966) Adolescent Boys in East London, London: Routledge

4 Crime, structure and conflict

Criminal damage?

Marxism has been one of the most influential perspectives in sociology. In the 1990s it began to lose support under the academic attacks of postmodernism and the more general criticism levelled against it after the collapse of most of the regimes which claimed to have followed a Marxist 'path'. In criminology Marxist analyses have continued to provide insights, but there has been a shift away from 'traditional' Marxist critiques, increasingly referred to as 'left idealism' by critics (meaning something like 'great in theory, lousy in practice') towards a much more thinned-down approach which accepts that inequalities of power, income and wealth provide the wider backdrop to criminality, but that other social factors are more important.

These newer approaches started in the 1970s with the so-called 'new criminology', and have matured into what the proponents call 'left realism' (or 'We may still be socialists, but let's roll up our sleeves and see how we can combat crime'). Ultimately, the major difference between left idealism and left realism is probably a moral one. Most left idealists would argue that youth crime reflects a cry for help or of resistance to capitalism and is at least partially good. Most left realists would argue that youth crime hurts the least powerful in society and is bad.

In the next two chapters we chart the history of the shift in Marxist or 'critical criminological' thinking. This chapter concerns itself with the more traditional Marxist approaches and focuses on corporate and white-collar crime. The following chapter considers the more innovative approaches.

Figure 4.1 Guidelines:
Marxist approaches

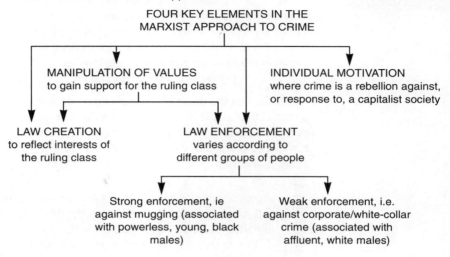

The traditional Marxist approach

The term 'Marxist' is much abused in sociology. It is often used to lump together a wide variety of sociologists who interpret Marx in different ways and whose sociological and political debts to him vary enormously. In this chapter, as elsewhere in sociological writing, a very broad school of thought has been summarised under the heading of 'traditional Marxism'. It is important to acknowledge this fact because Marx himself had very little to say about crime, merely seeing it as a product of poverty.

The traditional Marxist approach to crime and deviance has focused on the following four areas, which will be used as a framework for discussion:

- the manipulation of the basic values and morality of a society

- the process of law creation

- the enforcement of law

- individual motivation.

The manipulation of values

Marxists see society as dominated and controlled by those who own the 'commanding heights' of industry, commerce and finance. Control is maintained in two distinct but linked ways, through *socialisation* and *threat*.

In the socialisation process, people are persuaded from childhood onward of the naturalness and value of the capitalist system. This process involves a wide range of 'agencies', of which the most important are school and the mass media. These promote the values of freedom, self-interest, competition and the rights of private property. The result is a society in which the basic values guiding action support the capitalist political and economic system.

Threat is the fallback if socialisation fails. In this century it has been used in Britain on a number of occasions, for example to break the General Strike in 1926, in Northern Ireland since the early 1970s and against coal miners during the 1984–5 strike. On a smaller scale police violence has been used to control groups of youths deemed to pose a threat to the dominant order, for instance predominantly black and Asian youths in the inner cities and 'new age' travellers.

Marxists argue that the definition of what is criminal reflects the dominant social values. Causing the death of another person while in a fit of temper, for example during a street brawl, is regarded as murder. Yet the death of factory workers through exposure in their work environment to dangerous chemicals or asbestos is considered at worst as worthy of a fine – even when the management has been aware of the risks.

> Chemical giant Allied Colloids boasts that it has been chosen by the pollution inspectorate (HMIP) as the first UK partner to work on its so-called 'three Es': initiative emission, efficiencies and economies.
>
> The firm has plenty of experience in emissions. In 1993 it was fined £100,000 plus £60,000 costs after a huge chemicals blaze at its Bradford plant. It promised to tighten up procedures, but earlier this year eight workers from the same factory were hospitalised after a leak of dangerous chemicals.
>
> Allied Colloids, which has just been fined £15,000 plus £2,000 costs after again admitting breaching health and safety regulations, refuses to discuss health and safety issues with any trade union as unions are not recognised at the plant. Perhaps the pollution police will think again about who it is seen in public with.
>
> *Source: Private Eye*, 'Backbiter', 6 October 1995

One result of this ideological manipulation of society is that the law is only applied to less powerful groups such as the young, the working class and blacks. Such people are more likely to be arrested, convicted and sentenced to prison than members of more powerful groups, even though they may cause less damage and injury.

A further effect of the socialisation process, according to the Marxist view, is to create the belief that criminals are most likely to be drawn from the working class, the young and the black community, who generally live in inner-city areas. An important consequence is that there are far more police in these areas, and a disproportionate amount of police effort is concentrated on these groups.

Another result is that explanations of crime start with the assumption that criminality is highest among the less powerful groups in society, and therefore the causes of crime are sought in the shared characteristics of these groups – their culture, upbringing, housing patterns, etc. This ignores the fact that very similar deeds are being performed by members of the most powerful groups in society, yet these are not defined as criminal.

Law creation

You will recall that according to Durkheim law is a reflection of the will of the people. Marxists totally reject this contention; for them law is a reflection of the will of the *powerful*, although this may not always be immediately apparent.

Marxists argue that, as economic power guarantees political and social power, the rich are able to manipulate the rest of us and pass laws which benefit them. There are basically two ways in which the 'ruling class' ensures that laws favourable to themselves are passed.

First, the manipulation of values described above ensures that the debate on law and order is conducted within a framework of values sympathetic to the ruling class – this is known as *setting the agenda*. An example is the 1994 Public Order and Criminal Justice Act. This gave the state new powers to prevent gatherings of quite small numbers of people (if there was felt to be a possible threat to public order) and outlawed other activities which had previously been lawful, but which were annoying to more powerful sectors of society. In particular, the law on trespass, squatting and demonstrating was significantly tightened. The Act in effect takes away civil liberties from the majority of the population and severely limits the powers of protest. Yet during the debate before it passed into law the Act was portrayed as an attempt to deal with a small disruptive and anti-social minority.

On June 1, 1985, police ambushed a convoy of vehicles on its way to the 11th People's Free Festival at Stonehenge. Over 1,000 officers from five constabularies cornered travellers and festival-goers in a field on the Hampshire/Wiltshire border for several hours. Having refused to negotiate an alternative festival site, the operational commander ordered his men to attack the convoy.

Some of the travellers fled into an adjacent beanfield. The violence that followed was recorded by an ITN camera crew, headed by reporter Kim Sabido [who] described it as the worst police violence he had ever seen

Four hundred and twenty people were arrested and taken to holding cells throughout the south of England. Travellers' homes were systematically looted, smashed and burnt.

The convoy was portrayed by the media as a marauding army of crazed hippies. A row of ordinary household implements was described as 'weapons gathered up'. On ITN, fleeing drivers became virtually potential murderers.

The media coverage heightened public outrage against the travelling lifestyle, and eased the way for a new 'anti-hippie clause' to be added to the Public Order Act 1986. This restricted to 12 the number of vehicles that could travel or park up together. A new ban on processions meant that two or more people walking to Stonehenge could be arrested. The festival became an excuse for 'trashing' a lifestyle in which, for thousands of young people, a bedsit on wheels had become a viable alternative to scratching a living in a decayed inner city.

'The real reason was the threat to the state,' said Maureen Lodge, who had taken to the road during the recession of the late 1970s and who, like scores of others, was strip-searched in a police garage after the battle. 'The number of people who were living on buses had been doubling every year for four years. It was anarchy in action, and it was seen to be working by so many people that they wanted to be a part of it too.'

Since the beanfield incident the Government has spent millions of pounds hounding Britain's community of (what was then) approximately 15,000 travellers in attempts to make their lifestyle untenable.

Each public order situation has been exploited to create a climate of hostility towards travellers, and legislation has followed to criminalise the migratory lifestyle. Last year the Criminal Justice Act [CJA] abolished the 1968 Caravan Sites Act, itself set up to ensure official sites for nomadic people in the wake of over 100 Gypsy deaths at the hands of vigilantes in the 1960s. (In response to the disappearance of traditional sites, some travellers have attempted to buy their own land, only to be denied planning permission in 90 per cent of cases.)

The CJA made trespass a criminal offence, thereby extending police powers to prevent travellers from seeking alternative sites. The number of vehicles that can now park together has been limited to six. Failure to comply with any section of the law can result in travellers' homes being impounded and destroyed at the owner's expense.

Source: Neil Goodwin, 'Bean and gone', *Guardian*, 31 May 1995

1 Briefly describe the events portrayed in the extract.

2 In your opinion, could the police have dealt with the matter differently? How?

3 How did the media portray these events?

4 What was the outcome of the events and the media coverage of them in terms of legislation?

5 Analyse the events using a Marxist perspective, explaining why the police attacked and what the consequences were.

A second method of ensuring that the ruling class has its way is through the use of pressure group activity. Changes in the law are generally result from pressure group lobbying of the government. Organised pressure groups such as the Child Poverty Action Group, which carry out their activities in public, are the most visible, but Marxists point to the power of the City of London and its ability to lobby the government in informal ways behind the scenes. There is little publicity, but great influence.

Not all laws, however, are seen to be entirely for the benefit of the ruling class. Clearly, many laws do genuinely protect ordinary people – obvious ones would be the laws on rape, drunken driving and safety at work. Genuine concessions can be gained either when the interests of the powerful and of ordinary people overlap or

A threat to the state? Riot police forcibly prevent a vehicle from reaching Stonehenge.

when representative pressure groups are able to push through reforms in the interests of the wider population.

Finally, there are other occasions when the law does not obviously reflect the will of the powerful, most notably when there are divisions between members of the ruling class.

Law enforcement

Another focus of Marxist analysis concerns the different ways that the law is enforced.

Marxists argue, firstly, that certain *types* of crime are likely to be dealt with more rigorously than others. For example, 'street crimes' such as assault and theft are far more likely to be pursued by the police than much 'white-collar' crime, such as fraud or 'insider trading' in the City. In fact, white-collar crime is less likely to be reported to the police in the first place, as large financial institutions prefer to deal privately with crimes committed by their staff by sacking them, to avoid scandal.

Secondly, certain *groups* in the population are more likely to be on the receiving end of law enforcement. Inner-city areas have many more police on patrol than other areas. As crime is regarded as most common among the working class, the young and blacks, there is a much greater police presence among these populations than elsewhere, and the approach the police adopt towards them is also said to be more 'confrontational'.

Finally, the Marxists point to the differences in sentencing policies when it comes to certain types of crime. Property theft committed during burglary or robbery is punished by long terms of imprisonment. Financial swindles, if they come to court at all, are not regarded as serious and are not necessarily punished with prison sentences.

Source: The Times
Higher Educational
Supplement,
13 January 1984

Individual motivation for crime

The Marxist approach stresses the importance of placing individual actions within a wide framework, but it does not entirely neglect the question of why people decide to commit crimes.

In capitalist societies, according to the Marxists, the cultural stress is on competition (rather than cooperation) and the acquisition of wealth. The desire for money can lead those who are blocked off from legitimate chances of gaining wealth to turn to criminal methods. Note that this argument is very similar to Merton's version of anomie. The crucial difference between Merton and most Marxist writers is that, whereas Merton considers the stress on material success to be an aberration, the Marxists see greed as built into the very nature of capitalist society.

Although it is true that hundreds of thousands of people find employment in fighting crime, and hundreds of thousands find economic support through criminal offences and economic security while confined in prison, at the same time lowering the unemployment rate of the society, this does not mean that crime is necessary and inevitable. It means that under capitalism crime is generated within the capitalist mode of production. However, in no long-term way can crime be functional, even within capitalism. It results from the contradictions of capitalism and contributes further to these contradictions.

To reduce crime and thereby reduce the economic costs of crime would be to change beyond recognition the capitalist system. Crime in all its aspects, with all its economic costs, is the price paid for capitalism.

Social expenditures on criminal justice necessarily increase with the development of advanced capitalism. In the late stages of capitalism the mode of production and the forms of capital accumulation accelerate the growth of the relative surplus population. The state must then provide social expense programmes, including criminal justice, both to legitimise advanced capitalism and to control the surplus population.

Source: Quinney (1980)

1 What is the relationship between capitalism and crime, according to the extract?

2 Is crime inevitable in society?

3 Look back to the discussion of Durkheim's ideas on pp. 20–25. Is there any difference or similarity between his views and Quinney's?

4 According to Quinney, how can crime best be combated?

The creation and enforcement of law in action

Having looked at the theory of the Marxist approach to crime and deviance, we now consider two areas of discussion which bring out many of the Marxist issues. These are 'mugging' and corporate crime.

Mugging

The following is a summary of Policing the Crisis by Hall *et al.* (1979), a study of 'mugging' from a Marxist perspective.

In the early 1970s in Britain the crime of mugging became headline news. Mugging is generally defined as a robbery in the street where someone is threatened or harmed. The interesting point is that mugging was apparently a brand new phenomenon: until that time no one in the UK had heard of it. By 1972 the papers were filled with frightening stories of elderly people being attacked in the streets and savagely beaten. According to the Home Secretary, there had been a 129 per cent increase in muggings over the previous four years.

There were calls in Parliament and in the media for a strong police presence in the inner-city areas and for tough 'crackdown' on the groups of people most likely to be involved in mugging. Most newspapers declared or implied that the muggers were predominantly young black people.

However, according to Hall, violent street crime was not a new phenomenon at all. Indeed it had a long and 'honourable' history in Britain, certainly stretching well back into the last century. The sudden preoccupation with violent street crime in the early 1970s was rather odd, too, as the number of such crimes had increased quite steadily, by about 33 per cent in the 1950s and mid-1960s, but the rate of increase had halved by the late 1960s and early 1970s to about 14 per cent. A further interesting point is that there was no criminal act of 'mugging' at the time, and there is still no such crime today. The nearest legal category is 'assault with intent to rob'. The Home Secretary's figure of a 129 per cent increase was arrived at by adding together several different forms of street crime. Hall concluded, therefore, that the 'moral panic' was not based upon any real increase in crime. The explanation for the outcry over mugging must lie elsewhere.

In the early 1970s, according to Hall, Britain was entering a period of 'crisis', in which there was a massive increase in strikes, Northern Ireland was almost at the stage of civil war, and the inner cities were in a state of ferment. The ideological hold over sections of the population seemed to be weakening. This contrasted with the previous twenty years since the end of the Second World War when Britain appeared to be characterised by harmony and economic affluence.

Hall claimed that the public outcry over mugging, which was triggered by newspaper reports, based in their turn on information supplied by the police, served the useful purpose of justifying repressive policing in the inner-city areas. It also made the general point that there were subversive groups in society which needed to be confronted by force. The outcome was a greatly increased police presence in the inner cities, operating most forcibly against young blacks, and an increasing acceptance by the public of more repressive policing against potential threats to public order. The full impact of the stricter forms of policing was in fact felt elsewhere – in the actions of the police during the miners' strike of 1984–5.

There are two central elements of Hall's approach which distinguish it as Marxist. First, the focus of attention is the wider society within which the crimes took place, rather than on any attributes of the criminals. Therefore the approach is structural. Indeed, there is hardly any discussion of the reasons that would impel young blacks to commit street crime.

Second, crime is seen as a result of the very nature of capitalism (the crisis) and the need to maintain order. The police are seen as provocateurs, not agents of the law responding to offences committed against society.

It is important to point out that Hall did not claim that the police, the government and the media deliberately conspired to engineer the moral panic over mugging in order to justify increasingly oppressive policing methods, although that was the outcome. The situation arose from similar perceptions among these groups that 'things were getting out of hand', and mugging happened to be the issue that acted as the catalyst for action.

Criticisms of Hall

Many criticisms have been levelled at Hall's explanation of mugging. One is that, through its great stress on the wider situation, it almost completely ignores the people at the centre of the whole activity, the young muggers themselves. Their values and perceptions of the situation are ignored. To a large extent this is because they are seen as innocent victims of a process of *deviancy amplification* (see pp. 122–4).

A second problem is that there is a contradiction in Hall's study: on the one hand, an increasing police presence is said to be necessary to maintain law and order, which is supposedly under threat; yet Hall also claims that there was no actual increase in street crime. If there was no increase in crime rates, why was there a threat to the power of the capitalists?

Figure 4.2 The role of crime

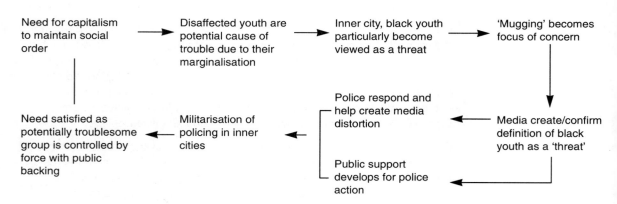

1 *Explain how the diagram illustrates the ideas explained above.*

2 *Could this idea be applied to the activities of Sinn Fein and the Provisional IRA in Northern Ireland?*

Criminalisation, the application of the criminal label to an identifiable social category, is dependent on how certain acts are labelled and who has the power to label.

Public support is more likely to be achieved for state intervention against 'criminal' acts than for the repression or suppression of political causes. Further, even where no purposeful political intention is involved, the process of criminalisation can divert attention from the social or political dynamics of a movement and specify its 'criminal' potential. If black youth is portrayed exclusively as 'muggers' there will be less tolerance of organised campaigns which emphasise that they have legitimate political and economic grievances.

Criminalisation is a process which has been employed to underpin the repressive or control functions of the state.

Source: Scraton and Chadwick (1991)

Marxism and street crime

Marxist approaches have a problem with explaining street crime, which is brought out most vividly by left realists (see pp.93–105). For Marxists tend to ignore the very real consequences for the victims of street crimes. In particular that it is the working class who are usually the victims, not the rich.

Marxist approaches seem to suggest that the working class or, in the example above, young blacks, are simply innocent people who are picked on by the police as they are seen as potential or real opponents of capitalism.

Or, secondly, that working class people who engage in crime are really (even if they do not realise it themselves) engaged in political action by opposing the capitalist system. Marxists take a very different view, however, of white-collar crime.

Corporate and white-collar crime

As we have seen, Marxists stress that much 'crime' committed by the working class is a legitimate defence against oppression. On the other hand:

● Powerful groups can manipulate the definition of what is considered to be crime in the first place. Only working-class crime is considered criminal.

● When they do commit crimes such as fraud or tax evasion, members of the privileged groups often escape punishment, or at most suffer less severe punishment. For instance, rather than being subject to the criminal law, the financial institutions of the City of London police themselves through various 'commissions'. It is argued that, as the police lack trained accountants and financial experts, such matters are best left to the 'experts'. If the same argument were put forward by thieves – that they know more about theft than the police and should therefore be left to control themselves – there would be a public outcry.

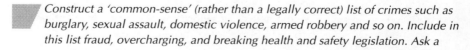

Construct a 'common-sense' (rather than a legally correct) list of crimes such as burglary, sexual assault, domestic violence, armed robbery and so on. Include in this list fraud, overcharging, and breaking health and safety legislation. Ask a

sample of students or people in the street to rank them in order of seriousness, or at least to name the three most serious. What do the results tell you about attitudes to corporate and white-collar crime? At the end of your survey, what criticisms would you make of your work? What would you do differently next time?

Corporate crime

The term 'corporate crime' refers to criminal acts committed by companies to increase their profits. Such acts range from breaking health and safety laws at work in order to increase productivity, to deliberate pollution of the environment to avoid the costly measures required by law to clear up or prevent the pollution in the first place. A second meaning of the term – and a more contentious one – includes activities that are harmful to others, but are not illegal.

Steven Box (1983) has argued for this wider definition. He points out that in terms of the harm caused to individuals and losses to the public in unpaid tax revenue, environmental costs, and costs in health and welfare benefits, corporate crime is a far more serious problem than street crimes and burglary. Estimates vary, but it has been claimed that the actual costs of corporate crime may be as high as £16 billion per year. Corporate crime has grown massively with the growth of the European Union, which has developed a complex system of financial supports for a wide range of commercial developments.

It is often unclear who is harmed by corporate crimes. For instance, pollution may harm everyone, but there is no individual victim, as we normally expect with crimes. Victims of corporate crime tend to be drawn from the following broad categories:

- Consumers in general: Examples include false or misleading claims in advertising, faulty, dangerous or poor-quality goods, and adulterated foods. The problem here lies in establishing the dividing line between sharp practice and illegality.

- Employees: The failure to enforce health and safety regulations at work is a common example. Over 500 employees each year are killed and 18,000 injured in 'industrial accidents'. It is estimated that over 300 of the fatalities and anything up to two-thirds of the injuries are the result of the failure of companies to observe health and safety regulations.

- The public: Here the harm is more pervasive and possibly more subtle than harm done to consumers. Companies which avoid taxation, or avoid paying their employees proper pensions or benefits, burden the general public with state welfare costs. Companies which manufacture products such as cigarettes kill their consumers directly, but they also cost the wider society huge sums in terms of health care provision. Pollution from factories harms the environment. Lead from car exhausts harms the health of all those living in cities.

Companies do not issue policy statements declaring that they intend to harm people in the interest of higher profits. The process of corporate decision making is complex: it involves a large variety of factors, including assumptions about the need for profit, the importance of the company's survival in the face of competition, individuals' desire for promotion, shareholders' pressure for higher dividends, and often simple incompetence. Therefore it is often difficult to find any single person or group of people to blame for corporate crime.

For instance, the cross-Channel ferry, *Herald of Free Enterprise*, sank in 1989 with the loss of over 100 lives. The ship sank because the bow doors were left open too long as it left harbour. The individual directly responsible had fallen asleep. He claimed he had worked long hours and was tired. It also emerged that it was normal practice to leave the bow doors open when the ship left dock in order to achieve a faster crossing time: this decision was made at a more senior level. The purpose of achieving a faster crossing time was to be more attractive to freight traffic in order to make more profits. The demand for higher profits and consequently also the drive for minimum staffing levels came from the Board of Directors. When the case came to court, no individuals were fined or jailed; no crime had been committed.

Who or what is to blame in a disaster such as this?

Corporations and organisations are goal-seeking entities operating in an unpredictable and contradictory environment full of competitors struggling over scarce resources. Consequently, their executives frequently find themselves in a situation where strict adherence to regulations governing their activities would not be a rational course of action to pursue. It would result in their corporation or even organisation failing to achieve its goal (or goals) and maybe even going out of existence. In these dire circumstances, executives investigate alternative means, including law avoidance, evasion and violation and pursue them if they are evaluated as more likely to lead to goals being achieved. In addition, corporations form powerful and, with the right government, persuasive pressure groups to change regulations and laws originally designed to limit corporate behaviour so that employees, consumers and the general public would be better protected.

Source: Box (1987)

1 Is Box suggesting that corporate criminals are necessarily evil people?

2 What is the direct link between the underlying logic of capitalism and corporate crimes?

3 The 1980s in the UK saw a continuing cut in funding for the government Inspectorate responsible for health and safety. In 1993 Prime Minister John Major insisted that government departments were going to be minutely examined for 'red tape', and, wherever possible, regulations would be repealed. What light does this extract shed on these facts?

White-collar or occupational crime

These terms refer to the types of crime committed by people in clerical, supervisory or managerial employment. The issue of white-collar crime was first raised by Edwin Sutherland in the early 1940s (though he was not a Marxist writer). He defined it as 'crime committed by a person of high social status and respectability in the course of his occupation'. However, such crimes are not always committed by people of high social status, and Croall (1992) has suggested the definition, 'crime committed in the course of legitimate employment involving the abuse of an occupational role'. The only problem with this definition is that it excludes related crimes such as tax evasion.

Like corporate crime, white-collar crime is often characterised by the invisibility of the victim and by its complexity. These two elements are particularly important in their effect on the levels of arrests and the extent of punishment.

You may like to research the case of Nick Leeson, the financier whose unauthorised wheelings and dealings were claimed to have caused the collapse of Barings Bank in 1995

● White-collar crime often occurs where a person with expert knowledge attempts to use their knowledge to steal or defraud. It can be extremely difficult for non-experts to uncover the crime and the means by which it has been committed. Moreover, the victims of white-collar crime often remain unaware that they are victims.

● Where white-collar crimes are detected and the perpetrators are found guilty, they generally attract relatively 'soft' punishment, given the amounts of money involved. There seems to be a moral issue here. White-collar crimes are not regarded as seriously as street crime or burglary. Terms such as 'technical offences' or 'errors of judgement' are commonly used. Marxists would argue that this is connected to the ability of the powerful to manipulate the values of society.

This failure of white-collar crime to fit the social construction of crime has many implications. Many theories of crime have sought to explain predominantly 'lower-class' crime and explore the relationship between crime and deprivation, unemployment or poverty. The existence of white-collar crime, however, means that these theories can only provide partial explanations of crime. White-collar crime also illustrates the wider political and ideological dimensions of definitions of crime. Few would describe fraud as a 'law and order' problem or see corporations as 'dangerous' criminals who need locking up. The fine line dividing acceptable business practices from fraud illustrates how the crimes of business executives are less 'criminalised' than the burglaries or robberies of lower-class offenders. Thus the definition and control of white-collar crime – and by comparison, that of conventional crime – are implicitly political issues. The sociological significance of white-collar crime is therefore far reaching.

Source: Croall (1993)

1 Explain what Croall means by 'This failure of white-collar crime to fit the social construction of crime'.

2 The extract refers to the way theories of crime concentrate on the relationship between crime and deprivation or unemployment. Explain why they tend to ignore wider political and ideological dimensions.

3 What explanations do Marxists provide for the criminalisation of 'the burglaries or robberies of the lower-class offenders'?

4 Obtain copies of newspapers such as the Financial Times, the Daily Telegraph, the Guardian or The Times. In small groups, go through the business pages looking for examples of what you decide is 'dubious practice'. Count how many examples you can find, and list them. Keep swapping the papers about between groups, so that all the groups have read and listed all the possible 'dubious practices', and equally some examples of what you

would consider (by your own definition) as excellent business practice. Finally, bring the groups together and compare your findings. Discuss the similarities and differences of your lists and explain why you categorised them as you did.

5 *For a more cynical view buy a copy of Private Eye magazine. What does this suggest (if anything) about business practices in Britain?*

Criticisms of the Marxist approach

The Marxist approach has been heavily criticised by both sympathisers and opponents.

One major problem has been the way it seems to ignore individual motivation. The stress is primarily on the nature of capitalism and how economic factors 'force' people to act in certain ways. Their perceptions, ideas and motivations are rarely discussed.

Second, Marxists seem to claim that the high rate of recorded crime among the working class, youth and blacks is solely the outcome of biased policing. At the same time they argue that the laws are biased against the working class, *forcing* them into crime. Critics point out that there seems to be a contradiction here.

Third, it seems implausible to explain all laws in terms of the interests of the ruling class; many laws appear to rest on genuine agreement. However, Marxists reject this argument, claiming that even laws which appear to be for the benefit of society are *in reality* of use ultimately to the ruling class. By providing a few laws that are of use to everybody, the real, repressive nature of the legal system is hidden. This reasoning is rejected by critics such as Mishra (1981), who has called this form of Marxist analysis 'left functionalism', by which he means that any law can be shown to be in some way 'functional' to the maintenance of capitalism. This makes any meaningful critical debate with Marxists impossible.

A final point that has often been raised is that societies which called themselves Marxist (whether they were or were not is a very different matter) appear to have had at least as high a crime rate as capitalist ones, yet in a Marxist society there ought to have been no crime.

Using the themes of

- *manipulation of values*

- *law creation*

- *law enforcement*

- *individual motivation*

compare the Marxist interpretations of white-collar crime and 'street crime'.

Summary

In this chapter we have examined an orthodox line of Marxist thought regarding crime and deviance. Orthodox Marxists attack the traditional concern of sociologists of crime and deviance with street crime – or, as they are more likely to term it, 'crimes of the working class'. They argue that crime arises from the definitions of criminality imposed by the ruling class. They focus on the extent of crime committed by corporations and white-collar employees, thereby demonstrating that crime is diffused throughout society.

Hall's work takes as its starting point the concept of 'relative autonomy'. By this he means that the ruling class do not manipulate and direct the activities of the various control agencies in society, such as the media or the police. These organisations are constrained and strongly influenced by the needs of capitalism, but they are to some extent autonomous. The job of sociologists, according to this view, is to uncover the links between the way control organisations operate, the effects upon the people being controlled and the benefits to the ruling class. Hall's work clearly illustrates these points.

Readings

Most non-Marxist criminologists argue that economic recession and rising unemployment lead to increases in street crime and burglary. However, Box (1987) argues that recession actually increases crimes committed by the powerful. Furthermore, recession leads the police to behave in 'illegal' ways which are subsequently sanctioned by changes in the law.

Source: Box (1987)

Research the debates leading up to the passing of the Criminal Justice Act 1994 by looking up contemporary newspaper reports on a CD-ROM. Use the results of your research to explain and illustrate the points made by Box on the right-hand side of Figure 4.3, ending with 'Police crimes increase'.

Now read the following extract and use it as a starting point to explain the left-hand side of Figure 4.3 which concludes that 'Corporate crimes increase'. You should use a CD-ROM to look up the two disasters referred to in the extract.

There was a general shift to the political right in many European countries during the 1980s, and this was usually accompanied by a diminished stress on health and safety in favour of production. Most of the inspectorates have had their staff reduced, political signals towards diminished enthusiasm for restricting entrepreneurialism have doubtless affected regulators' approaches. One consequence – though not necessarily a logically necessary one – is disasters like the *Piper Alpha* oil rig or the sinking of the *Herald of Free Enterprise* near Zeebrugge ... there has been a tendency in the UK to make most efficient use of scarce resources by concentrating them upon high risk, untrustworthy areas, leaving the major corporations increasingly to self-police. Given resource constraints this may be rational, for the results of studies of corporate crime tend to show that large, profitable bureaucracies do generally exhibit greater safety-consciousness, perhaps encouraged by their greater profit cushions.

Source: Levi (1991)

Examination Question

Critically discuss the Marxist argument that deviance ought to be explained in terms of a person's social class position.

AEB, Summer 1995

Figure 4.3 Recession and crimes of the powerful
Source: Box (1987)

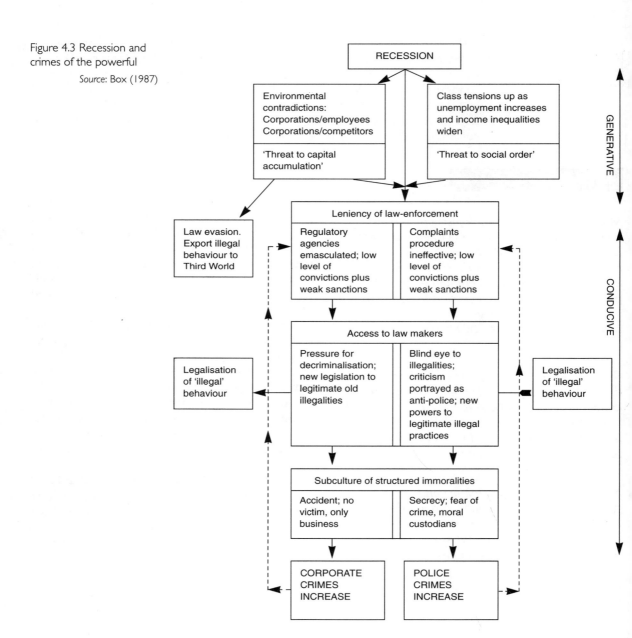

Bibliography

Box, S. (1983) *Power, Crime and Mystification*, London: Tavistock

— (1987) *Recession, Crime and Punishment*, London: Macmillan

Croall, H. (1992) *White Collar Crime*, Milton Keynes: Open University Press

— (1993) `White-collar crime', Sociology Review, November

Hall, S. et al. (1979) *Policing the Crisis*, London: Macmillan

Levi, M. (1991) 'Developments in business crime in Europe', in Heidensohn, F. and Farrell, M. (eds) *Crime in Europe*, London: Routledge

Mishra, R. (1981) *Society and Social Policy*, London: Macmillan

Quinney, R. (1980) *Class, State and Crime*, London: Longman

Scraton, P. and Chadwick, K. (1991) 'The theoretical and political priorities of critical criminology', in Stenson, K. and Cowell, D. (eds) *The Politics of Crime Control*, London: Sage

5 Post-Marxist approaches: making sense of the structure

In this chapter we examine theories which, although claiming to based upon a Marxist analysis, move away from the rather rigid Marxist approach and shift their emphasis much more on the construction of the beliefs and ideas that lead young males into crime. Essentially the ideas in this chapter come from linking, in various ways, the theories of subculture we looked at in Chapter 3 with the Marxist structural perspectives we reviewed in the previous chapter.

What all the ideas in this chapter share in common is that they stress the importance of exploring how groups of people create sets of values and ways of acting which, in their eyes at least, allow them to solve the problems they face in their everyday lives. Crucially, though, the problems they are solving are created by capitalist society. The two levels of analysis are related.

The first set of post-Marxist approaches examined in this chapter – known as Marxist subcultural theory – moved beyond traditional Marxist thinking by attempting to understand the activities of working-class youth, both criminal and non-criminal, by interpreting their actions as responses to the oppression of capitalism. Although the approach is distinct from traditional Marxist approaches discussed in the last chapter, it shares the beliefs that crime and deviance still emanate from the inequalities of capitalism and that only by eliminating capitalism can crime be eradicated.

The second part of the chapter covers an approach which is currently holding sway in academic circles in Britain. It has become known as left realism, and although it draws upon Marxist ideas it does not accept that the only way to resolve social problems is first to abolish capitalism. Left realists believe that the problems of crime can be alleviated within capitalist society if the police, central government and local authorities take positive action to create safer cities and communities.

Figure 5.1 Guidelines: post-Marxist approaches

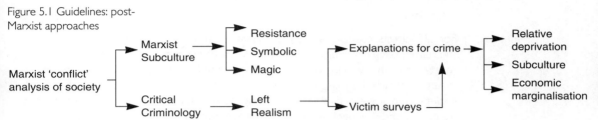

The Marxist subcultural approach

The Marxist subcultural approach to crime and deviance spread far wider than an examination of the law. It also extended into an analysis of the more extreme, perhaps deviant, working-class youth cultures. This presented a clear alternative to the traditional subcultural theories we examined on pp. 50–57.

Before examining the approach in detail, it is worth briefly discussing the functionalist view of youth culture, which provides a more conservative explanation for deviant behaviour among youth.

Traditionally, sociologists have regarded 'youth' as a period of transition from childhood to adulthood. The emphasis of the analysis provided by the functionalist school is that all youths have to find a way of moving from the secure, cosy world of the family into the competitive adult world of work, where individual talent and sharp competition with others bring financial rewards.

The role of youth culture is to smooth the path from childhood into adulthood by providing a link between the conflicting values (or 'pattern variables') of the home (childhood) and work (adulthood). Eisenstadt (1956), for example, suggested that most young people seek to distinguish themselves from their parents, yet being different leaves them emotionally insecure. In response to this emotional insecurity young people create distinct sets of values and styles of dress. These serve the twin purposes of setting them apart from their parents (fulfilling the function of independence) and also providing them with a model or standard against which they can measure their behaviour. If I am a 'casual', for example, I know how I ought to dress, the music I ought to listen to, and possibly the sort of behaviour expected of me. Each generation of young people faces the same problem of transition and therefore creates a distinctive youth culture.

Two points need noting here for comparison with the Marxist approach. First, the actual *contents* of the youth culture (for instance, the style of clothes adopted and the patterns of behaviour) are unimportant and need no further analysis. Second, *differences in the backgrounds* of young people and between the various youth subcultures are unimportant too. The functionalist approach stresses that all youth need some kind of 'transition mechanism', no matter what subcultural form it takes.

Features of the Marxist subcultural approach

The Marxist approach to youth begins where the functionalists left off. Marxists stress the importance of the contents of youth culture and the differences in class backgrounds. The Marxist subcultural approach is generally associated with Birmingham University's School of Contemporary Cultural Studies.

Hegemony

For all Marxists, capitalist society is characterised by *class conflict*, which arises from the ruling class's determination to retain control over the rest of society and the resistance of the working class. According to the Marxist view, one of the major means by which the ruling class control people is to manipulate the cultural values of society to their benefit – for example, by claiming the 'right' to have private medical treatment and the 'right' to pass on wealth from one generation to another. This is achieved through control of the mass media and of the values taught in schools. In Marxist terminology, the imposition of the ruling class's values on the rest of society is known as *hegemony*.

Youth

Most people in British society are so trapped by mortgages, credit repayments and general family commitments that they are extremely nervous of any serious resistance to the status quo. The relative security of the contemporary capitalist system is seen to be better than the alternatives. In this way the ruling class has successfully imposed its hegemony.

The least 'locked-in' group in British society is youth. Young people are relatively free of long-term financial commitments, have less allegiance to the family and are increasingly likely to be unemployed. They are therefore the weakest point in the structure of hegemony.

Resistance through style

As we have noted, functionalists argue that each generation faces the same problem of the transition from childhood to work. Marxists see the situation very differently. Each generation of *working-class* youth faces similar problems – of entry into routine, low paid employment, or no employment at all – but they do so in *different circumstances*. For example, the youth of the 1950s grew up in the aftermath of the Second World War, within very different cultural and economic circumstances from the youth of the 1980s.

Writers such as Mike Brake (1980) and Dick Hebdidge (1979) argue that the different generations of working-class youth develop their youth culture as a means of coping with their problems, and the styles they develop reflect the particular cultural and economic circumstances of their generation. However, youths only solve their problems temporarily and only to their own satisfaction: the solutions they devise do not really alter anything. For example, if you think you are unattractive and decide to combat this with lots of make-up, this does nothing to alter the structure of your face and body. Youth culture does not alter the power and economic differences in society, which created the problems for working-class youth in the first place. Brake therefore uses the term 'magical' to describe the solutions provided by working-class youth culture.

However, youth culture is about more than just 'coping': there is a strong sense of *resistance*, according to the Centre for Contemporary Cultural Studies. Youths actively show disdain for the dominant values of society through their choice of clothes and forms of behaviour. Working-class youth culture, which is often regarded as deviant and a threat to the wider society, is in fact an aspect of the class struggle.

A key element of the Marxist approach is that the styles the various youth cultures adopt are not meaningless, as the functionalist school would argue, but are deeply imbued with meaning. Through style working-class youths work out their problems and express their resistance.

By 'style', sociologists mean the choice of clothes, haircut, hair colour, music, argot (slang) and 'ritual' forms of behaviour. Compare the contrasting hair styles of contemporary male youth, from short-crop to long hair. Are these simply hair style preferences, or do they indicate wider lifestyle choices, including possibly clothes, music and political views? Much of the work of the Marxist subcultural school is concerned with decoding the hidden meaning of youth cultural style in an attempt to see how the style denotes resistance.

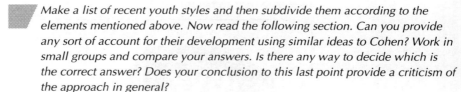

Make a list of recent youth styles and then subdivide them according to the elements mentioned above. Now read the following section. Can you provide any sort of account for their development using similar ideas to Cohen? Work in small groups and compare your answers. Is there any way to decide which is the correct answer? Does your conclusion to this last point provide a criticism of the approach in general?

An example of the Marxist subcultural approach

One of the earliest studies using this form of analysis was that of Phil Cohen (1972), who analysed youth in East London in the early 1970s. Cohen suggested that the only way to understand the meaning of youth cultures was to examine them in (a) their immediate context, and (b) the wider context.

The *immediate context*. Cohen argued that during the 1960s the fabric of East London society had been ripped apart as a result of the following factors:

- Redevelopment. Large numbers of people had moved out to new towns, or if they remained they were likely to live in high-rise apartments. Partly as a result of this, the close-knit street life was lost. Also, the price of property rose as developers began to realise the potential of an area so close to the centre of London. Small workshops and businesses were driven out as rents and rates rose.

- The loss of jobs on the docks. The economy of the traditional East End had been based on the docks, and the closeness of housing to employment had helped to create the feeling of belonging and community. After the decline of the docks in the 1960s both the economic structure and one of the props of the community were destroyed.

- Decline of the extended family. Partly as a result of the other two factors, the working-class extended family also declined. This had consisted of a network of family members who provided each other with mutual support. Youth in the

1960s had therefore grown up without the traditional East End community to support them.

The wider context. During the 1960s the benefits of greater affluence percolated through to large sections of the population. Ownership of houses and consumer goods had risen sharply over the previous decade and a whole new ideology of affluence had begun to develop. This ran alongside the continuing existence of poverty and deprivation in inner-city areas.

Youth cultures develop, according to Cohen, to cope with the loss of community, but they also reflect the divisions of society as a whole. The working-class youths of his survey therefore split into different youth subcultures, one looking back to working-class values and the other embracing the new, more affluent society).

Many of the factors which Cohen found to affect working-class white youth in the 1970s in the UK have also been at work more recently among poor black youth in US cities. In both cases there was major urban redevelopment and a move away from the city centres. Like Britain, the USA experienced a decline in well-paid employment as a result of wage deregulation, and there was a massive increase in the number of lone mother families. The lyrics of rap music reflect the division of US cities along racial lines, and describe an urban landscape in which violent crime and drug usage are common.

The lyrics of Ice T's *Cop Killer* caused outrage in the United States when the song was released in 1994.

The music and the style of dress associated with it make clear statements about young black males' experience of life, attitudes towards the police and feelings about other racial groups. Paradoxically, the commercial success of the music itself has provided a means of escape from this reality for the most popular rap performers.

Figure 5.2 illustrates how these contrasting types of behaviour produced a variety of youth subcultural styles.

Figure 5.2 Marxist subcultural explanations

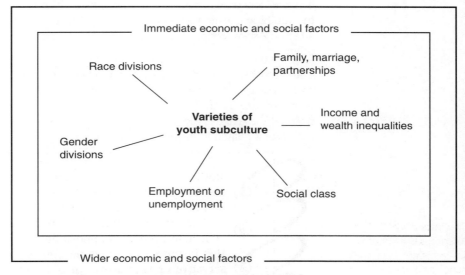

Immediate economic and social factors

Race divisions

Family, marriage, partnerships

Varieties of youth subculture

Income and wealth inequalities

Gender divisions

Employment or unemployment

Social class

Wider economic and social factors

Summary of Marxist subcultural theory

First of all, it is important to remember that the vast bulk of crime (as conventionally defined) is committed by youths. Any theories that can explain the motivations of young males correctly will also provide the key to understanding crime.

By the 1960s traditional subcultural theories were no longer appropriate, as they could not provide convincing explanations for the deviant activities of youth. The new Marxist-inspired approaches added important insights. First, they stressed that the activities, styles of dress and behaviour of youths all had *meaning*, which could be interpreted by sociologists. Second, they maintained that the activities of youths could not be understood without referring to the wider *structural* context of the economic and political system. Third, the impetus of the new subcultural approach led sociologists to examine a range of groups and activities.

Criticisms of the approach

Feminist writers argued that the Marxist subcultural approach ignored women. In defence of the Marxist subculturalists it should be pointed out that the overwhelming bulk of criminal activity among youth is committed by males. The subcultural theorists were merely trying to find out why particular groups of males rebelled. Feminist writers have since used the insights of the subcultural approach to examine the culture of adolescent girls (see pp. 178–9). Not all the writers accepted the perspective provided by the new Marxist approach, but it did provide the framework within which the debate took place. Moreover, as we will see later, considerable attention has now been given to women and blacks by Marxist subculturalists, notably by McRobbie (1978) and Griffin (1985).

Stanley Cohen (1980) criticised this whole school of thought on the grounds that its followers believe they have a special insight into 'decoding' the meaning of the styles adopted by the working-class youth cultures. For example, in his study of racial attacks (Paki-bashing) in Lancashire, Pearson (1975) suggested that it was 'misdirected heroism', and drew a parallel with the Luddites. It could just as well be argued that the youths in question were simply racist (a traditional working-class value) and attacked Asians for that reason. Why is one interpretation more correct than the other?

The Marxist subcultural approach has also been criticised because it implies that the sociologist always knows best. For example, the youths themselves may well give their own explanations for their behaviour, but the Marxist sociologists would discount these and argue that the real, *underlying* reason (of which the youths are unaware) is related to elements of the class struggle.

> Both these themes of *resistance* and *symbols* are rich and suggestive. I have only the space to mention, somewhat cryptically, a few of the problems they raise.
>
> The first arises from the constant impulse to decode the style in terms *only* of opposition and resistance. This means that instances are sometimes missed when the style is conservative or supportive. In other words, not reworked or reassembled but taken over intact from dominant commercial culture.
>
> There is also a tendency in some of this work to see the historical development of a style as being wholly internal to the group – with commercialisation and co-option as something which just happens afterwards. In the understandable zeal to depict the kids as creative agents rather than manipulated dummies, this often plays down the extent to which changes in youth culture are manufactured changes, dictated by consumer society.
>
> An allied problem is the often exaggerated status given to the internal circuit of English working-class history. The spell cast on the young by American cultural imperialism is sometimes downgraded.
>
> This is inevitable if the subculture is taken to denote some form of cumulative historical resistance. Where we are really being directed is towards the 'profound line of historical continuity' between today's delinquents and their 'equivalents' in the past.
>
> Historical evidence is cited to prove that mass proletarian resistance to the imposition of bourgeois control did not after all die out. It lives on in certain forms of delinquency which – though more symbolic and individualistic than their progenitors – must still be read as rudimentary forms

of political action, as versions of the same working-class struggle which has occurred since the defeat of Chartism. To justify this claim, a double leap of imagination is required. In Pearson's example, the 'proof' that something like Paki-bashing is a 'primitive form of political and economic struggle' lies not in the kids' understanding of what it is they are resisting but in the fact that the machine smashers of 1826 would also not have been aware of the real political significance of their action.

This seems to me a very peculiar sort of proof indeed.

Source: Adapted from Cohen (1980)

The above extract from Folk Devils and Moral Panics by Stanley Cohen attacks the way that Marxist subcultural theorists interpret the 'style' and activities of the deviant youths. Summarise Cohen's (rather difficult) criticism under the headings:

1 bias in interpretation of a) style, b) actions
2 the lack of interest in 'commercialism'
3 the romantic search for evidence of 'working class resistance'.

Marxist subcultural theory has recently come under more radical attack on the grounds that it is based on the erroneous belief that subcultures have (political) meaning. Whereas Stanley Cohen had complained that the meaning assigned by Marxist subculturalists to the activities of delinquent youth was biased, post-modernist critiques deny that there is any intrinsic meaning to be found. For instance, in his examination of the rave subculture closely associated with the drug Ecstasy, Redhead (1991) argues that the style of clothes, the language or argot and the music are all built up from a melange of previous fashions and musical styles, commercial pressures, wider social circumstances, chance happenings and a host other factors which exert varying degrees of influence. In short, fashions and subcultures are really devoid of any meaning.

Left realism

Left realism has developed in the last 15 years as probably the mainstream form of criminology. It is one of the most 'complete' form of sociological thinking in that it seeks to avoid the age-old division between sociologists who start their analyses by looking a the structure of society (for example Marxists and functionalists) and those who begin with the perceptions of individuals (for example social constructionists). Left realists set out an agenda which includes all levels of analysis, and then tries to complete this agenda.

The origins of left realism

The origins of left realism lie in:

● the newer Marxist approaches examined in the last chapter, in particular a group of writers who argued for a 'new criminology' in the mid-1970s

- the decline of social class as an organising principle for sociological research

- the impact of local crime surveys, which showed that traditional assumptions about the victims of crime and the impact of crime on individuals underestimated how bad the situation was for the least powerful in society

- the desire to move away from 'pure' theory to more applied research which could be put into action

- the desire to escape from 'romanticism', by which left realists mean the way that sociological research had romanticised and excused the crimes committed by youth.

Critical criminology

In the late 1970s a group of writers – in particular Taylor, Walton and Young (1973) – began to modify the then dominant Marxist approach in criminology. They felt that there was too much emphasis on the study of powerful groups who created laws for their own benefit. These writers did not dispute the general Marxist framework that crime resulted from the control of society by an unrepresentative group, but they felt they needed to draw some lessons from the social constructionist or labelling school of thought and include a much clearer analysis of action and reaction by criminals and law enforcers. The result was the 'new criminology'.

Taylor, Walton and Young (1973) suggested that sociological theories of crime ought to cover all of the following points:

- *The wider origins of the deviant act.* This refers to the normal Marxist point that all actions in society need to be understood in relation to the economic structure of society.

- *The immediate origins of the deviant act.* This refers to the need to understand why individuals are motivated to commit crime. For example, it may be poverty or the desire for 'fun' that drives a person to commit a criminal act.

- *The act itself.* Why should a person choose a particular act as opposed to any other? For example, why does one individual choose solvent abuse and another football hooliganism?

- *The immediate origins of social reaction.* Why do people respond in different ways to a particular deviant act? For example, do police officers respond differently to black offenders?

Figure 5.3 Critical criminology

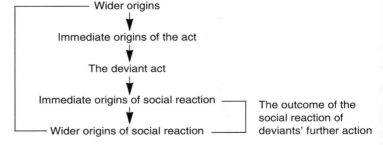

- *The wider origins of deviant reaction.* This refers to the need to explain the wider background to law creation and enforcement – for example, studying the circumstances leading to the criminalisation of certain forms of picketing.

- *The outcome of the social reaction on deviants' further action.* This refers to the need to understand how the 'labelled' criminals respond to their labelling. Clearly here the 'new criminologists' have been influenced by interactionist approaches.

- *The nature of the deviant process as a whole.* This final point concerns the need to appreciate the sheer complexity of social action and not to force it all into simplistic models, as happens with 'left functionalism'. If this makes the explanations exceedingly complex, that is the price to be paid for fully understanding the nature of crime.

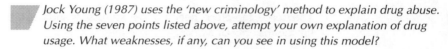
Jock Young (1987) uses the 'new criminology' method to explain drug abuse. Using the seven points listed above, attempt your own explanation of drug usage. What weaknesses, if any, can you see in using this model?

Decline in class analysis

Marxist approaches stress above all else the importance of social class. Society is said to be characterised by class conflict as a result of the ownership of production and commerce by a small ruling class. The ruling group seeks to maintain control over the bulk of the population by dividing it into competing groups, by constructing and maintaining values to its own benefit if necessary by force.

All Marxist approaches use social class as a starting point for analysis. However, in sociology generally there has been an acceptance that there may be other divisions which are of great significance, such as gender and race. The newer Marxist approaches have 'grafted on' the analyses of race and gender in a way that has not been to everyone's satisfaction. Left realism has responded to this by tackling class, race and gender as equally important elements of analysis – in essence they are looking at differences in power in society, and in doing so draw more from the work of Weber than Marx.

Local crime surveys

The significance of the last point was reinforced by the results of several local crime surveys – in particular studies conducted in Islington (North London) and Merseyside – which gave a rather different picture of crime from the British Crime Survey.

The original BCS (which is discussed in detail in Chapter 10) suggested that, for the majority of the population, street crime and burglary were unusual, not to say remote, occurrences. Furthermore, it was demonstrated by the use of national data that women and older people had a much lower likelihood of being victims of crime than young men. In some ways this concurred with the traditional Marxist argument that the really important (and ignored) crime was corporate crime, or 'crimes of the powerful', which we discussed on pp. 78–81.

However, the local surveys suggested that in fact in certain geographical areas, such as inner-city areas, women and older people really were more likely to be victims. But, even more significantly, the impact on their lives of being 'victims' of crime was very, very powerful indeed. So it seemed that crime was a real concern of people living in inner cities and that it was not just a class issue – crime hit both working-class and middle-class people, but women and older people especially.

The role of the police

The Marxist analysis of society suggests that the primary role of the police is to control the working class, particularly working-class male youth (see for example Hall 1979, which we mentioned on pp. 75–6). The police can best be seen as enemies or oppressors, according to this view. But the left realists suggested that, if the results of the local crime surveys were true, people in inner cities and social housing developments actually wanted higher levels of policing to protect them. Furthermore, this was as true for those of Afro-Caribbean origins as any other groups, as long as the policing was fair and just.

The police, therefore, need not be oppressors and could potentially be of great help for the majority of working-class people.

 How do people view the police? Design and implement a small-scale survey to investigate the attitudes of a cross-section of the public to the police in your locality. What differences in attitudes (if any) emerge between different ages, social classes and racial groups?

The flight from romanticism

This is possibly one of the most contentious areas of left realism. Left realists suggest that Marxists have *romanticised* working-class youth, and particularly black youth, so that their acts are explained away or justified. The consequences for victims – themselves largely working class and black – are thereby overlooked. Left realists argue that this can only be viewed as romanticism.

 Realism must trace accurately the relationship between victim and ofender. Crime is not an activity of latter day Robin Hoods – the vast majority of working-class crime is directed within the working-class. It is intra-class not inter-class in its nature, and inter-racial crime is (in fact) overwhelmingly intra-racial. This is not to deny the impact of crimes of the powerful or indeed of the social problems created by capitalism. Rather, left realism notes that the working class is a victim of crime from all directions. It notes that the more vulnerable a person is economically and socially, the more likely it is that both working class and white-collar crime will occur against them.

Source: Adapted from Matthews and Young (1986)

1 *Explain the meanings of the terms realism and idealism as used in criminology.*
2 *How and why does realism reject the idealist approach?*

The causes of crime

The points we have made so far help us to understand the underlying principles that motivated the left realists, but they do not yet provide us with an explanation of why crime occurs. There are three key elements to such an explanation:

● relative deprivation

● subculture

● marginalisation.

Relative deprivation

One of the most interesting arguments advanced by Jock Young (1987) is that unemployment and poverty are not directly the causes of crime. The unemployment–crime link has become a cherished refrain for most liberal and socialist politicians in recent years, and the rejection of the link has caused a considerable stir on the left.

Young explains his argument by pointing to the old notion of relative deprivation. People measure their situation against social expectations provided by society. A person may well be poor in some objective sense, but may not feel poor if all those around him or her are in the same financial situation. On the other hand, by making a different comparison the same person could feel poor and aggrieved. The feeling of being deprived is relative to one's expectations.

Young points out that in the 1930s the levels of unemployment were roughly the same as in the mid-1980s, yet the level of crime was 15 times higher in the 1980s than in the 1930s. Poverty cannot be the cause for this, as one of the poorest groups in society is the elderly, yet they commit the lowest number of crimes of all groups.

According to Lea and Young (1984), contemporary youth feel frustrated and bitter because of the disparity between their high expectations and the reality of what they can actually obtain, given the levels of unemployment and the low-wage jobs on offer.

As we saw earlier, the values of a subculture are not sharply distinct from the general set of values in society. Working-class youth accept the dominant values of society and accept those aims too – but their behaviour is modified by the circumstances in which they find themselves: to put it simply, they are at the bottom of the heap. Therefore they develop strategies to enable them to solve their problems, and these can include crime.

Subculture

The model of society proposed by the theories of left realism consists of a multiplicity of groups which have developed their own variations of value, within the mainstream culture, as a response to their own problems. So the police have their own subculture (as they face particular problems) just as much as working-class black youths have theirs.

The subcultural model proposed by Lea and Young has a number of distinguishing features:

● *Subculture as a response to problems.* Those who are most likely to commit street crime have developed their own cultures as a response to their particular problems and position in society. They are not necessarily aware of this, nor is it necessarily true to say that the subculture provides them with a real solution; nevertheless the subculture is a means of solving their problems.

In North Philadelphia, teenage drug dealers return from a shopping spree. Money is spent on leather coats and gold jewellery – indications here of cultural status.

● *The macro–micro dimension.* The 'problems' which people face are not randomly distributed. They are the precise results of a political and economic system. Capitalism ensures that some people are far worse off than others and considerably less powerful. (This is quite clearly a structural model; see pp. 4 and 97.)

● *The objective–subjective balance.* The views of the members of a subculture are important but not necessarily the 'reality' of the situation. On the other hand, it is not right for sociologists and other observers to read into the actions of the members of the subculture the meanings they would like to exist there. (This is a reference to the criticisms of the Marxist youth culture approach made by Stanley Cohen, discussed on pp. 92–93 above.) A balance has to be struck between the views of sociologists and those involved in the subculture, though one needs to ask just how Lea and Young propose to do this.

● *The subculture is not completely separated from the values of the wider society.* The distinctive values of subcultures are not divorced from the wider society; rather they are closely enmeshed in those values. They are distinct but not separate. This is important, because Lea and Young argue that it is precisely because of the acceptance of British society's material goals that young blacks, for example, feel relatively deprived. (See the discussions on Matza and subterranean values on pp. 54–5 and race and crime on pp. 244–8.)

● *The historical dimension.* The subculture is not passed on from one generation to the next, but is created anew by each generation according to their experiences and the context in which they live. These contexts change over time. So the working class do not have an alternative set of values, as Miller suggested (see p. 53); rather they have constantly changing sets of values reflecting the broader changes in society.

Marginalisation

The third element of the left realist approach concerns the concept of marginalisation. This means the process by which certain groups find themselves 'on the edge' of society, in both an economic and a political sense. White and black working-class youth, especially in inner-city areas, face particular problems in terms of their high rates of unemployment. However, Young points out that there is a political dimension beyond this.

A number of pressure groups and political organisations have developed over the years to force the voice of the working class to be heard and some of their demands to be met. The strength of the working class lay in its economic muscle, for example the strike, and to some extent in the feeling of community in working-class districts. However, youths have no such economic muscle, nor do they have political or community organisations. They are marginal to both the economic and the political system.

Before the extension of the franchise towards the end of the last century, there were no legal channels through which the working class could influence political decisions. Their outlets were political demonstrations and riots. For Lea and Young, this is true of 'marginalised' youths, particularly black youths, today.

Alternative approaches to unemployment and crime

Unemployment does lead to increased criminal behaviour, according to a new report ('Unemployment, school leaving and crime', Farrington *et al*, in the *British Journal of Criminology*, Vol 26, No 4).

Theoretical and common-sense hypotheses that increases in unemployment will lead to rising crime have previously been dogged by the difficulty of establishing causal links between aggregate crime and unemployment rates. Other intervening factors, such as the validity of unemployment statistics and changes in the exercise of police discretion in dealing with offenders, have also made interpretation extremely difficult.

But this new study by Farrington and his Cambridge colleagues has circumvented most of these difficulties. Using a group of 411 mostly working-class males, studied since they were eight or nine years old, the researchers analysed data from the period before and after leaving school when the youths were 14, 16 and 18 years old. They were therefore able

to compare the youths' educational and job histories with their officially recorded criminal behaviour over time. This demonstrates quite conclusively that unemployment does lead to greater offending, though the nature of the relationship is not straightforward.

Not all types of offending were increased by unemployment, and neither were all unemployed youths prone to react criminally. Unemployment led to a significantly increased number of offences for material gain (theft, burglary, fraud and so on), but other offences (such as assault, criminal damage and drug offences) were unaffected.

It was also clear that higher levels of offending during unemployment occurred only with those youths who were already at greatest risk – those with low-income parents, from large households, in poor housing, with relatively neglectful parents, and of low educational achievement.

Farrington is careful to remind his readers that these data were collected in 1968–72 when unemployment was relatively low. The group studied were also almost entirely white. Nevertheless, the message is stark, particularly for the inner cities.

Source: Morgan (1986)

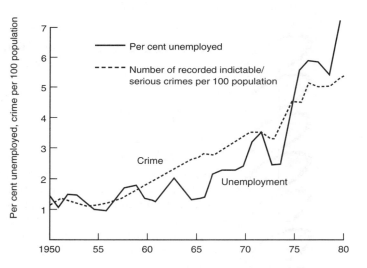

Figure 5.4 Crime and unemployment

Source: Tarling (1982)

There is no evidence that absolute deprivation (e.g. unemployment, lack of schooling, poor housing, etc.) leads automatically to crime. The crime rate was minute in the 1930s, despite very high levels of poverty. Left realist criminology points to relative deprivation in certain conditions as being the major cause of crime: that is, when people experience a level of unfairness in their allocation of resources and turn to individualistic means to attempt to right this condition.

The common problem of mechanistic notions of crime causation is that they assume an immediate causation. But if we consider that it takes time for people to evaluate their predicaments and even longer for them to build up alternative solutions, then the notion of an immediate causation becomes ludicrous. Unemployment now does not relate to crime the day after tomorrow. Youth subcultures, for example, build up and develop appraisals of their situation, but they may not flourish until several years after the initial problem of unemployment. Perhaps even more significantly, the development of a hidden economy including a level of illegal activity will take a considerable time to build up.

Source: Young (1994)

1 Explain how the two extracts above interpret the information provided in Figure 5.4 differently.

2 What do left realists mean by:
● mechanistic notions of crime causation
● absolute deprivation
● relative deprivation?

3 Explain the meaning of the term 'youth subculture'. How would left realists and contemporary Marxists explain the origins of youth subculture?

4 In Chapters 1 and 3 we used the term 'positivistic' to describe the development of criminology in the UK. Explain how the first extract is an example of 'positivism'.

5 The first extract makes use of a 'longitudinal study' to understand the causes of crime. Explain the meaning of the term, illustrating with material taken from the extract. What advantages and disadvantages are there in using longitudinal studies?

The framework of crime

Left realism offers a clear explanation for street crime with very obvious origins. But the approach aims to be a total theory of crime which includes all the better elements of previous theories and packages them in such a way that policies to combat crime will emerge. The explanation for street crime is only one part of this wider project.

Left realists argue that their approach can help understand the entire range of crime and allows us to shift away from stereotypes of young males driven to crime by factors beyond their control. These theorists accept the importance of wider factors, but concentrate on the rational process of the individual making choices within a subculture and then in response to official agencies of control. So structure and meanings are combined.

Figure 5.5 The square of crime

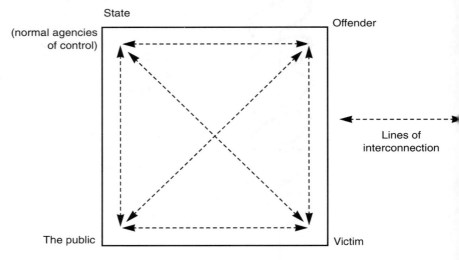

State
(normal agencies of control)
Offender
Lines of interconnection
The public
Victim

The starting point in understanding this wider analysis is what Young, Lea and Matthews all call 'the square of crime' (Figure 5.5). This illustrates the interplay between the offender, the victim, the public (agents of 'informal control'), and the agencies of formal control (sometimes referred to as 'the state'), all of which are involved in crime in some way. It is only by understanding the complex interrelationships between the various elements of the square that we can begin to grasp the complex nature of crime.

The victim

In one sense, being a victim of crime depends upon reporting the crime. It is generally the victim who decides a crime has taken place and then further decides whether to report it or not.

Depending upon the crime, victims are often not randomly chosen but have some sort of relationship with the offender. It may be close, such as a partner in domestic violence, or distant, such as a person of similar race and class living in a local neighbourhood.

The idea of an 'average spread' of crimes portrayed by official statistics, which suggests that most people have an equal chance of becoming victims, is inaccurate. In reality, people who are victims once have significantly higher chances of becoming victims a number of times.

The offender

As we saw earlier, the factors suggested by left realists to explain street crime include the development of a subculture within a wider context, the influence of beliefs about relative deprivation, and economic marginalisation. These beliefs and values are of course related to the role of the state in structuring inequalities and in the activities of wider groups of the public in terms of the development of values which permit or encourage crime.

A point which tends to be ignored in most analyses of crime, according to left realists, is the *trajectory* of crime over time. In essence this means that offenders become involved in criminal acts, make choices about the types of crime they will commit, and then (for the overwhelming majority) move out of crime at different periods in their lives. Research is needed to determine the influence on the trajectory of factors such as the judicial system, stable relationships and employment.

The state

The state shapes the nature of political, social and economic forces which partially provide the context of crime. This includes defining what is crime, and making decisions about enforcing the laws. The role of the police and the judicial system is crucial to an understanding of the motivations of offenders in committing crime in the first place, but also in continuing to commit crime. Left realism has engaged in considerable research on the impact of different styles of policing and their effect on crime levels.

Informal control

In many ways this has become the most important area of analysis. Left realists have pointed out that the various forms of informal control have the greatest impact on levels of crime.

Fear of stigmatisation and rejection by family, peer groups and neighbours has been shown to be one of the most powerful determinants of behaviour.

Informal controls also exist *within* formal agencies of control, affecting how the formal control operates. An example is the belief that there is a high level of racism among police officers. It is argued that police officers on patrol duty reinterpret and subvert the formal rules, and in so doing they fail to carry out the official aims of the police service. This seems to be true when police officers choose individuals for 'stop and search'.

Informal controls also link victims and offenders. Most crimes of theft are committed by one group of local people against others in the same locality. The victims are therefore in some way failing to gain control of informal social control. One example of how victims and offenders are linked is that in many inner-city areas or social housing developments crime is perpetuated because people are willing to purchase stolen goods at low prices. The public who are purchasing the goods are also providing the pool of victims for the theft.

Table 5.1 The multiplicity of agencies involved in crime control

Stages in the crime	Factors	Agencies
Causes of crime	Unemployment	Central government
	Housing	Local authority
	Leisure	Business
The moral context	Peer group values	Schools
	Community cohesion	Family
		Public
		Mass media
The situation of commission	Physical environment	Local authority
	Lighting	Public
	Home security	Police
The detection of crime	Public reporting	Public
	Detective work	Police
The response to the offenders	Punishment	Courts
	Rehabilitation	Police
		Social services
		Probation
The response to the victim	Insurance	Local authority
	Public support	Victim support
		The public groups
		Social services

Left realism explores the relationship between the immediate social factors which lead to crime and wider social factors. It also stresses that something needs to be done about crime, and that this task is not solely for the police.

1 Explain in your own words the significance of the various 'Stages in the crime' in Table 5.1.

2 Explain how the agencies mentioned in the table can contribute to combating crime.

3 Arrange to interview a representative from your local authority on what they are doing to limit crime in your town or city. If possible, also arrange to speak to a member of your local Police Commission. (Names and addresses can be found in your local library.)

Criticisms of left realism

Left realism has provided a different way of approaching the understanding of street crime, but in doing so it has gathered a considerable number of enemies.

The first criticism is that much if not all of the theory is drawn from previous approaches. It is less of a breakthrough than a pulling together of ideas, sometimes failing to acknowledge the origins of the work.

Secondly, the theory has developed in complexity (it is much more detailed than outlined above), yet it has not delivered the goods in terms of successful research using a very clear left realist structure. How good is a theory which cannot be tested?

Thirdly, it ignores white-collar and corporate crime. It does so because surveys show that it is street crime and burglary which most people worry about – but this does not mean that they are more important phenomena than white-collar crime. In a sense this reinforces the Marxist argument that the 'ruling class' scapegoats youth crime to draw attention away from white-collar and corporate crime.

The fourth criticism some critics would make is that the concentration on street crime has, to an extent, supported the racialisation of the street crime debate. According to Solomos (1989), the emphasis on this form of crime has led to a belief that street crime is 'black crime'. Others have gone further, and suggested that the left realist explanation of street crime is actually racist.

A final, and perhaps rather difficult, criticism is that left realism falls back on the common-sense definition of crime prevalent in capitalist society. It accepts that street crime is of real concern to working-class people, and concludes that it must be studied and combated. Brown and Hogg (1992) argue that this lack of critical reflection over the nature of crime is not good enough. Marxists have claimed that crime is defined by the ruling class and that the emphasis on street crime is in the ruling class's interest, so left realists are supporting an ideologically biased definition of crime which helps to sustain capitalism. In their own defence, Lea and Young have claimed that they only study street crime because it really does harm working-class people. However, the critics remain unconvinced, alleging that left realists happily ignore other things that do significant harm to the working class such as poor housing and environmental pollution.

Summary

In this chapter we have explored how the ideas of Marxism have been developed in different ways. The Marxist subcultural school was the first real development. It tried to enliven the traditional approach with dynamic and innovative insights. It sought to understand the activities of youth and explain their behaviour as both rational and as a form of inarticulate political protest. However, the approach was heavily and effectively criticised by Stanley Cohen, who pointed out its ideological bias.

A second development, known as critical criminology, tried to infuse new life into Marxism by drawing upon the insights provided by labelling or social constructionist theories. It tried to relate the specific motivations of individuals to the wider social context in which a crime is committed, and to include in the analysis the social reaction of those affected by the crime and the consequent effect on the future behaviour of the perpetrator.

Critical criminologists split among themselves. One group developed what they call 'left realism', which is very far from traditional Marxism. It is mainly concerned with exploring the impact of crime upon the daily lives of 'ordinary' people and in developing strategies to ease their burden.

I was a housewife drug dealer

'You can always get women to buy knickers, and sex toys are good for a laugh. So the sexy lingerie parties seemed like a good idea when I needed some money two years ago.

'My husband Mark, who's in computers, thought of the idea of selling drugs as well. I'm 35 now and have had a casual drug habit since I was at college – mainly dope and E and occasionally coke and crack just to be experimental – nothing heavy. We have always passed on drugs for friends. Mark has contacts from years back and so it's never been a problem getting hold of them.

The knickers and stuff became a bit of a cover. I could make much more money on the drugs. It was a quiet area in the suburbs and most of the women who might have taken drugs ages ago just didn't get the opportunity any more. It was an untapped market – the kind 'pushers' would never have the inclination to go out and get.

'I never felt guilty about it. Smack heads living on the streets is one thing but this was a few house-wives having a good time.

'Those parties were a hoot. I don't think any group of women ever found knickers so funny as we did when we'd all lit up. There was the odd po-faced person who didn't do the drugs but most of them were glad of something to take them away from it all.

'So you could say I was more than a little peed off when somebody shopped me to the police. They just visited me one day, said they 'had reason to believe' I had drugs and started ransacking the house. I had stuff there but fortunately not as much as sometimes and no class A. I was only done for possession – all I got was a fine and a ticking off – as I just admitted my guilt and tried to look like a sappy housewife with a sad life. I had a £300 fine and had to go for counselling to teach me what a bad girl I'd been and that a woman with two kids should be a good influence!

'It cut back my confidence for a while ... but a year on I still get stuff if people ask me – nothing like as much as I used to, but enough to make a bit on the side.

'It just feels too risky now. I know that if I get caught again I could end up inside.'
Source: The Big Issue, No 150, 2–8 October 1995

Demonstrate how a left realist framework can help us to understand the activities of the woman in the above extract. First briefly explain what happened, and then discuss the following elements:

1 *The wider origins of the deviant act: What cultural and economic factors created the situation in which the offence could take place?*

2 *The immediate origins of the act: What specific factors led to the decision to act illegally?*

3 *The particular choice of that act rather than another: Where is the rationality involved?*

4 *The career or trajectory of the deviant activity: Did it start and finish in the same way? Did it grow in size? Why did things change?*

5 *What social reactions took place initially to the deviant acts?*

6 *How did this affect the deviant activities?*

7 *What further reactions took place from the 'public'?*

8 *What were the reactions of the official agencies of control?*

9 *What was the deviant's response to these reactions?*

10 *Finally, explain how the concepts of subculture, relative deprivation and marginalisation can all apply to this situation.*

Examination Question

Evaluate the contribution of the 'New Criminology' to a sociological understanding of crime.

AEB, Summer 1994

Bibliography

Brake, M. (1980) *The Sociology of Youth Culture and Youth*, London: Routledge

Brown, D. and Hogg, R. (1992) 'Law and order politics – left realism and radical criminology: a view from down under' in Mathews, R. and Young, J. (eds) *Issues in Realist Criminology*, London: Sage

Cohen, P. (1972) *Subcultural Conflict and Working Class Community*, Working Papers in Cultural Studies No. 2, University of Birmingham

Cohen, S. (1980) *Folk Devils and Moral Panics*, London: Martin Robertson

Eisenstadt, S. (1956) *From Generation to Generation*, New York: Free Press

Griffin, C. (1985) Typical Girls? *Young Women from School to the Job Market*, London: Routledge

Hall, S. and Jefferson, T. (eds) (1977) *Resistance through Rituals*, London: Hutchinson

Hall, S. et al (1979) *Policing the Crisis*, London: Macmillan

Hebdidge, D. (1979) *Subculture: The Meaning of Style*, London: Methuen

Lea, J. and Young, J. (1984) *What Is to Be Done about Law and Order?*, Harmondsworth: Penguin

Mathews, R. and Young, J. (1986) *Confronting Crime*, London: Sage

McRobbie, A. (1978) 'Working-class girls and the culture of femininity', in Centre for Contemporary Cultural Studies, *Women Take Issue*, London: Hutchinson

Morgan, R. (1986) 'Jobless turn to crime, study shows', New Society, 14 November

Pearson, S. (1975) '"Paki-bashing" in a North Lancashire cotton town: a case study and its history', in Mungham, G. and Pearson, S. (eds) *British Working Class Youth Culture*, London: Routledge

Redhead, S. (1991) *Rave Off: Youth, subcultures and the law*, Social Studies Review

Solomos, J. (1989) *Race and Racism in Contemporary Britain*, London: Macmillan

Tarling, R. (1982) *Crime and Unemployment*, Home Office Research and Planning Bulletin, 12

Taylor, I., Walton, P. and Young, J. (1973) *The New Criminology*, London: Routledge

Young, J. (1994) 'Recent paradigms in criminology', in Maguire, M.R. and Reiner, R. (eds) *The Oxford Handbook of Criminology*, Oxford: Oxford University Press

6

Social constructionism

'How do other people see me?' The looking-glass self

Social constructionism or labelling theory derives from the 'symbolic interactionist' school of sociology. This originated towards the end of the last century in the writings of Cooley and later Mead. In essence, symbolic interactionism was a revolt against the positivist approach which viewed society as objective and 'real'.

In the positivist model people were seen to be totally controlled by society and had little autonomy. They were like puppets with 'society' pulling their strings. Symbolic interactionism stressed the way that people actively go about creating their own worlds, making choices and altering their behaviour according to their own perceptions of situations. Far from being some all-powerful controlling force, society was seen as the product of people's interactions.

The use of the word 'symbol' in the term 'symbolic interactionism' suggests that the world consists of symbols to which we attach meaning and then respond. A simple example of a symbol is a red traffic light. This 'tells' us to stop if we are driving a car. There is of course nothing intrinsic in a red light that says we *have* to stop. It is merely a symbol which we understand and respond to. Furthermore, the symbol can be ignored in certain situations – by an ambulance racing to the scene of an accident, for example.

A red traffic light is an inanimate symbol, but we respond to symbols attached to people as well. We have expectations and particular ways of behaving towards a doctor, a mother, a next-door neighbour and so on, even though this may be the same person in different roles.

Symbolic interactionists argue that we are brought up to recognise symbols attached to things and people and to respond in what we regard as appropriate ways. The responses are not fixed, or determined by society, but are open to negotiation by us. Society consists of people responding to, and negotiating over, symbols.

This may well be interesting, you say, but what are the implications for crime? More positivistic approaches start from the viewpoint that only a small proportion of the population commit deviant and criminal acts. If we make the assumption that people act the way they do because they are 'propelled' by social forces beyond their control, then presumably if we can isolate those social forces we can find the 'causes' of their antisocial behaviour. The result of this approach is to blame parental upbringing, a delinquent peer group, the nature of the capitalist economy, etc.

The alternative approach which developed from symbolic interactionism has been called *labelling theory*. This is generally associated with the work of Howard Becker and to a lesser extent Edwin Lemert.

Becker argues that the central questions for the study of deviance and rule-breaking are:

● how an individual becomes labelled as a deviant and the consequences for that person of being so labelled: these are the processes of labelling and the deviant career

● how certain acts come to be defined as deviant and the consequences of this process: this is the process of law creation.

The following sections of this chapter will explain and develop these issues, applying them to a range of apparently disparate areas including the changing concepts of sexuality, child abuse, homelessness and 'juvenile delinquency'. We will also look at a classic study of how and why laws were introduced in the USA to make marijuana use illegal, and also on the issue of drug use we will look at the contemporary British situation. The intention is to illustrate the significance of social constructionism in the study of deviance and to highlight how different the insights of this approach are from those of other approaches.

The labelling of individuals and groups

Writers such as Becker (1963) and Lemert (1972) have pointed out the important fact that most of us commit deviant acts at one time or another and yet we continue to regard those who are caught as somehow different from the rest of us. For labelling theorists the only difference between the bulk of the population and criminals is that criminals get caught!

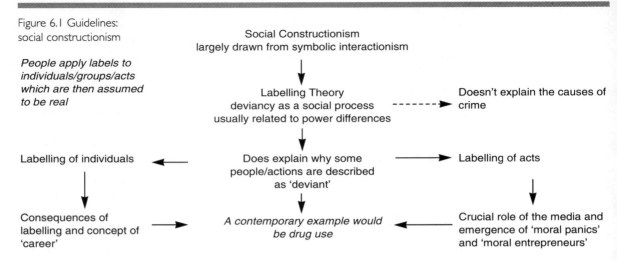

Figure 6.1 Guidelines:
social constructionism

People apply labels to individuals/groups/acts which are then assumed to be real

A story from Box's book *Deviance, Reality and Society* (1981) will illustrate this. Box once found himself selected for jury duty. The trial was fairly mundane and consisted of a theft charge concerning a very small amount of money. After a short deliberation the jury agreed that the defendant was guilty. Having finished their duty as citizens, the members of the jury then relaxed and in a matter of fact way began to discuss how they would fiddle their travelling and out of pocket expenses by claiming inflated amounts. Box points out that most people on the jury actually 'fiddled' more money than the woman they had just convicted of theft had stolen!

The difference, then, between being a criminal and being an upright citizen is the fact that a person is labelled as such. The application of a label to someone has significant consequences for how that person is treated by others and perceives himself or herself.

The labelling process: how individuals and groups are labelled

We live in a world in which we categorise people and then respond to them according to the label. Teachers label pupils as 'good' or 'troublemaker' and then act accordingly by rewarding and punishing; the casual acquaintance is labelled as 'interesting' or 'boring' and we seek out their company or avoid them on this basis.

Lemert (1972) drew a distinction between primary and secondary deviance. In a study of stuttering, he found that this speech impediment was common in only one Native American nation living on the Pacific Coast, and was unknown in all the others. Lemert observed that public oratory was extremely important among the nation that displayed high levels of stuttering; indeed, to attain the status of 'manhood' a mastery of oratory was necessary. If young boys showed any speech defect the parents reacted with such concern and horror that the child became sensitised to his defect and worried about it. His nervousness would be so great, argued Lemert that it would *cause* him to stutter.

We can see here that the primary deviance of a speech defect was not particularly important, but the effect of the worried parents *labelling* the child a stutterer was important, and caused the nervousness that actually led to the stuttering (the secondary deviance).

Thus people are labelled in various ways by others and then treated accordingly. This has consequences which labelling theorists suggest are more important than the original deviance.

 There are a number of ways of finding out how people respond differently to awkward, embarrassing or deviant situations. You could devise a simple questionnaire consisting of two stages: first, ask what they define as deviant or odd, and second, investigate how they would respond to hypothetical 'deviant' situations which you suggest to them.

A more radical (and more difficult) activity is to set up an experiment. Create a deviant situation (a loud argument in public, or a pretend fight, perhaps). Observe the various responses of the 'audience'. Interview them afterwards to see how they interpreted the situation.

Variability

The process of labelling someone is not straightforward or based on clear-cut laws; after all, the person who interests you may bore me and *vice versa*, while the unemployed youth who steals from a large chain store may evoke sympathy in one person and anger in another. Labelling can be said to be variable, with the application of a label to someone varying with such diverse factors as place, gender, age and so on.

An example of this is John Kitsuse's study of responses to homosexuals (Kitsuse 1962). He asked mature students about their responses to homosexuals whom they had met, or who had made advances to them. The definitions of what constituted 'typical' homosexual behaviour, or what actions had signified homosexual advances, varied astonishingly. One student claimed that when he was in the army he knew an officer was homosexual because he had been pleasant to ordinary troops. Another student claimed that a man he had met in a bar was obviously homosexual because he had wanted to talk about psychology! Yet other students had defined acquaintances kissing them as merely signs of friendship. Responses too varied considerably, from violent rejections of presumed advances to no change in attitude whatsoever. One note of caution here: Kitsuse assumed that the respondents in his research were themselves heterosexual; it is possible that part of the variety of responses could be linked to the sexual preferences of the respondents.

Figure 6.2 Variety of possible responses to trouble

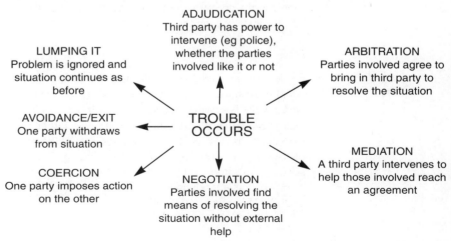

LUMPING IT
Problem is ignored and situation continues as before

ADJUDICATION
Third party has power to intervene (eg police), whether the parties involved like it or not

ARBITRATION
Parties involved agree to bring in third party to resolve the situation

AVOIDANCE/EXIT
One party withdraws from situation

TROUBLE OCCURS

COERCION
One party imposes action on the other

NEGOTIATION
Parties involved find means of resolving the situation without external help

MEDIATION
A third party intervenes to help those involved reach an agreement

Social constructionist theories do not make the assumption that there is any one response to social problems or 'troubles'. Instead they argue that there are numerous possible responses, ranging from ignoring a troublesome act to calling the police. This means that *responses* can be as important as causes of the initial act. Take the example of domestic violence. Traditionally this was ignored by the police, or the victim of violence either left their partner or simply accepted the violence – however gradually the police have begun to take domestic violence very seriously indeed and now are very likely to arrest the perpetrator. This has had a very significant impact on the numbers of arrests for violent crime. But what has actually happened is that the response has changed.

Understanding the variety of responses also helps us to see how counsellors, clergy and social workers are all agents of social control who are using different methods to police officers but still responding to 'trouble'.

Explain how the different responses may (or may not) apply in different ways to the following:

- *drug abuse by a daughter giving 'trouble' to a mother*
- *violence of a male against a female partner on a regular basis*
- *loud music played by householder giving 'trouble' to neighbours*
- *sexist comments/harassment by males in the street causing 'trouble' to females.*

Negotiability

We often change our minds about people and then decide as a result to re-label them. After half an hour with the 'bore' we may realise he or she is actually quite interesting, but shy. People also have some control over the labels placed upon them by others. Labelling theorists point out that some people may have the power to reject a negative label, while others are unable to muster enough resources to deny the negative label and so must accept it.

An example of how labels can be rejected comes from Reiss's work on boy homosexual prostitutes. The boys developed a strict code of honour in which they were not allowed to enjoy their activities and anyone who did was immediately thrown out of the group. The boys perceived themselves, and were perceived by others in the group, as heterosexual, finding little difficulty rejecting the label of homosexual through their aggressiveness and a code of honour.

Master status

Becker (1963) used this term to describe how, once a label is applied to someone (child-molester or violent criminal, for instance), all the actions that a person performs or has performed in the past are interpreted in the light of the label. For example, we may stop talking about 'a dedicated father', 'a committed charity worker', 'an honest politician' and think only of the man as a paedophile, thereby discounting his other 'positive' aspects. The significance of the concept of master status is illustrated by the surprise that most people show when prisoners engage in some charitable fundraising activity, as if the fact that they have committed a crime excludes them from such behaviour.

Effects of labelling: how people perceive themselves

Cooley, writing near the end of the last century, had suggested that a good way to describe how we see ourselves is *the looking-glass self*. By this he meant that we build our identity primarily as a result of how others act and respond towards us. If people comment on how ugly I am, what a large nose I have and how spotty my skin is, I am likely to see a big-nosed, spotty, rather ugly man in the mirror and to think of myself that way. This view of myself will influence how I act towards other people. For example, I will probably lack confidence in my dealings with the opposite sex and may revert to writing books as a result!

Career

Becker (1963) suggested that the process by which people take on an identity given to them by others could be regarded as a 'career'. We normally use the term 'career' when we are talking about employment, and it means a gradual climb up the ladder to reach the point where one can finally say 'I made it'. At this stage the person may have achieved his or her aim in life.

Becker suggested that this process is going on all the time in the area of deviance, as people gradually attain the status of being anything from a drug addict to a child abuser.

Figure 6.3 The deviant career

	Initial situation	Label applied to individual: people act differently	Responses of individual seen as proof of oddity	Alter behaviour in an attempt to conform
Ms X				Unable to escape from deviant career
Person's perception	'I am the same as everyone else'	'Why are they treating me like this?'	'I don't appear to be the same as everyone else. Maybe I am odd'?	

> 1 *Why did Ms X get labelled in the first place? Surely she must be odd to be picked out?*
>
> 2 *Why do some people escape the deviant career and others remain trapped in it?*

Clearly the career cannot progress without other people labelling a person and then responding to them in such a way that eventually they accept that this is their identity (or master status). They then begin to act in a manner which reflects this perception of themselves. In turn this final acceptance of the label and adjustment of behaviour will confirm to others that they were right all along.

A fatal case of labelling

One day an outbreak of wailing and a great commotion told me that a death had occurred somewhere in the neighbourhood. Kima'i, a young lad of my acquaintance, of sixteen or so, had fallen from a coconut palm and killed himself.

He had broken the rules of exogamy [with] the daughter of his mother's sister. This had been known and generally disapproved of but nothing was done until the girl's discarded lover, who had wanted to marry her and who felt personally injured, took the initiative. This rival threatened first to use black magic against the guilty youth, but this had not much effect. Then one evening he insulted the culprit in public, accusing him in the hearing of the whole community of incest and hurling at him certain expressions intolerable to a native.

For this there was only one remedy; only one means of escape remained to the unfortunate youth. Next morning, he put on festive attire and ornamentation, climbed a coconut palm and addressed the community, speaking from among the palm leaves and bidding them farewell. He explained the reasons for his desperate deed and also launched forth a veiled accusation against the man who had driven him to his death, upon which it became the duty of his clansmen to avenge him. Then he wailed aloud, as is the custom, jumped from a palm some sixty feet high and was killed on the spot. There followed a fight within the village in which the rival was wounded; and the quarrel was repeated during the funeral.

Whether an act is deviant depends on how other people react to it. You can commit clan incest and suffer from no more than gossip as long as no one makes a public accusation: but you will be driven to your death if the accusation is made. The point is that the response of other people has to be regarded as problematic. Just because one has committed an infraction of a rule does not mean that others will respond as though this had happened. (Conversely, just because one has not violated a rule, does no mean that he may not be treated, in some circumstances, as though he had.)

Source: Becker (1963)

Construct a chart with these headings and then break the above 'story' into the relevant sections:

1 the events
2 the crime

3 *normal attitudes to crime*
4 *moral entrepreneur*
5 *the label*
6 *the consequence of the label.*

Sexuality

Traditional accounts treat homosexuality as deviant and abnormal, even if studies (such as Wellings *et al* 1994) suggest that at least 6 per cent of males and 3½ per cent of females in Britain engage in a homosexual activity at least once in their lives. Historically homosexuality has been common, if not normal, in many societies, and homosexual love (between males) was widely regarded by the Ancient Greeks as a higher form of love than that between heterosexual partners.

Today, homosexuality is illegal in many countries, including Pakistan, which punishes transgressors with whipping. In the UK the law still distinguishes between heterosexual and homosexual activity, with the latter only being legal for consenting males over the age of 18, compared to over 16 for heterosexuals.

Protesting for an equivalent age of consent, 1994

Explanations for homosexual preferences have been provided by biologists and by psychologists, both groups seeking to show how homosexuals are different from heterosexuals. However, sociologists such as Jeffrey Weeks and Michel Foucault have suggested that sexual identities are not as clear cut as generally believed, and that there is a case for arguing the normality of bisexuality.

Change of meaning over time

Weeks (1986) suggests that there are three key stages in the development of current notions of sexuality in the Western Christian world. In the first stage of early Christianity the disciples of Christ preached against the idea of sex as an activity to be undertaken purely for pleasure. It was almost 1,000 years before there gradually emerged, in the twelfth and thirteenth centuries, the belief that the only true form of acceptable sexual activity was between husband and wife for reproductive purposes. During the nineteenth century the only accepted form of sexuality became defined as heterosexual sex. Other forms of sex were regarded as deviant.

The term 'homosexuality' was only devised in 1860, both reflecting the emergence of, and helping to construct, a clear-cut sexual identity. Weeks argues that the sexual act between two people of the same sex moved from a form of particular, specific sinning *act* to a specific psycho-social *identity*.

A different, but not incompatible, historical perspective was devised by Foucault (1976–84). He pointed out that the first time governments became interested in population and birth control was in the eighteenth and early nineteenth centuries. As a result of this interest, 'discourses' or ways of thinking and discussing sexuality were developed. Discourses are key elements of Foucault's thinking: for him ways of thinking, categorising and discussing an issue have extremely important implications for the social definitions of what is normal on the one hand and deviant, perverse and unnatural on the other

The discourses that developed as a result of the government interest in population control divided sexuality into four types, with clear views on each. These types were: women's sexuality, children's sexuality, married sex, and homosexuality.

Women were not supposed to have the same sexual drive and needs as men. Children were removed from sexuality altogether. Married sex was normal (though not necessarily pleasurable). Finally, homosexuality was clearly a form of perversion, engaged in by 'perverts'. So Foucault, like Weeks, claimed that a category of person – the homosexual – was 'invented' at this time. Foucault also showed that the ability to construct a discourse reflects differences in power, so that the discourses on sexuality reflect the power of heterosexual males. The very construction of the discourse is part of a process of controlling homosexuals (and women).

Categories of homosexuality

Plummer (1975) examines the situation of male homosexuals in contemporary Britain. He argues that homosexuality falls into four categories, depending upon a variety of factors. These categories are:

1. *Casual homosexuality*. This refers to a brief encounter or passing homosexual act, often happening in periods of sexual experimentation during youth.

2. *Situated activity*, where people whose preference in most circumstances would be heterosexual turn to homosexual actions because of various constraints. This occurs in prisons, for example.

3. *Personalised homosexuality*, where homosexuality is the preference of the person, but he or she is unable to express it openly. Homosexual activity therefore become furtive and occurs in hidden encounters.

4. *Homosexuality as a way of life*, when people have 'come out' and have integrated into alternative gay or lesbian cultures which provide a network of links and social relationships.

The significance of the labelling approach

The labelling or social constructionist perspective is particularly useful in the study of homosexuality. As we can see from the work of Foucault and Weeks, homosexuality can be viewed less as a deviant form of personality caused by psychological or biological 'abnormalities' than as a social status imposed upon certain categories of acts.

Moreover, sexual acts between people of the same sex are more common than the stigmatised category of 'homosexual' would suggest. Such acts are not uncommon among those who are defined at some point in their lives as heterosexual.

Third, Plummer's categorisation of homosexual activity allows us to see quite clearly the power of labelling and the response to it. People can switch from one form of sexuality to another, depending upon how it is defined by others. For example, in both female and male prisons homosexuality is normal, even though the majority of people involved would define themselves as heterosexual. On release the majority of former prison inmates resume heterosexual activities. Another of Plummer's categories, casual homosexuality, refers to a stage that many young people go through which involves experimenting with peers of their own sex. This is a passing phase, and the individuals do not generally retain the label of homosexual.

One of Plummer's categories is particularly significant: the 'homosexuality as a way of life' category shows how a group can develop strategies to change the way that society views them. Labelling theory has often been criticised for implying that groups labelled as deviant are always powerless and must accept the stigma of the label. Yet since the 1980s gay and lesbian pressure groups have been extremely effective in demanding equal rights and challenging the traditional negative view of homosexuality. Indeed, in Foucaultian terms they are attempting to 'shift the discourse'. To some extent their efforts have been successful because it is increasingly accepted that there is a wide range of sexualities which do not necessarily have to be classified as 'right' and 'wrong'.

The labelling of acts as deviant

We have just examined the way in which people can be labelled as deviant and seen how that process has important consequences for them. However, any understanding of why *people* come to be labelled as deviant must be related to why some *acts* are considered deviant. After all, a deviant is merely a person who is believed to have committed a deviant act.

Most of us can construct a list of acts which we would argue are deviant in themselves – for example, the killing of another human being. Yet we can also see that in certain circumstances this judgement changes. The obvious example is the killing that occurs in wartime. So it is not the act of killing itself that is bad (or good) but the circumstances in which it takes place.

This *relative* element of morality prompted Becker (1963) to argue that there are no such things as actions which are deviant in themselves, merely acts that people define as deviant in certain circumstances.

The labelling perspective centres on two propositions. First, what is considered deviant and criminal varies. Second, social rules are not fixed and natural, but are created by people for various reasons.

According to Becker, there is little point in studying why people break laws until one understands why the rules exist in the first place. Laws vary according to a number of circumstances, including the following:

- *Who commits the act.* For example, if a child gets drunk it is deviant; in an adult drunkenness may be acceptable, although a drunken woman is frequently regarded as being far worse than a drunken man.

- *When the act is committed.* Twenty years ago child abuse was generally ignored, but today it is regarded as a major evil of society.

- *The places where acts are committed.* Bathing naked in Majorca is different from entering the local swimming pool (un)dressed in a similar way.

- *The society or culture in which the act takes place.* One society may well accept an act which another considers deviant. For instance, the emancipation of women in Western societies enables women to do things which in Muslim societies would be labelled deviant.

- *The historical and political context.* For example, the deliberate killing of another person in wartime may be 'good', but in peace it is generally classed as murder.

If we accept that acts are not good or bad in themselves, but that they are defined as wrong or illegal in a variety of circumstances, the next stage must be to explain the variation.

1 Give your own examples of the variation of deviance according to the points mentioned here. Are there any other headings you could suggest?

2 Does everyone regard the same acts as deviant? Construct a brief attitude questionnaire, then ask different groups of people (for example, divided by occupation, gender, age, etc.) if they regard the acts as 'bad' or not. What do the results indicate? What does this tell us about labelling theory?

The process of rule and law creation

According to Becker, what is considered deviant is neither a reflection of the 'will of the people', as the functionalists claim, nor is it necessarily a reflection of the interests of the ruling class, as the Marxists argue. Instead, Becker claimed that individuals or groups set about making certain acts illegal because they see it as in their own interests, or they genuinely believe it to be in the interests of the rest of society.

Becker advanced an essentially pluralist argument to explain the creation of rules in society; he claimed that interested groups, or 'moral entrepreneurs', attain law changes by mobilising enough support to alter social rules.

1 '... social groups create deviance by making the rules whose infraction constitutes deviance' (Becker 1963). What are the implications of Becker's statement for the study of deviance?

2 *What comments would:*
- *functionalists*
- *Marxists*
- *subcultural theorists*
- *positivist theorists*
  make in response to this quotation?

3 *Could you suggest any acts which are intrinsically deviant?*

4 *Look up the pluralist model of the state in a textbook. Compare the interactionist and pluralist models. Do any clear conclusions emerge?*

As we have just seen, labelling theory provides us with considerable insight into how the individual is affected by being defined as a criminal. But labelling theory goes beyond this and argues that rule creation is the result of a labelling process too. We will look at two examples to show how this model of law creation works: the development of laws in the United States against cannabis use, and the origins of the juvenile courts there.

The Marijuana Tax Act

Until 1937 smoking marijuana or cannabis was legal in the United States, even though opiates had been banned for a considerable time before that. Becker suggested that underlying the ban on drugs were three American values:

- *The Protestant value of self-control and responsibility.* In Protestant-based societies considerable stress is placed on the fact that people make decisions on the basis of rational choice, and should then accept the responsibility for the consequences of their original decision. Drugs distort this relationship, as people are not in full self-control when they commit acts, therefore the question can arise whether they are actually responsible for their acts.

- *Disapproval of states of ecstasy.* In American culture the idea of 'states of ecstasy' provokes feelings of unease, even in a religious context. Achieving these states through drugs is seen as wrong, and an example of the search for selfish pleasure.

- *Humanitarianism.* Anything which enslaves people, depriving them of their right to free choice, is seen as abhorrent. Drugs (and alcohol) do just that and therefore stand condemned.

These three values led to the banning of alcohol during the period of Prohibition and to the Harrison Act (1937) which banned the use of a range of drugs including cannabis and opiates except for approved medical purposes.

However, the existence of values does not in itself lead to the passage of legislation. What are needed are 'moral entrepreneurs' to wage a moral crusade on behalf of the enforcement of the values in a specific context. In this case it was the Treasury Department's Bureau of Narcotics that launched the moral crusade because, according to Becker:

> they perceived an area of wrongdoing that properly belonged in their jurisdiction and moved to put it there. The personal interest they satisfied in pressing for marijuana legislation was one common to many officials:

the interest in successfully accomplishing the task one has been assigned and in acquiring the best tools with which to accomplish it.

Moral crusades, according to Becker, usually involve enlisting the support of other interested organisations and developing a favourable public attitude towards the proposed rule. The first part of this strategy was to win over another powerful branch of the Federal bureaucracy, the National Conference of Commissioners on Uniform State Laws, which attempted to coordinate the implementation of laws in the various US states (American states have the right to create their own legislation within certain constitutional limits). When there was some delay in assistance from the National Conference, the Bureau of Narcotics applied some inter-bureaucratic 'blackmail' by threatening to bypass the Conference altogether. This posed a threat to the prestige and power of the Conference, which promptly offered full support to the Bureau.

When it came to winning over the public, the Bureau ran a long campaign, releasing selected information to the press concerning the terrible effects of marijuana, which sensitised the public to the issue of marijuana use and helped to create a strong climate of opinion in favour of legislation. Here is an extract of a magazine article, based on information provided by the Bureau:

> An entire family was murdered by a youthful [marijuana] addict in Florida. When officers arrived at the home they found the youth staggering about in a human slaughterhouse. With an axe he had killed his father, mother, two brothers and a sister. He seemed to be in a daze … He had no recollection of having committed the multiple crime. The officers knew him ordinarily as a sane, rather quiet young man; now he was pitifully crazed. They sought the reason. The boy said he had been in the habit of smoking something which youthful friends called 'muggles', a childish name for marijuana. [Quoted in Becker 1963]

The Bureau's campaign began in 1932, and by 1937 Congress was debating a bill that would outlaw the sale and use of marijuana.

The only opposition came from manufacturers of hempseed oil, who argued that they used the marijuana seed as an essential element of their manufacturing process. After some discussion with the organised hempseed lobby, the government modified its bill to allow its continuing use by the manufacturers, as long as the seed was sterilised. Marijuana smokers, as an unorganised group, had no say. In July 1937 the Act was passed.

The juvenile courts

Much of the content of labelling theory centres around the contention that how people define deviants and respond to them is less a result of the act they have committed than of other factors. A good example of this is the way we treat young people who commit theft. Instead of treating them as criminals who need punishment, they are (at least initially) treated as young delinquents who need help and treatment.

The origins of special courts and penal institutions for youth in late nineteenth-century USA was the subject of study by Platt (1969), who was interested in why they developed at that particular time.

Underlying the debate on delinquency and crime were two values which had tremendous influence on thinkers during this period:

● *The 'nature versus nurture' debate.* The traditional idea that criminals were 'born bad' was giving way to the newer explanations of psychology and sociology. In particular, the belief was growing that people were 'made bad', or corrupted, by bad family or peer-group influences. This theme is still common in much writing on juvenile crime.

● *Urban disenchantment.* There was a growing dislike of the huge US cities with their high levels of crime, poverty and slum districts. Middle-class commentators argued that many of the social problems were a direct result of city life. If only people could be removed from its corrupting influences, the social problems might be overcome.

These two values led many reformers to believe that, if they could only take young offenders out of the cities to the countryside where they could be put in reformatories and set to work in the clean, pure outdoors, away from the corrupting influence of the city, peer groups and family, they would learn to become 'good' people.

Platt pointed out the tremendous influence of women on the development of the juvenile justice system, and explained it by reference to the way that middle-class and upper-class women had been edged out of any major employment role at that time. Their role was to run the household for their husbands and families. Clearly this left large numbers of intelligent, articulate women unfulfilled. The outlets for their energies were rather limited, but one possibility lay in charitable work, and within this field the most 'appropriate' area for a woman was to work with children.

Although the women were generally motivated to help young people, there were advantages for them as a result of their campaign. Most importantly:

> it had … considerable practical significance for legitimising new career openings for women. The new role of social worker combined elements of an old and partly fictitious role – defenders of family life – and elements of a new role – social servant. Social work was thus both an affirmation of cherished American values and an instrument for women's emancipation. [Platt 1969]

The women pursued their campaign with vigour, lobbying at all levels of the legislature. However, their most powerful weapons were their husbands, who were generally well connected in business and politics. It was through them that the reform movement channelled its pressure. The result was a new system of justice for youth, who were thereafter tried in separate juvenile courts and sent to separate penal institutions in order to reform rather than punish them.

Using the headings of 'values', 'moral entrepreneurs' and 'moral crusade', investigate the passage of one bill (successful or not) through Parliament.

Conclusion

The two examples we have examined show that labelling theory provides a very clear model of law creation based on the concept of a moral crusade waged by moral entrepreneurs. Most rules, formal or informal, follow this pattern. This model is, as Becker says:

> equally applicable not only to legislation in general, but to the development of rules of a more informal kind. Wherever rules are created and applied, we should be alive to the possible presence of an enterprising individual or group ... Whenever rules are created and applied we should expect to find people attempting to enlist the support of coordinate groups and using the available media of communication to develop a favourable climate of opinion; where they do not develop such support, we may expect to find their enterprise unsuccessful. [Becker 1963]

 Construct a chart comparing the main factors invoked by the Marxist and labelling approaches to explain the process of law-making. Is there any way that a researcher could substantiate one or other of the two approaches?

Crime and the media

You may have noticed from the quotation above the importance Becker placed on the use of 'the available media of communication' in running a successful moral crusade. Labelling theorists have been particularly interested in the role of the media and crime, and have identified two processes which they associate with the media:

- *sensitisation*: the process by which the media develop an awareness of an issue among the general public, and

- *deviancy amplification*: the process of distortion and manipulation of a real or imagined deviant group, such that the 'problem' is magnified with consequences for the labelled.

This element of labelling theory has been very influential in sociology and has had a strong impact on other perspectives, such as Marxism.

Creating folk devils

The best-known (and probably still the best) study of deviancy amplification and the media is Stanley Cohen's *Folk Devils and Moral Panics* 1972). Cohen studied the fighting between the Mods and Rockers in 1964. Mods can reasonably be seen as the originals of such diverse groups as skinheads and 'casuals' of the 1970s and early 1980s. They were distinguishable by their taste for soul music, 'Parka' ex-army coats and motor scooters. The 'Rockers' were the original 'Bikers'. They wore leather jackets, rode motorbikes and listened to rock and roll.

During Easter Sunday 1964 some spasmodic and isolated incidents of fighting broke out among bored youths in the coastal resort of Clacton. The fights were neither serious nor noteworthy but they resulted in 24 youths being arrested. Coinciding with these innocuous events, however, journalists on national newspapers found themselves short of hard 'news' material and exaggerated and distorted what had

Trouble brewing for Mods in Brighton

occurred. The newspapers stressed that violence was caused by clearly identifiable groups of Mods and Rockers, who hated each other and had gone to Clacton deliberately to cause trouble. Feature articles contained interviews with Mods and Rockers and discussions of their lifestyles. Yet Cohen comments that before the media coverage, although divisions between Mods and Rockers existed, they were weak and of little significance to the youths themselves. After the coverage, however, British youth polarised sharply into those associating themselves with either the Mods or the Rockers.

During the following Whitsun Bank Holiday the newspapers predicted scenes of blood and violence in certain 'target' towns. Although the Mods and Rockers (and other youth) turned up in large numbers, they mainly milled around uncertain of exactly what they were supposed to do. Nevertheless, newspapers still managed to create headlines suggesting excitement and violence.

The newspaper predictions influenced the police and magistrates too, and the police were strongly reinforced to deal with the violence. As the police had been 'sensitised' by the press, they reacted at the slightest hint of trouble. The result was that more people than usual were arrested – not necessarily because there was significantly more trouble, but because the police were more likely than usual to arrest youths who seemed to fit the stereotype of Mod or Rocker. This process of sensitisation also affected the magistrates, who imposed heavier penalties than normal in order to combat the crime wave.

According to Cohen, this was a process by which the media actually created crime through its exaggeration and distortion. Cohen used the term *deviancy amplification* to describe this process. The distortion of events and the labelling by the media of a group of youths as troublemakers (*folk devils*) created the stereotyped image held by police officers and the public, which led them to respond forcibly against the perceived threat to law and order (*a moral panic*).

Crime waves

Is the situation described by Cohen typical of crime reporting in general? The answer appears to be 'yes'. Studies indicate that the amount of crime being reported in the newspapers does not indicate the real extent of crime, but is a reflection of other factors.

Armstrong and Wilson (1973) studied the relationship between crime reporting and the actual amount of crime in Glasgow. They concluded that crime had become a local election issue, and local newspapers devoted large amounts of space to juvenile crime as a means of supporting Conservative political candidates and discrediting the Labour-controlled council. This factor was more important in the newspapers' reporting of crime than the real amount of crime.

Fishman (1973) examined an apparent crime wave in New York which consisted of muggings on elderly people. At the height of the media's reporting of this crime wave, the actual amount of mugging of the elderly was *decreasing*.

Fishman found that the reported crime wave rose and fell depending upon other major stories. If there was a particularly newsworthy non-crime event, the reporting of muggings would decline. When other events were thin on the ground, the crime wave built up again.

Fishman argued that editors are daily faced with a wide range of very disparate items of information which they need to weld together into some form of cohesive news. They search for 'themes' which will act as an umbrella to tie news items together. The theme of street crime allowed a wide range of stories about crime, the police, politicians and elderly people to be welded together into a coherent sets of stories. The result was an apparent crime wave.

The crime wave spreads across the media because all the stories feed off one another. Newspaper editors and television news editors check the news output of all the other media to 'steal' information and stories. As a result, reports in different media tends to have similar contents.

Newspapers' sources

Chibnall (1977) examined how crime reporters obtain the information that eventually comprises the news. He pointed out that newspapers do not always reflect the full range of crime, but a combination of what the reporter considers interesting news and what the police are prepared to divulge.

Both these factors mean that most white-collar crime and corporate crime is ignored because the police feel that it is not in their area of responsibility. Also, marital violence, routine theft and shoplifting are generally regarded as unimportant by the police and dull by crime reporters.

The material that does emerge is generally what is normally regarded as (exciting) material by the reporters and 'real' crime by the police – particularly serious crimes such as bank robbery, murder and rape. These crimes are therefore brought to the attention of the crime reporters by the police who are also usually the only available source of information. Hence the output of the press could be regarded as a reflection of police attitudes and priorities.

Reporting crime

What in fact we are dealing with is the relation between three different *definitions* of crime: the *official*, the *media* and the *public* definitions of crime. Each of these definitions is socially constructed – each is produced by a distinctive social and institutional process. The *official* definition of crime is constructed by those agencies responsible for crime control – the police, the courts, the statisticians, the Home Office. This definition is the result of the rate of reported crime, the clear-up rate, the focused and organised police response to certain crimes, the way the patterns and rates of crime are interpreted by judges and official spokesmen in the crime control institutions and so on. The *media* definition of crime reflects the selective attention of news men and news media to crime, the shaping power of 'news values', the routines and practices of news gathering and presentation. The *public* definition of crime is constructed by the lay public with little or no direct experience or 'expert' knowledge of crime. It is massively dependent on the other two definitions – the official and the media definitions. The selective portrayal of crime in the mass media plays an important part in shaping public definitions of the 'crime problem', and hence also (through further feed-back) in its 'official' definition. So we must replace the simple equation, crime = apprehension = news about crime with a more complex model, which takes full account of the shaping power of the intervening institutions. Thus:

crime
volume and incidence unknown
↓
'crime'

product of institutional definition by crime control
agencies
↓
news values
the selective institutional practices of 'news making'
↓
'crime-as-news'
the selective portrayal of crime in the media
↓
public definition of crime
the consequences of information provided by official
and media sources

Source: Adapted from Cohen and Young (1981)

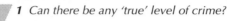

1 *Can there be any 'true' level of crime?*

2 *What is the relationship between the public's perception of crime and the various definitions?*

3 *Using information from this chapter and the above extract, what impact may the reporting of crime have on the public's behaviour? Can this actually increase crime? If so, explain how.*

4 *Is there an argument for censoring the reporting of crimes, so that members of the public are not alarmed?*

Social constructionist approaches tend to explore issues of deviance as much as criminality and in doing so they point us in different, usually interesting, directions. An example of this is the research on youth homelessness.

The media and homeless youth

Homelessness among young people has grown considerably during the 1980s as a result of changes in the housing market and exclusion from state benefits, and as young people have increasingly refused to remain in family situations where they were abused.

The young homeless are a group of people who have been viewed ambivalently by the majority of the population. They have often been the object of media reporting, which has had the effect of confirming them in a stigmatised role. The majority of people have not experienced homelessness themselves, and have been bemused at the rapid increase in the numbers of young people begging on the streets and sleeping rough. These youths do not fit the more traditional category of middle-aged alcoholic males who have been a common sight on the streets since the 1950s. These men had been labelled as homeless and impoverished as a result of their own failings. They were treated with amused contempt by passers by.

However, the new homeless are clearly very different in terms of age, their different begging techniques and the causes of their homelessness. In a situation of ambivalence like this the media play a crucial role: they help to provide explanations for homelessness, explore the relationship with prostitution, street crime and drugs,

and offer possible solutions. Unlike the organised gay culture discussed earlier, the young homeless have been less organised and far less powerful, so the labels attributed by the media are far more likely to stick.

According to the analysis presented by Susan Hutson and Mark Liddiard (1994), the following seven themes are important in determining the public's perception of the issue:

● *The presentation of an unfamiliar problem*: This refers to the process explained earlier in which the media present an issue to the public and help them to come to a definition.

> Men and women live in second-hand worlds … The quality of their lives is determined by meanings they have received from others … The mass media is now even more central in the creation of their images in our heads of the world outside. [C. Wright Mills, quoted in Negrine 1989]

● *The presentation of negative themes*: Negative themes are much more of a basis for 'news' than positive themes. It is in the interests of newspapers and television to stress the elements of crime, drug usage and prostitution than of the actual causes and nature of homelessness.

● *The presentation of contrasts*: A common journalistic technique is to contrast the problem under review with the norm. This emphasises the differences between the young homeless and 'normal' young people.

● *The presentation of human interest stories*: Most journalists will attempt to inject 'human interest' into their reports by personalising the issues. The 'facts' of the case will then be illustrated with a particular person's story – and the more spectacular the better. The point is that stressing the individual may obscure the structural causes.

● *The presentation of stereotypes*: The definition of what constitutes homelessness is a matter of considerable debate among academics. In terms of news value, reporters tend to concentrate on extreme homelessness (the majority of young homeless are actually to be found sleeping on friends' or relatives' floors), thereby stereotyping what homelessness is and who the homeless are.

● *The presentation of ambiguity*: Readers and viewers engage in a filtering process, drawing the information they want to hear from articles and programmes. Often there is ambiguity in reporting, enabling readers to seek out the information that best accords with their own views.

● *The presentation of structural issues and statistics*: Charitable or voluntary organisations sympathetic to the homeless can provide the media with information, statistics and analyses of the nature of the structural problems. How the paper or programme presents the information, and how it is interpreted, varies widely. Nevertheless, Hutson and Liddiard found significant evidence of structural issues and statistics emerging in the media reports they studied. This can be compared with the treatment of most crimes. The media will turn to the police or sources in court for information. These will give a view that is rarely sympathetic to the criminal, and therefore the social construction of the offender is usually negative.

Hutson and Liddiard's work demonstrates that there is a greater complexity to news reporting, presentation and interpretation than was suggested by Cohen's early work or Hall *et al's* study of 'mugging' (see Chapter 4). This complexity also shows through in Kitzinger and Skidmore's work on child sexual abuse which we examine in the next section.

Find out the backgrounds of a sample of homeless people, and investigate how they perceive themselves. If you live in a large town or city there will be young, homeless people on the streets. Interview them, if they are willing to cooperate. Try to find out the reasons for their homelessness, their plans and how they are managing.

Applying social constructionist approaches

In this section we look at two examples of social constructionism in practice. First we will examine the changing meanings applied to child sexuality, and then we will explore the use of drugs.

Child sexual abuse

Much like mental illness or homosexuality, child sexual abuse can be viewed as a social construction which tells us a great deal about changing attitudes to sexuality and childhood, and equally about the nature of professional power.

It has been argued that ideas on the sexuality of children have been created in just the same way that discourses on homosexuality and lesbianism have altered over time. According to Aries (1973), in medieval society children were not excluded from sexual activity and there was no concept of protecting them from being defiled by knowledge of sex. Physically, children were beaten more often than adults, and at least as violently. Violence was very much a part of life. Aries maintains that childhood as we know it only began a long process of development in the latter part of the sixteenth century, and did not evolve into a form recognisable form for us until the eighteenth century. Foucault, as we saw earlier, also pointed to the way that children's sexuality was classified and limited in much the same way as homosexuality.

Given this background, social constructionist approaches have thrown some light on the debate about the notion of sexual child abuse, which can be seen less in terms of an absolute sexual aberration and rather more as a product of defining and outlawing certain acts.

Moral entrepreneurs

Concern about child abuse only emerged as significant issue in the 1970s in the case of physical violence and the in the 1980s in the case of sexual abuse. Parton (1991) suggests that much of the explanation lies in the emergence of the Right in politics in Britain and the USA. Right-wingers have strong opinions and concerns about the changing nature of the modern family on the one hand and the role and power of social workers as representatives of the 'interfering state' on the other. The issue of child abuse can be seen as part of a broad social terrain in which wider battles are fought over the role of the state and the level of interference in individuals' lives. It also acts as a catalyst for fears about the changing nature of society and its apparent 'disintegration'.

Parton argues that the 'disease model' dominated early discussions of child abuse: the search for explanations began with the notion of pathological families with parents who were abnormal or mentally ill. The job of preventing these people engaging in abusive acts was one for social workers, and their repeated failure to prevent such problems drew considerable public abuse onto their heads. This fitted the agenda of the Right, who claimed that social workers' activities – like any form of state intervention – were likely to fail. The Right argued that child abuse is a natural if 'pathological' element of human nature; it was an unfortunate but inevitable outcome of the differences between people. State interference, and social work in particular, was a waste of time, and might even make matters worse if it weakened the traditional family.

The moral panics which erupted over child abuse have focused, according to Parton, on the role of social workers and their failings. He argues that there was no attempt to look at the wider context, which indicates that poverty and unemployment are key factors in cases of violence against children. Criticism has undermined the role of social workers while at the same time shifting attention away from these wider social factors.

The role of the media

Parton sees the role of the media as relatively straightforward: they appear to reflect the views of the most powerful groups in society. However, Kitzinger and Skidmore (1994) decided to try to unravel the way in which news of sexual abuse was constructed and trace its effects on readers and viewers. They argue that the construction and representation of news is more complex than Cohen and Parton suggest. In particular they claim that there are often competing interests attempting to get their version of reality propagated through news reporting.

Kitzinger and Skidmore compared the way the news was constructed in similar cases of 'ritual' child abuse in 1986 and 1991. What emerged were quite different accounts of similar activities as a result of the increasing ability of social work agencies, and organisations sympathetic to social work, to project their own view of events.

In 1986 the actions of the social workers were the focus of the news reporting – and most of it was critical. The subject-matter was classified as 'crime', and the police emerged as the neutral upholders of truth. By 1991, however, the stories were more often seen as 'human interest', the social services were the focus of more sympathetic attention, and the views of police officers were less often quoted.

Kitzinger and Skidmore suggest that there are several elements in the process of gathering and reporting news which together create a competition for 'definitional power':

- *The reporters* are more likely to be male than female, and to be non-specialists. As males, according to Kitzinger and Skidmore, they are not likely to be sympathetic to the idea of child sexual abuse by parents, and as non-specialists they have to rely for all their information on specialist agencies such as charities, the police, social work departments and academics.

- *The agencies* that were approached were those with 'source credibility', which meant the more 'respected' or traditional agencies. Groups with more radical views – Kitzinger and Skidmore suggest this includes most feminist organisations – were excluded.

- The law and the issues relating to child abuse are particularly *complex* and thus beyond most journalists' understanding. The effectiveness of organisations in giving background briefings that fitted a commonsense interpretation of the events was significant in altering the contents of the media reports.

Moral abuse or moral clampdown?

Kitzinger and Skidmore argue that the model of moral panic suggested by Cohen is the very opposite of what happened around ritual child sexual abuse. They suggest that the three factors they identified – reporters, agencies and complexity – combined to minimise the reality of child abuse. Rather than there being a moral panic over the issue, they see a moral clampdown, which may conceal the extent of the problem

Figure 6.4 The media presentation of issues

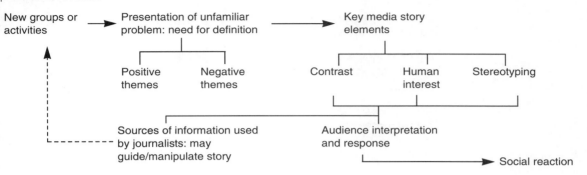

Using Figure 6.4, analyse the approach of the mainstream media to drug use. A particularly useful example was the 'scare' in 1996 over the use of ecstasy and the deaths associated with it by the media. Use a CD ROM to search the newspapers for that year. Alternatively, select another topical issue.

Drugs

To end our discussion of social constructionist approaches, we will use the issue of drug use to pull together and illustrate many of the points we have made.

Street dealing

The first point is that it is not how dangerous or addictive a drug is which determines its legality. Two of the most harmful drugs in use in the world – alcohol and tobacco – are legal, and provide enormous profits for internationally reputable companies, while other drugs which are possibly less harmful, such as cannabis, cocaine or Ecstasy (MDMA), are illegal and those who supply or manufacture them risk imprisonment.

Second, those who use drugs are routinely labelled as addicts, yet evidence in Britain points to the fact that the majority of users of illegal drugs do so in a 'recreational' manner, increasing or restricting their use depending upon the availability and cost of the drugs and their own desire to use them.

Third, traditional law enforcement activities have arguably had no impact upon drugs usage, but may actually have led to an increase in crime associated with drug supplying.

Fourth, the media have consistently given a false portrayal of drugs use and effects, through a succession of moral panics.

Legislation

Opium was widely used in the UK in the nineteenth century and was regarded as socially acceptable among certain sections of the upper class. Its derivative heroin was only made illegal in 1923. One of the reasons for the change in the law was that a link was made between heroin usage and fears about the Chinese immigrants who were alleged to import the material. A second important influence was the attempt by doctors and pharmacists to extend their control over drugs. They were aided by others with strong beliefs about the immoral characteristics of drugs. One particularly influential pressure group was the Society for the Suppression of the Opium Trade.

Cocaine had been outlawed in 1916, partially because of fears about its effect on British soldiers' morale and fighting ability in the First World War.

Cannabis was made illegal in the UK in 1925, but not until 1937 in the USA. Becker's classic study of the introduction of the Harrison Act, which we looked at on p. 119, clearly illustrates the way social values and pressure group activities combined to lead to the passage of legislation which made the sale and possession of marijuana illegal.

Explanations for drug use or 'addiction'

Traditionally, explanations for the use of drugs have covered an enormous range of different approaches, ranging from the biological, in which the individual drug user is seen as in need of drugs, to the psychological, which suggests that the individual has some personality weakness which leads him or her to compensate for the deficiency by turning to drugs. More sociologically oriented explanations have ranged from explanations based on poor family upbringing through to the more sophisticated approaches of Merton's 'retreatist' adaptation to anomie (discussed on pp. 27) and Hirschi's concept of 'control theory' (discussed on pp. 30–1).

Despite their differences, these explanations share the belief that illegal substance misusers are somehow *different* from the majority of the population. But this claim does not seem to fit the facts. The difference between a legal drug and an illegal one is very much a matter of pressure group activity, as we saw earlier. Even if we confine ourselves to illegal substances, drug use is a normal recreational activity for young people. It is estimated that approximately 500,000 people currently take Ecstasy (MDA or MDMA) every weekend, and even more use cannabis. On the other hand, estimates of heroin and cocaine use suggest that only a very small number of people routinely use these drugs. So the use of illegal drugs is very widespread, and integrated into young people's typical recreation patterns. Most research indicates that drugs are used selectively, with drug users making choices about which drugs to use.

The significance of labelling theory for explanations of why people choose to take drugs is that explanations based upon distinguishing between drug users and non-users are likely to be flawed as they assume that use of drugs is in some way abnormal. The more interesting question then becomes why a small minority tend to take the more expensive and possibly more harmful drugs such as heroin or crack cocaine.

Table 6.5 Percentage of males and females who said they had taken drugs at some time

Source: Graham and Bowling (1995)

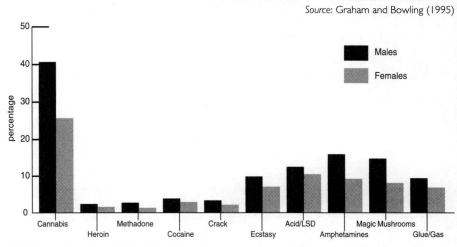

1 *What does Table 6.5 tell us about the extent of drug use by the young?*

2 *What differences emerge between male and female drugs use?*

3 *Is there pattern in the types/extent of drugs used?*

4 *Suggest different methods of obtaining information on the extent of drug usage in your institution, and comment on the strengths and weaknesses each approach might have.*

5 *If you first obtain the agreement of the institution, conduct the research. Do your results tally with Table 6.5? Suggest reasons if they do not.*

Law enforcement strategies, drug use and criminality

An early example of the effects of policing on drug use was provided by Jock Young in *The Drug Takers* (1971). Young studied drug users in North London and found that the actions of the police actually confirmed them in their use of drugs and may even have contributed to the move from cannabis to other drugs such as heroin.

Young argued that strict policing of drug use meant that young people who wished to use drugs on a regular basis had to become very secretive, developing an exclusive subculture which helped them to escape the attentions of police and reduced the risk of arrest. Casual drug use became less of an easy option as one was either a part of the drug subculture or excluded from it. So people who would previously have been more recreational in their pattern of drug use were drawn into greater proximity to heavy drug users. As the members of the drug subculture became increasingly isolated from the broader society, they increasingly focused on drugs and drug usage. The result was a greater propensity to use drugs and to try 'harder' drugs.

Partly as a result of studies like Young's, the police have developed far less interventionist strategies and generally accept that people found in possession of small amounts of drugs should not be prosecuted. In effect, possession of some types of drugs for personal use has become decriminalised.

Nevertheless, the effects of policing has been to ensure that street prices of illegal drugs remain high, and supplying drugs becomes an attractive proposition, both in terms of income and because of the low levels of risk for professional criminals who are seeking alternatives to crimes such as armed robbery which have become increasingly risky through changing police tactics and decreasingly lucrative because of a move away from the use of cash in payment and salaries.

Learning to enjoy drugs: the career of a drug user

The concept of 'career' which we met earlier is particularly useful in understanding drug use. Most drug users point out that the first use of most substances, whether legal or illegal, is not particularly pleasurable. Usually the aspiring user must learn to appreciate the pleasant effects of the drug and distinguish it from the less pleasant elements.

For example, injecting heroin gives an intense rush of pleasure, but the down side is that it often makes you feel nauseous. Cannabis can make the person using it feel disoriented and frightened, or there may be no appreciable difference in the mental state of the user. Generally, more experienced drug users will guide the learner through the process of learning to derive pleasure.

This is particularly important in countering the idea that simply by using illegal substances a person will soon become an addict. The majority of people who try heroin only ever use it once, and of those who do continue relatively few will choose to inject or become addicted. Drug use is a social activity the meaning of which is created by the user. The physical or addictive element is only part of the pleasure of drug use.

Drug addiction

To reach a state of resonance, users must work at it hard, for a long time. One obstacle they must overcome is heroin's side effects. After taking an intoxicating dose of heroin the user typically gets nauseated and often vomits. Learning the joy of nausea takes fortitude.

If a person takes a lot of heroin frequently and for a long time, the drug may engage in a 'physical resonance' with the user's body. In such a development, continued use of heroin is necessary to maintain the body's physical stability, otherwise the user feels sick. Resonance is often called 'physical dependence', but that latter term is wrong – and

inaccurate terms can mislead our thinking. A diabetic is physically dependent on insulin. Without it, the person gets sicker and sicker. Heroin users do not become physically dependent on their drug [because they] never have an organic need for the substance.

Physical resonance is different from heroin addiction. Resonance is only one part of the latter condition [and] we can say that ending addiction is much harder than ending resonance. The ease of withdrawing from resonance is important, however, because some people believe that heroin users take the drug and accept a life of crime and debasement simply to avoid the withdrawal syndrome. Addicts take heroin for other reasons.

Source: Miller (1994)

1 What is 'resonance', according to the writer of the extract?

2 In what way can resonance be said to have a social element of learning or labelling in it?

3 How does the author view the concept of 'addiction'?

4 Can you suggest why the concepts of addiction and the difficulties of withdrawal have become accepted as facts?

Drugs: a contemporary moral panic

Drugs scares appear regularly in the media, and provide especially good stories when they can be linked with the famous or royalty. However, they have helped create and perpetuate the myth of 'pushers' preying upon weak or innocent victims. The reality for the majority of drug users is that, as they obtain supplies, they are likely to sell some of the drugs they buy on to friends and others in the network. Sellers and buyers are often the same people in different times.

Using the model presented above, analyse the approach of the mainstream media to drug use. A particularly useful example was the 'scare' early in 1996 over the use of ecstasy and the deaths associated with it by the media. Use a CD ROM to search the newspapers of that period. Alternatively, choose a topical current issue and follow out a similar analysis.

Criticisms of the labelling approach

The first criticism of labelling theory is that it fails to explain why people commit crime in the first place. Labelling theorists suggest that all of us commit criminal acts, but only a few of us are caught. This is partially true. Many people have at some time broken the law – for example, driving over the speed limit, 'stealing' free telephone calls at work, etc. – but virtually all research has shown that there are significant differences in the likelihood of different groups of people committing crime.

In reply, the British interactionist Ken Plummer (1975) has argued that labelling theory does not *claim* to explain different rates of crime, nor does it say that everybody breaks the law equally. Instead it examines the importance of *some* of those people being labelled as criminal in terms of how they are treated and how they perceive themselves.

A second criticism is that Becker and Lemert seem to suggest that people who commit crime but are not labelled are not deviant and that there are no consequences for their view of themselves. People are aware that they are committing deviant acts, and the knowledge they can do so without getting caught or labelled can influence their future behaviour. Becker has accepted this criticism but, as he and Plummer point out, the very real consequences of having a deviant label attached to a person remain.

A criticism which Taylor, Walton and Young (1973) put forward in their Marxist critique of labelling is that it offers no adequate explanation of the role of power in the creation (and enforcement) of criminal laws. Plummer robustly rejects this, pointing out that labelling theory does have a clear model of law creation. This model may not be a Marxist one, but the whole concept of moral entrepreneurs opened up, for the first time, a realisation that laws were the result of the actions of power groupings.

A further problem raised by Taylor, Walton and Young was the failure of labelling theory to link deviance to the (capitalist) structure of society. This is true, but then, if labelling theory did that, it would simply be a variation of Marxism. Indeed, contemporary Marxist writings on deviance, particularly left realism, owe a considerable debt to labelling theory.

Summary

In this chapter we have explored one of the most fruitful and interesting approaches to the sociology of crime and deviancy. Labelling theory opened up a range of new questions and challenged the rather simplistic ideas about what constituted crime that had previously dominated the literature. Labelling theory emphasised that what academics regarded as fixed and given – criminal and deviant behaviour – was in fact very much socially constructed. Instead of asking why some people commit crimes, they asked why some people make rules which made others into criminals and deviants. They then applied insights derived originally from social psychology to look at the impact that being labelled as a deviant had on the person so labelled.

It could reasonably be argued that the question of law construction had been central to all Marxist approaches, and that the idea that laws make criminals was hardly new. However, the Marxists approached the construction of laws through the blinkers of their ideological bias. Social constructionist theories have offered a range of possible explanations, suggesting more complex and confusing but nevertheless more plausible explanations for law construction. They have gone on to show how the effects on individuals can influence further activities of law makers and enforcers.

Readings

Looking after tobacco

The tobacco industry has developed a very effective parliamentary lobby: it retains the services of a number of members of parliament as its paid consultants. It also provides sympathisers on both sides of the House with selective information to support its case and these members are well placed to bend the chancellor's ear in the run-up to the budget. It has the resources to buy goodwill: the Minister of Health in 1982 said he was 'pleased to announce' a grant of £11,000,000 from the tobacco industry to establish the Health Promotion Research Trust. Its terms of reference required that it promote health in the UK through research to encourage people, especially the young, to take responsibility for their own health and to promote research into factors which might affect the consequences of a more responsible attitude to health. However, the terms of reference specifically excluded 'studies designed directly or indirectly to examine the use and effects of tobacco products ...' Thus, while the Trust may promote much worthwhile research, in so doing it will also inevitably shift public attention away from smoking as a cause of illness and death, by the emphasis which its work will give to other, relatively less important factors.

The anti-smoking lobby is a pauper in comparison to the tobacco industry. It is led by ASH (Action on Smoking and Health), which was set up in 1971 by the Royal College of Physicians and depends on an annual grant from the government for most of its funds. It relies on the enthusiasm and commitment of a very small number of staff, although it has a large number of subscribing supporters.

When the tobacco industry approaches senior civil servants, it is direct and effective. An investigative journalist, Peter Taylor, has given a detailed and disturbing account of this aspect of the industry's activities. He notes that the industry approaches all government departments which may be influential in their case, and they entertain officials at major sports and arts events, which they are involved in sponsoring. The events include the tennis championships at Wimbledon, the cricket cup finals at Lords, Formula One grand prix racing and the opera at Glyndebourne.

Source: Norris (1991)

1 *In what way does the extract help us to understand the reasons why some drugs are legal and others illegal?*

2 *How does this 'fit' with labelling or social constructionist approaches?*

3 *List the methods used by the tobacco companies to defend their interests.*

4 *The interest group defending the 'right' to smoke is FOREST. Contact them to hear their arguments for smoking. Could these arguments be applied to cannabis or Ecstasy use?*

Examination Question

Examine sociological explanations of the contribution of the mass media to the process of deviance amplification.

AEB, Summer 1994

Bibliography

Aries, P. (1973) *Centuries of Childhood*, Harmondsworth: Penguin

Armstrong, G. and Wilson, M. (1973) 'City politics and deviance amplification', in Taylor, I. and Taylor, L. (eds) *Politics and Deviance*, Harmondsworth: Penguin

Becker, H. (1963) *The Outsiders*, London: Macmillan

Box, S. (1981) *Deviance, Reality and Society*, London: Holt, Rinehart & Winston

Chibnall, S. (1977) *Law and Order News*, London: Tavistock

Cohen, S. (1972) *Folk Devils and Moral Panics*, London: MacGibbon & Kee

Cohen, S. and Young, J. (eds) (1981) *The Manufacture of News*, London: Constable

Cooley, C.H. (1902) *Human Nature and the Social Order*, New York: Charles Scribner's Sons

Fishman, J. (1973) 'Crime waves as ideology', in Cohen, S. and Young, J. (eds) *The Manufacture of News*, London: Constable

Foucault, M. (1976–84) *The History of Sexuality*, Vols 1–3 (in French); English paperback edn, Harmondsworth: Penguin

Graham, J. and Bowling, B. (1995) 'Young people and crime', *Research Findings*, Vol. 24, December

Hutson, S. and Liddiard, M. (1994) *Youth Homelessness*, Basingstoke: Macmillan

Kitzinger, J. and Skidmore, P. (1994) 'Playing safe: media coverage of child sexual abuse prevention strategies', *Child Abuse Review*, Vol. 3, No. 4

Kitsuse, J. (1962) 'Societal reaction to deviant behaviour', *Social Problems*

Lemert, E. (1972) *Human Deviance, Social Problems and Social Control*, Englewood Cliffs, NJ: Prentice-Hall

Littlewood, R. and Lipsedge, M. (1982) *Aliens and Alienists*, Harmondsworth: Penguin

Mead, G.H. (1934) *Mind, Self, Society*, Chicago, IL: University of Chicago Press

Miller, J.M. (1991) *The Case for Legalising Drugs*, Praeger Publications

Moore, S. (1995) *Sociology Alive!* 2nd edn, Cheltenham: Stanley Thornes

Negrine, R. (1989) *Politics and the Mass Media in Britain*, London: Routledge

Norris, A. (1991) 'Government and tobacco: economies, ethics and epidemics', in Cochrane, R. and Carroll, P. (eds) *Psychology, Social Issues*, Brighton: Falmer

Parton, N. (1991) *Governing the Family: Child Care, Child Protection and the State*, London: Macmillan

Platt, J. (1969) 'The rise of the Child Saving Movement', *Annals of the American Academy*, January

Plummer, K. (1975) *Sexual Stigma: An Interactionist Account*, London: Routledge

Taylor, I., Walton, P. and Young, J. (1973) *The New Criminology*, London: Routledge

Trowler, P. (1996) *Investigating The Media*, 2nd edn, London: Collins Educational

Weeks, J. (1986) *Sexuality*, London: Ellis Horwood/Tavistock; paperback edn, London: Routledge

Wellings, K., Field, J., Johnson, A.M. and Wadsworth, J. (1994) *Sexual Behaviour in Britain*, Harmondsworth: Penguin

Young, J. (1971) *The Drug Takers*, London: Paladin

7

Perspectives from the right

In this chapter we will explore the theoretical perspectives which I have loosely categorised as 'on the political right'. The term covers a range of approaches which share some common ground, but which have quite distinctive features. Some of these approaches have been extremely influential in terms of British crime policy, and have supplanted more traditional liberal or 'welfare-based' approaches to combating crime.

The right should not be seen as a coherent grouping; as with left-wing thinking, there is quite a fragmentation of thought which can lead to very different attitudes to crime. For example, the 'liberal' or 'radical' right would argue for the complete abolition of controls on any drugs on the grounds that it the right of anyone to purchase and consume what they please (as long as no harm comes to others). On the other hand, 'traditional' or 'paternalistic' conservatives insist that drugs should be banned as they are harmful to individuals and morally wrong.

In order to gain a clear overview of the range of thought contained within the right, it is simplest to categorise the variety of approaches into the following headings:

● right libertarians

● rational choice

- administrative criminology

- paternalistic conservatives

- right realism.

Before we examine each of these approaches, it will be useful to explore their common background.

Figure 7.1 Guidelines: New
Right perspectives

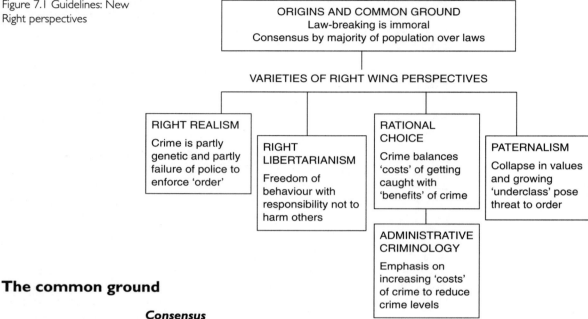

The common ground

Consensus

Most conservative thinkers argue that society is based on a common set of values which everybody shares, and the laws derive from these. Laws are therefore a reflection of the will of the people. This idea of consensus in society is a common thread among most conservative sociological writers, and underlies their approach to the rule of law and the necessity of punishment.

From Durkheim onwards the belief that the law reflects the majority consensus in society has meant to conservatives that those who break the law are acting incorrectly in moral terms. This stands in contrast to most subcultural, Marxist and labelling approaches which do not necessarily see the criminal as acting immorally. Indeed, Marxists believe that criminals may be striking a blow for freedom.

The inherent nature of mankind

Human beings are considered to be naturally selfish and self-seeking. However, people are aware that there needs to be regulation, so a framework of laws reflecting the generally accepted morality is instituted. As long as the laws are respected, society can operate. Without obedience to the laws, society would fall into a state of anomie.

Rationality

In the conservative model of society, it is assumed that people are rational in their actions, making choices and being aware of the consequences. This is the model of 'economic man' who decides whether the benefits of a line of action outweigh the penalties, and then acts accordingly. This belief in the essentially rational person is the basis for much right-wing writing in economics, where people operate in a 'market' based on rational responses to supply and demand. Individuals take jobs or leave them, purchase goods or not, on the balance of the benefits to themselves.

If people really do make economic choices as the conservatives suggest, they are best left to do so within a society that ensures minimum regulation and maximum 'freedom'. Conservatives disagree with the introduction of laws into areas of personal decision making where no clear moral issue is at stake. For example, the imposition of laws requiring the wearing of seat-belts in cars is held to be wrong (there is no morality here), but laws restricting violence are necessary and right (reflecting the moral 'consensus' of society) as harm is caused to others.

The concept of rationality is extremely important as it is closely linked to the conservative approach to punishment. The argument is that if people commit crime when the benefits outweigh the costs, then the costs must be increased proportionately over the benefits. This requires heavier, but appropriate punishment and greater policing of the streets to increase the likelihood of being caught.

The role of the government

Although conservatives castigate the state in their writing, it still plays a key part in containing crime. However, they reject the idea that its role is to alter social conditions, which liberal and socialist writers claim cause crime. Instead they believe that the role of the government is to ensure that people can go about their lawful business (of amassing wealth) with minimum intervention.

Furthermore, they point to the fact that during the 1960s, when radical measures were taken to alleviate poverty in Britain and America, there was the greatest leap in the number of crimes committed since official recording began. The statistics appear to indicate that increases in wealth for the majority of the population are actually linked to an increase in crime, not a decline as most socialist thinkers had traditionally argued. This leads conservatives to the conclusion that the state cannot eliminate crime through tackling its causes, it can merely make the costs to the potential criminal outweigh the benefits.

The importance of community

The rule of law is merely a back-up to a far more important form of social control, that of the community. Informal controls imposed by neighbours and fear of 'what others would think' are far stronger in restraining people from committing illegal or anti-social activities than anything the state can do.

A central theme in conservative writing from Durkheim onwards has been the idea of the *loss of community*. It is only through strengthening the social bonds that constrain people, based on religion, tradition and a sense of belonging (usually to a nation), that crime can be held down to a low level.

The ubiquity of crime

We have just seen that informal controls can help *limit* crime, but not *eliminate* it. This is because, following Durkheim once again, most conservative writers see the eradication of crime as impossible. This is in contrast to socialist writers, who blame social problems on the capitalist system, and who argue that the elimination of crime will follow the end of the capitalist system. Crime, according to the conservatives, will always exist, therefore the aim is to limit its impact.

The importance of order

Conservatives stress above all else the importance of *social order*, that is, the feeling of individuals that they can live without disturbance by others. This may seem obvious and desirable at first, but conservatives go further in asserting that, in certain circumstances, order is more important than strict observation of the law.

Most right-wing commentators believe they reflect the majority view on the causes of crime and the best ways to combat it. Are they right?

Administer to a cross-section of people a questionnaire which contains the following questions (or your versions of them). Aim to categorise the answers you receive according to certain characteristics of the respondents – possibly age, political affiliation or gender. You will need to design your questionnaire with this objective in mind.

In your opinion, which of the following are (in rank order) the two biggest causes of crime?

- *Poverty*
- *Greed*
- *Poor upbringing by parents*
- *Can't be bothered working for a living*
- *Led astray by friends*
- *Drugs*
- *Decline of the traditional community*
- *Too few police officers*
- *Other – please specify*

What do you think would be the most effective way to limit crime?

- *More police*
- *More spending on deprived areas*
- *Harsher prison sentences*
- *Better parenting*
- *Punishing parents of youth offenders*
- *Government action to reduce poverty and inequality*
- *Other – please specify*

Classify your answers. Do this work as you are working through this chapter. At the end of the chapter, as a group decide which of the above are indicators of right-wing views. What do you conclude about what the majority of your respondents want?

Right libertarians

Right libertarians emphasise two concepts above all others: freedom and responsibility.

Freedom

This approach stresses above all else the freedom of individuals and their right to choose to do whatever they reasonably wish. Freedom results in a wide variety of behaviours and has a multitude of different consequences for individuals, including becoming rich or poor, and engaging in activity that others might deem to be personally immoral. Nevertheless, as long as others are not deliberately and knowingly harmed, such activities should be permitted.

Defining crime becomes a very important issue, for the law must permit the widest possible range of behaviour while at the same time providing people with protection from others who would harm them. Crime is defined by Rothbard (1982) as 'violent invasion or aggression against the property of another being (including his property in his own person)'.

The stress on individual freedom and the resulting definition of crime has important implications for the so-called 'victimless crimes' such as those related to pornography, prostitution or drug taking, for these are simply choices made by individuals which we may regard as foolish or immoral but are not our business, as they are freely chosen activities.

This approach turns the tables on most other analyses of crime and claims that, far from the government being the defender of people against criminals, it is the government itself which is the main perpetrator of crime by passing laws which constrain individual freedom.

Debating in the House of Commons. Does the government actually constrain individual freedom?

Individual responsibility

A second core element of this approach is the idea that when the government steps in to make decisions on behalf of people it destroys the idea of individual responsibility. In particular, it fosters the idea that there are overwhelming social forces which lead certain people inexorably to commit crime. According to the 'statist' approach it is not the criminals' fault – the culprit is the system, the lack of education, poor housing, racism, patriarchy, etc.

Right libertarians reject all this, insisting that people are responsible for their actions, and do make decisions. If they were solely driven by social forces, how is it that the majority of poor people and those from 'problem families' do not turn to crime?

Those who break the law, as defined earlier, should be punished, and furthermore there should be restitution to the victims of crime. By this libertarians mean that victims of crime should be compensated in some way by the convicted criminals, so there is a direct relationship between the punishment of the transgressor and the victim.

Criticisms

There are problems with this approach. The main difficulty lies with the stress on the rational actor, making decisions and then being expected to live by those decisions. Most sociologists would dispute the extent to which decisions are freely made. People make choices, but the circumstances within which they make these choices are limited and to some extent prescribed by factors outside their control. The more affluent and the better educated individuals are, the greater their freedom of choice.

The paternalistic argument features prominently in the case for the prohibition of drugs since drug users are believed to be incompetent in the judgement of their own best interests.

In principle, there is no reason why an informed adult should be prevented from using mind-altering substances, provided that no harm is caused to others. Legal prohibition makes drug use more dangerous than it need be and hands the control of drug markets to criminals.

This paper proposes that drugs could be bought and sold in much the same way as most other goods. Users would choose from a range of products of certified purity in much the same way that drinkers choose between beer, wine and spirits.

Source: Adapted from Stevenson (1994)

The above is an example of the libertarian approach to a social issue. Readers may be quite shocked at this rather radical argument, which people rarely associate with the 'right-wing' of politics.

1 Explain why this is an example of a libertarian approach.

2 *What, in your opinion, would be the effect of Stevenson's proposals for law enforcers and the level of crime?*

3 *Do you agree with this proposal?*

4 *In his book, Stevenson uses the example of abortion as a successful libertarian policy (abortion was illegal until 1969). What other illegal acts do you think could be legalised with beneficial results for society?*

5 *Carry out a small random sample to see if there is general agreement to legalise drugs (though, for clarity of research, you may have to separate them into categories or identify a few specific ones). Make sure you assess the age of the people replying. What differences emerge between age groups, if any?*

Rational choice

Rational choice theorists apply the concepts and rules of classical economics to an understanding of human action. When it comes to crime, the more simple versions claim that any person will work out the costs and benefits of an action. If the benefits outweigh the costs they will carry out the act. Therefore, individuals will commit criminal acts if the benefits are perceived to be greater than potential costs.

Meiselman and Tullock (1973) argue that, in this sense, 'crime, far from being the result of a sickness or mental disorder, in most cases is simply a business oriented economic activity which is undertaken for much the same reasons as other types of economic activity'. The way to limit or stop crime, according to this analysis, is to increase the costs – through harsher penalties and by making it more difficult to steal.

Indirectly, rational choice theory has had a significant impact on criminology in Britain, in that it has provided some of the framework for administrative criminology, which we examine next.

Administrative criminology

Sociologists who subscribe to the approach known as 'administrative criminology' may consider themselves ill served to be categorised in the chapter on the right. However, many aspects of the right's approach fit with their views – in particular, the virtual abandonment of theory and the desire to restrict crime levels without looking at the wider factors which might lead certain groups in the population to commit crime.

The rejection of theory

According to Clarke (1980), the writer primarily associated with this type of criminology, most sociological approaches to crime and deviance had searched for the factors or causes which make some people turn to crime – what is known as the search for 'dispositional factors'. Clarke, the originator of administrative criminology, argues that this is a mistake. Rather than search for causes to distinguish criminals from law-abiding members of the public, it is more useful to conceive of criminals as only hazily (if at all) distinct from the general public. Rather than dispositional factors,

Figure 7.2 Administrative criminology

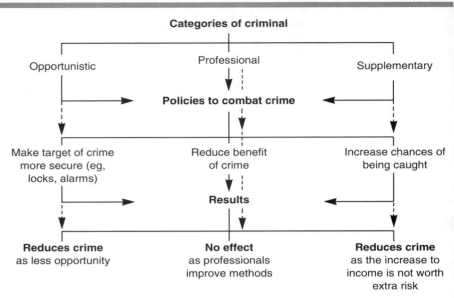

it is better to look for 'opportunistic' factors to explain why some people commit crimes and other do not.

Most young men who commit crime are not strongly disposed to criminal behaviour, but if the chance to steal arises, in the right circumstances and with limited risk, then a high proportion of young males will take the opportunity. If the opportunity is not there, then equally they will not scheme or plan to commit crime.

Clarke argues that specific explanations for 'crime' are mistaken in the same way that finding one explanation for all diseases would be a mistake. Crimes are very different in terms of motivation and explanation. Instead Clarke argues that crimes are usually the outcome of 'immediate' choices and decisions made by an offender, arising from the opportunity to commit crime. The choice he (or, to a lesser extent, she) will make is based upon a whole range of variables including the specific situation at that moment (might be drunk), the specific features of the individual's life history (might have a criminal parent) and current life circumstances (might be unemployed), These will combine to give what Clarke calls a 'repertoire' of responses to situations, so a successful criminal act may influence the perpetrator's actions the next time a similar situation arises. This links to the concept of a 'criminal career', commonly discussed by sociologists of crime and delinquency (see Chapter 6).

The answer to tackling crime, according to Clarke, is therefore not to look at generalised causes, but instead:

● ensure that there are fewer opportunities

● increase the risks of being caught.

Limiting the opportunities

Clarke argues that, simply by limiting the opportunities to commit crime, very significant reductions in levels can be achieved. One extreme example of this was Hassal and Trethowan's study of suicide by gassing. They discovered that when the poisonous content of the gas used in domestic cookers was reduced, the numbers of suicides decreased significantly. Suicide is normally regarded as requiring strong motivation, so it would be expected that, if gassing failed, would-be suicides would turn to another method. However, this did not seem to happen in a significant number of cases. So, according to Clarke, even where there is great motivation, limiting opportunities or even limiting favoured opportunities can reduce the level of a 'crime'.

Clarke suggests that crimes can be categorised in terms of motivation, as follows:

- *Opportunistic.* Many crimes are committed on the 'spur of the moment', when someone sees an opportunity and commits an offence. If the target of the crime is made more difficult in situations like these, the offence is unlikely to take place, as there is no great motivation.

- *Professional.* This is the other extreme to opportunistic, in that professional criminals live off the proceeds of crime. If there is an increase in protective measures the criminal is likely to put in greater effort towards developing alternative or more sophisticated means of committing crime.

- *Supplementary.* The majority of burglaries and street crimes for profit fall somewhere between the professional and the opportunistic. The offender has gone out deliberately to commit a crime, but the proceeds of the crimes are used to supplement other incomes, so one can argue there is an intermediate level of motivation to commit crime. Again, Clarke argues that by careful thought much of this crime can be controlled by some form of 'target hardening'. For example, burglar alarms on properties, wheel and steering locks on cars, high-quality locks on bicycles and marking electrical goods with postcodes all deter those who are not absolutely determined to succeed.

Increasing the risk of being caught

This is significantly harder to achieve than target hardening, but Clarke suggests that improvements can be made nevertheless.

British research indicates that putting more police officers 'on the beat' has a marginal effect on the numbers of offenders caught. However, there is evidence that where there are employees who oversee possible targets of crime, the increased risk of being caught may limit criminal activities. According to Clarke, housing estates with caretakers, buses with conductors, shops with a significant number of sales assistants and public telephones placed in situations where there is some supervision by staff (in launderettes, for example) all have significantly lower levels of theft or vandalism then where there is no supervision.

In line with this approach, the Home Office has encouraged Neighbourhood Watch Schemes, the introduction of closed-circuit television systems in public areas and the use of private security companies.

The role of sociology

Clarke's work raises a particularly important point regarding the purpose of sociology. As a sociologist employed by the Home Office, Clarke is concerned to employ sociological approaches to produce practical ways to reduce the incidence of crime. He shares that concern with left realists and most of the New Right. But the question needing to be asked is whether this should be the role of sociology? An alternative interpretation of the activities of sociologists is to continue to understand the nature and cause of crime and deviance, irrespective of the practical consequences.

Some theoretical difficulties could be avoided by conceiving of crime not in dispositional terms, but as being the outcome of immediate choices and decisions made by the offender. Common-sense as well as the evidence of ethnographic studies of delinquency strongly suggest that people are usually aware of consciously choosing to commit offences. This does not mean that they are fully aware of all the reasons for their behaviour, nor that their own account would necessarily satisfy a criminologically sophisticated observer, who might require information at least about: (i) the offender's motives, (ii) his mood, (iii) his moral judgements concerning the act in question and the 'techniques of neutralisation' open to him, (iv) the extent of his criminal knowledge and his perception of criminal opportunities, (v) his assessment of the risks of being caught as well as the likely consequences, and, finally, as well as of a different order, (vi) whether he has been drinking.

These separate components of subjective state and thought processes which play a part in the decision to commit a crime will be influenced by immediate situational variables and by highly specific features of the individual's history and present life circumstances, in ways that are so varied and countervailing as to render unproductive the notion of a generalised behavioural disposition to offend.

Source: Adapted from Clarke (1980)

1 *Clarke writes about 'dispositional' and 'situational' approaches to crime. Can you explain the meanings of these terms?*

2 *Clarke suggests that some of the problems normally associated with 'dispositional theories of crime can be eliminated by 'conceiving of crime as being the outcome of immediate choices and decisions made by the offender'. Explain the meaning of this and the implications for criminology.*

3 *What evidence can you find in the extract to suggest that Clarke's approach can be classified as being influenced by the 'right'?*

Paternalistic conservatives

Paternalist approaches to crime derive almost exclusively from Durkheim. The basic argument is that crime results from a weakening of the social fabric which binds society together. Social control through socialisation and punishment is important in helping to locate a clear boundary between acceptable behaviour and the unacceptable. At the same time, paternalists recognise that crime is inevitable in an unequal society.

Van den Haag

The most famous proponent of the paternalistic approach to crime is Van den Haag, who argues in *Punishing Criminals* (1975) that inequality is inherent in the capitalist system, as the whole basis of the system is to reward people on the basis of the risks they are taking and the abilities they have to offer. Of course, Van den Haag believes that this is a good thing and is to be preserved. However, inherent in this system is the temptation for the losers in the race for wealth to 'cheat' and try to deprive the affluent of what they have obtained, or to overturn the entire economic system. Therefore laws are needed which will restrain them from doing so.

Van den Haag argues that those who believe the law generally imposes itself on the poor rather than the rich and who claim that this is a sign of unfairness are completely mistaken. It is obvious, he points out, that the law is going to deal mainly with the poor, because there is little reason why the more successful should commit crime. The entire purpose of the law is and *should* be to prevent the poorer sections of the community from taking from the affluent or trying to bring about revolutionary change.

The basis of the law is coercion against the poor, and this is absolutely necessary. It is not, however, that the law is unfair or applied unequally, it is merely that those who are most likely to break the law come from the poorer sections of society. There is little interest in white-collar or corporate crime in Van den Haag's writings.

Van den Haag's explanation for law-breaking is therefore based on an awareness that crime is the inevitable outcome of capitalist society. However, it can be limited (apart from through punishment) by strict emphasis on moral rules and family discipline.

On social policy, Van den Haag argues for a strengthening of moral codes and a penal code based on proportional punishment for the crime, taking into account the social position of the transgressor. Perhaps an example will make this clear. If a police officer and an unemployed man commit a burglary, strictly speaking they have both committed the same offence and therefore ought to be punished equally. However, conservative notions of justice (which pervade our judicial system) argue that the police officer must be punished more severely because of his or her position in society. It is not just the offence that is important, but also who commits the offence.

The main aim of the law is *deterrence*, and therefore publicity is needed to point out what happens when the limits of acceptable behaviour are breached. There are clearly links to Durkheim. The principle of deterrence is the reason why so many conservatives are in favour of capital punishment.

Reading Van den Haag's work, there may not appear to be a big gap between paternalistic and libertarian approaches – but there is in fact a chasm. For paternalistic conservatives drug taking, pornography and other deviant acts are morally wrong and seriously damaging to the moral fabric holding society together. Whereas libertarians regard the state as damaging to individual morals and even actively encouraging criminality, paternalistic conservatives argue that the state has a role to play in holding society together, and that it should exist to uphold central values against those who would seek to undermine them. Whereas libertarians argue that victimless crimes are unfairly penalised by the state, paternalistic conservatives hold that there is a moral issue involved and that it does not matter if individuals are harmed or not – what is important is the general moral standard of society.

Upholding the values of society?

The decline in morals

A similar approach is put forward by Christie Davies (1992), who argues that in nineteenth-century Britain there was very little crime because of the strength of the prevailing morality based on personal responsibility, the role of the free market and a stress on individualism. Increases in crime were the direct result of ever-increasing interference by the state in the workings of the economy and in the social structure of British society.

For Stephen Davies (1987), only the re-moralisation of society through the values of individualism and personal responsibility allied to a return to the free market could lower crime levels.

The family and crime

Within the paternalistic tradition, great stress is placed upon the role of the family in providing a set of moral standards by which children are brought up. The family also provides an emotional refuge and a physical base where young people can feel secure. Writers such as Denis (1993) argue that there is a direct link between the decline in the 'traditional family' and the growth in youth crime. In essence, Denis' argument is a form of control theory (see pp. 30–2); everyone is potentially criminal, it is just that the controls placed on most of us by such things as the family, the community and our employment all limit our tendencies to deviance. For Denis, however, the key to the situation lies in the family, or at least, the heterosexual, two-parent family:

> Thirty or forty years ago two features of everyday life in England began their extraordinary transformation, the results of which are now beyond all denial. One was in the prevalence of criminal conduct. The other was in the attitudes and activities associated with family life, as that term had been understood for at least the preceding one hundred years.

The specific blame for the increase in criminality lies, according to Denis, in the changes in fatherhood. He cites three examples:

- *Increase in fathers leaving their families.* Denis argues that there has been a decrease in the moral approbation that was put on men who left their families. He suggests that the legal changes which have made divorce easier, both reflect and confirm the change (or decline, in his view) in moral values.

- *Cohabitation.* Another element in the decline of the family (and the role of the father within it) is the decline in the idea that marriage is for life. The growth in cohabitation marks the decline in the public statement that the 'private project of living together' requires the 'public statement' of marriages signifying a 'binding commitment'.

- *Domestic circumstances.* The increasingly dominant role of the mother in the household has led to the marginalisation of the father. The result has been a decline in the role of the father, such that it is now expected that fathers are peripheral figures in the home. In certain parts of the UK, young males have grown up to view child-raising as a female activity which is to be undertaken by women, with no commitment from the male needed, or even expected.

The impact of these changes in the family has been to weaken the external patterns of social control based on families and communities. In the past, these prevented young males from committing crime and, secondly, alerted the internal forms of social control which had traditionally occurred through family socialisation.

Denis's and Van den Haag's arguments bear similarities to the views of Durkheim. In what ways can they be said to have based their arguments on Durkheim? Give explicit examples.

Crime, welfare and equality

Milton Friedman is an economist rather than a criminologist, but he has commented on crime in relation to the general philosophy of 'market liberalism'. In *Free to Choose* (1980) Friedman discusses the impact of the 'drive to equality' which he claims marks the policies of various post-war governments before Mrs Thatcher's. According to him, most people do not believe in the movement towards greater equality, and consequently have felt justified in evading the law, for example by tax evasion. Lack of respect for laws is infectious in that once people see others breaking the law and 'getting away with it' they ask themselves why they should continue to respect the law. Again, once one set of laws is treated with disdain, disrespect for other laws increases – even laws which people generally believe are right and proper, such as those prohibiting vandalism, theft and violence. The end result is that crime becomes widespread. Friedman concludes that, 'hard as it may be to believe, the growth of crude criminality in Britain in recent decades may well be one consequence of the drive for equality'.

Why does Friedman see equality as such an evil thing? The answer goes back to our discussion earlier of freedom. Freedom and equality are incompatible, for any government's attempt to eliminate extremes of poverty and wealth must inevitably infringe the 'liberty' of the citizens by imposing the will of the state on them. Furthermore, equality eliminates the incentive required to create a dynamic wealth-producing nation, and this is one of the major reasons for Britain's economic decline since the 1940s, according to Friedman.

Friedman, following Hayek (probably the most important New Right thinker of all), sees the welfare state as the primary cause of the problems faced by society, and holds that crime rates could be brought down by *reducing* welfare provision. This runs against most other liberal and left arguments that dominate sociology. Friedman and most of the New Right argue that the growth of 'welfare-ism' has undermined the social bonds that hold society together. The primary units of family and community have become redundant as the welfare state has provided an 'easy option' for those who do not want to meet their social obligations. As the state will take over when problems arise, it is no longer necessary for family members to provide care for the old. As the family is seen as the very basis of society, its undermining pulls down the entire structure.

A relevant example is the way that everybody 'minds their own business', and what goes on in the street outside is nothing to do with them. This is a licence for criminals to operate. On top of this, people see it as the role of the police to control crime, failing to see that it is a general social obligation. The message is not to look for others to provide solutions to social problems. As Mrs Thatcher put it in *Let Our Children Grow Tall* (1980), a healthy society is one where 'people ... care for others and look first to themselves to care for themselves'.

 Compare the views of Friedman with those of the Marxists analysed in Chapters 4 and 5. In what key ways do they differ?

The underclass

This approach has been closely linked to the US writer, Murray (1990), and in a number of ways it ties in closely with the writings of Denis. Murray argues that in both the USA and the UK there is a division within the poor. This division lies between those whom we might term the 'respectables' – those who try to get employment, who adhere to the law and who do their best to provide a responsible family life for their children – and those who are not interested in employment, responsible child-rearing or marriage. The result is a generation of young people who do not share the values of the wider society and who are much more likely to commit crime.

Figure 7.3 The underclass and crime

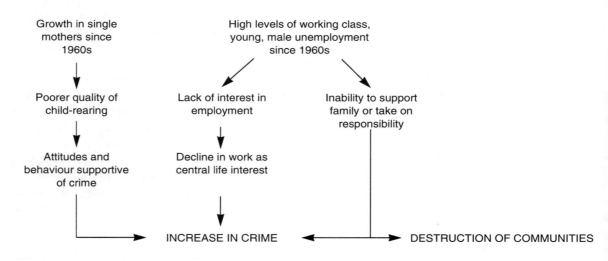

Murray's arguments are a mixture of subcultural theory and traditional conservatism, concentrating on the following three main areas which distinguish the underclass. One point worth noting is that Murray specifically argues that the concept of the underclass is not related to race.

- *Crime*. Murray looks back to the late 1960s for clues regarding changes in society, arguing that the numbers of crimes in England and Wales (he gives no figures for Scotland or N. Ireland) have risen much more sharply than those in the United States. In particular he finds this reflected in the proportion of crimes such as burglary.

- *Illegitimacy*. Murray believes that there are clear distinctions between the socialisation of children in certain single-parent families (by which he means never-married mothers, usually in poorer neighbourhoods) and in two-parent families. Like Denis, he sees neighbourhoods where single-parent families are in the majority, as stimulating a move towards crime or at least forms of social disorganisation:

  > The key to the underclass is not the individual instance [of single motherhood] but a situation in which a very large proportion of the entire community lacks fathers, and this is far more common in poor communities than in rich ones.

- *Dropping out of the workforce*. Murray argues that the values of British society which saw employment providing self-respect, have been lost by certain groups of young, predominantly working-class males. In Murray's view, the answer to this does not lie in providing better training or higher-paid employment. The problem has progressed beyond that, since the communities in which these young men are brought up have now been destroyed by both the lack of interest in work and the consequent collapse of the family and its associated values.

By remaining out of the workforce during the crucial formative years, young men aren't just losing a few years of job experience. They are missing out on the time in which they need to have been acquiring the skills and the networks of friends and experiences that enable them to establish a place for themselves – not only in the workplace, but a vantage point from which they can make sense of themselves and their lives.

Furthermore, when large numbers of young men don't work, the communities around them break down, when large numbers of young, unmarried women have babies. The two phenomena are intimately related. Just as work is more important that merely making a living, getting married and raising a family are more than a way to pass the time. Men who do not support families find other ways to prove that they are men, which tend to take various destructive forms.

Source: Adapted from Murray (1990)

1 *According to Murray, is it unemployment* per se *which causes the social breakdown in the family which can lead to crime?*

2 *Murray refers to the growth of poverty and the related growth of an underclass in the UK. Is poverty the cause of the underclass?*

3 *Do single-parent families subscribe to different values from married couples regarding their children's activities? In the full text of Murray's book, he cites several examples, including:*

- *having no set bedtime*
- *letting very young children play unsupervised in the street*
- *leaving children in the home unsupervised by an adult (or child over 14)*
- *allowing children to be physical and aggressive.*

Try to organise a small-scale survey of parents, comparing single-parent mothers (that is, never-married) with married couples. Is there any evidence to support Murray's assertions?

Criticisms

When discussing issues such as the decline in moral values or in the 'moral fabric' of society, the right tend to ignore issues of power and assume that crime consists of offending against consensually based laws. They dismiss the possibility that laws reflect the values of the more powerful groups in society and, furthermore, that the values upon which the criminal law is based are once again reflections of differences in power. A call for the re-moralisation of society is in effect a call for the majority to accept the values of the powerful.

Right realism

In the USA in the 1960s President Lyndon Johnson launched possibly the most expensive and comprehensive programme to combat poverty that has ever existed in a capitalist society – the 'War on Want'. The aim of this multi-billion dollar initiative was to eliminate poverty and inner-city deprivation through a targeted crash programme to combat problems such as illiteracy, lack of skills and poor housing. The programme was initiated for a variety of reasons – genuine concern for the poor, a desire to counterbalance the increasing disillusionment of US youth with the Vietnam War, and an attempt to combat crime. By the early 1970s there was a general agreement among intellectuals that the programme was a failure. Poverty had not been eradicated and crime rates were soaring.

Emerging from the ruins of the policy, a considerable number of liberals engaged in a radical critique of the whole welfare-orientated approach to solving the problem of crime. These ex-liberals did not approach the problem of crime from the same direction as conservative writers, but gradually their analyses merged into a radical right critique of welfare and crime.

James Q Wilson

The most prominent figure to emerge has been James Q Wilson, author of *Varieties of Police Behavior* (1968) and *Crime and Human Nature* (Wilson and Hermstein 1985).

Wilson commands an ambiguous position when discussing the causes of crime: although he does not deny that there are causes of crime, he does reject the idea that there is much a government can do about them. He suggests there are three factors affecting 'long-term crime rates':

- *Numbers of young males*. The most likely criminal is a young male, so demographic changes in this group influence the amount of crime. An increase in this age group will therefore lead to a proportionate increase in crime.

- *Cost/benefits*. Changes in the benefits of crime such as the ease of accessibility of goods to be stolen, the value of these goods, and the counterbalancing costs of crime (such as increased detection rates and the costs of missing employment opportunities), will have a particularly powerful effect upon property crime.

- *Social and cultural change*. Wilson argues that the motivation to crime cannot be solely that individuals weigh up the costs and benefits rationally, as the chances of being caught are so small that crime almost always pays. Instead he argues that the more important factor affecting crime is socialisation during childhood, which is then reinforced during adulthood. This leads to an internalised self-control which leads to rule-conforming behaviour.

Given this analysis, there would appear to be very little in the short term that can be done to limit crime. But Wilson argues that marginal improvements can be made, and that these can be very significant. In particular he argues for different policing, consisting of three elements:

- public service

- order maintenance

- law enforcement.

Public service consists of such things as traffic control and helping old ladies who are lost. This function, according to Wilson, should be handed over to other agencies as it is not a sensible use of police time.

Wilson and Kelling (1982) discuss the other two aspects of police work. First, they point out that disorder in the streets leads to a breakdown of the social bonds of the community. If people are frightened to go out, the streets become deserted and petty criminals are free to prey on those who do venture outdoors. Eventually law-abiding people move out of the area, leaving it to those too poor to leave and to the petty criminals. The result is a huge increase in crime. Thus disorder leads to crime as it weakens the informal social controls of the neighbourhood.

Second, Wilson and Kelling suggest that too much attention has been paid by the police to a law enforcement model of policing. A crime is committed, the police are called and they attempt to apprehend the culprit, usually without success. Instead, they suggest, the police should be encouraged to engage in policing disorder, even where no crime has been committed. By this they mean that the police officers 'on

The Red Hook housing project in South Brooklyn where a crack epidemic broke down the resident community.

the beat' should be encouraged to keep the streets clear of gangs of loitering youths, drunks, etc. It is not that they are necessarily going to commit crime, but that they destroy the social fabric and sense of community in the neighbourhood:

> Public drunkenness, street prostitution, and pornographic displays can destroy a community more quickly than any team of professional burglars.

The implication is rather shocking since Wilson appears to be arguing that it does not necessarily matter if the law is adhered to by the police, as long as public order is maintained.

A further point made by Wilson is that increasing the numbers of police officers, as usually championed by the right, is a pointless activity. The role of the police is not necessarily to be crime fighters, but to regenerate the desire and ability of the public to impose informal controls on those engaged in deviant activities. The police should provide the 'kick start' for communities to police themselves. Wilson argues that this will not necessarily occur in all neighbourhoods, and that police activities will only be effective in areas where 'the public order is deteriorating but not unreclaimable'. So neighbourhoods with extreme rates of crime and a collapse in the social order are not good candidates for this sort of police action.

Wilson points to the fact that a very large proportion of crimes are committed by a small number of people. This being the case, the point of the criminal justice system should be to 'incapacitate' these people. By this term Wilson means that it is better to punish transgressors on the basis of their whole criminal record rather than for the one specific offence with which they are currently charged. While criminals are in prison they are not going to commit other offences.

Criticisms

The first criticism of Wilson's work is that it would appear to completely ignore the rule of law. One of his arguments is that it is more important to *maintain* order than it is to enforce the law. This is a very dangerous path to go down, as the arbiters of what is acceptable behaviour become the police, who are being encouraged to interpret the law as they think fit.

Wilson argues that to some extent disorder and crime are inevitable in a free society and that the benefits of capitalism, including freedom and the possibility of wealth, outweigh the disadvantages for many of inequality and poverty. Therefore the causes of crime need not be tackled – instead there should be more effective ways of preventing crime. But for the majority of people it is a matter for debate whether the benefits of a free society outweigh the costs. Related to this are the costs to the freedom of those individuals who are defined as undesirable (the young, blacks, the poor) in the sort of control society which Wilson appears to advocate.

> We suggest that long-term trends in crime rates can be accounted for primarily by three factors. First, shifts in the age structure of the population will increase or decrease the proportion of persons – young males – in the population who are likely to be temperamentally aggressive and to have short time horizons. Second, changes in the benefits of crime (the accessibility, density, and value of criminal opportunities) and in the costs of crime (the risk of punishment and the cost of being both out of school and out of work) will change the rate at which crimes occur, especially property crimes. Third, broad social and cultural changes in the level and intensity of society's investment (via families, schools, churches, and the mass media) in inculcating an internalised commitment to self control will affect the extent to which individuals at risk are willing to postpone gratification, accept as equitable the outcomes of others, and conform to rules.
>
> *Source*: Wilson (1986)
>
> The patrolman's role is defined more by his responsibility for maintaining order than by his responsibility for enforcing law. Any intervention by the police is at least under cover of the law and in fact might be viewed as an enforcement of the law. A judge, examining the matter after the fact, is likely to see the issue wholly in these terms. But the patrolman does not. Though he may use the law to make an arrest, just as often he will do something else, such as tell people to 'knock it off', 'break it up' or 'go home and sober up'.
>
> *Source*: Wilson (1986)

1 What three factors does Wilson suggest lead to increased levels of street crime?

2 How does Wilson see the role of the police officer (patrolman)? Explain how this differs from the judge's perspective. What are the implications for policing?

3 *In Chapter 5 we examined the approach known as 'left realism'. Explain how left realism and right realism differ.*

Criticisms of the New Right

The New Right has come in for a number of criticisms, particularly – and fairly predictably – from the left. These criticisms derive from the fundamentally different assumptions of the left. The left argue that the conservative approach is merely a justification for keeping people unequal. Some conservatives would agree with this and would then justify inequality from their perspective. This is less a debate over the rights and wrongs of the conservative viewpoint and more a debate over morality.

This is also true of the conservatives' belief in the natural greed of individuals. Marxists argue that this greed exists because of the way capitalism socialises people. There does appear to be a massive contradiction in the conservative position, however, in that conservatives elevate the search for success to a central moral value of capitalism, stressing the need to compete and look after oneself rather than others. On the other hand, they lament the lack of community and the selfish way people behave. Community and self-seeking greed appear to be opposites rather than complementary values (as the conservatives see them).

A further criticism is that if financial gain is promoted as a morally praiseworthy goal, it is not surprising that people try to achieve it through any means open to them, such as 'crime'. Merton (1938) recognised this contradiction in his discussion of anomie over 50 years ago, yet the lesson appears to be ignored by many conservatives today.

Summary

In this chapter we have explored the variety of perspectives that draw their explanations of criminality from politically right-wing and conservative thinking. These approaches have in recent years been highly favoured by policy makers in Britain and the USA.

The starting point for their analyses is that laws reflect the will of the people in democracies and therefore criminals who break the laws (and harm others) are acting against the good of society. This contrasts with Marxist and some liberal and feminist analyses, which argue that the law can be oppressive.

Although a variety of explanations for crime is provided by right-wing theorists, they would all agree that most people act rationally. Therefore, a crime is committed once a deliberate choice has been made; crime is not the result of social conditioning beyond the criminal's control. All right-wing analysts believe that punishment, rather than state-provided help or welfare, is the answer to crime.

Beyond these basic ideas, however, there is considerable divergence in right-wing analyses. The blame for the increase in criminality is laid variously on the Welfare State, the decline in the family or the failure of the police to maintain order. At the time of writing, the Home Office, which is responsible for law and order policies in the UK, subscribes to what we have called 'administrative criminology'. However, the writings of James Q Wilson are having an increasing impact on the two main political parties in Britain, particularly his argument that the role of the police is to enforce order, as opposed to the traditional belief that their role was to enforce *law* and order. Equally influential is his view that the role of the criminal justice system is to incapacitate criminals, another way of saying that criminals should not be punished for the particular offence for which they are charged but for their pattern of misbehaviour. In the USA this has led some states to introduce laws which send people to prison for life if they commit three offences, two of which involve violence or drugs.

Readings

The influence of the right

Labour's 'get tough' law and order policy was dramatically made clear yesterday when the Shadow Home Secretary, Jack Straw, urged that the streets be reclaimed 'for the law-abiding citizen' from the 'aggressive begging of winos, addicts and squeegee merchants'.

The spokesman went on to attack windscreen cleaners at traffic lights – the squeegee merchants – who bullied women into paying for a service they had not asked for. He said they were a prime example of the brutalisation of Britain's streets.

Mr Straw said he was not concerned whether a policy sounded 'harsh or horrible'; what mattered was whether it worked and carried community support.

Mr Straw's speech on the need to reclaim the streets from crime openly borrowed from a strategy developed by the police commissioner of New York, William J. Bratton, and the city's new mayor, Rudolph Guiliani.

Source: A. Travis, 'Straw takes on "addicts and winos"', *Guardian*, 5 September 1995

This extract reports the current views of the Labour Party – generally accepted to be to the left of centre in political terms.

1 *What is Mr Straw arguing is currently wrong with the situation in the UK?*

2 *What links can be found with the writings of James Q Wilson?*

3 *More radical sociologists have suggested that right-wing crime theories tend to lay the blame for problems at the feet of the powerless. How does this extract illustrate this argument?*

4 *If you live in or near a city, carry out a small survey to see if Mr Straw's views are supported. Construct a small-scale survey which involves asking shoppers and workers in your local city centre their views on beggars. Do they consider them a nuisance? Do they distinguish between types of beggars? Do they give money for services such as busking, windscreen washing, etc.? If they do object to begging, what would they like to be done about it?*

Examination Question

'The existence of a value consensus in society ensures that deviant behaviour is confined to a minority and that such behaviour is punished.' Explain and discuss this view.

AEB, Summer 1995

Bibliography

Clarke, R. (1980) 'Situational crime prevention: theory and practice', *British Journal of Criminology*, Vol. 20, No. 2, pp. 136–147

Davies, C. (1992) 'Moralization and demoralization: a moral explanation for change in crime, disorder and social problems', in Anderson, D. (ed.) *The Loss of Virtue: Moral Confusion and Social Disorder in Britain and America*, London: Sage

Davies, S. (1987) 'Towards the remoralisation of society', in Loney, M. (ed.) *The State or the Market: Politics and Welfare in Contemporary Britain*, London: Sage

Denis, N. (1993) 'Rising Crime and the Dismembered Family', *Choice in Wefare, Series 18*, London: Institute for Economic Affairs

Friedman, M. (1980) *Free to Choose*, New York: Avon

Hayek, T. (1972) *Law, Legislation and Liberty*: The Mirage of Social Justice, London: Routledge

Meiselman, D. and Tullock, G. (1973) Preface in Rottenburg, S. (ed.) *The Economics of Crime and Punishment,* Washington: American Enterprise Institute

Merton, R.K. (1938) 'Social structure and anomie', in Lemert, C. (1993) *Social Theory: The Multicultural Readings*, Boulder, CO: Westview Press

Murray, C. (1990) 'The Emerging British Underclass', *Choice in Welfare, Series No. 2*, London: Institute for Economic Affairs

Rothbard, M. (1982) *The Ethics of Liberty*, New Jersey: Humanities Press

Stevenson, R. (1994) 'Winning the War on Drugs: To Legalise or Not?', *Hobart Paper 124*, London: Institute for Economic Affairs

Thatcher, M. (1980) *Let Our Children Grow Tall*, London: IEA

Van den Haag, E. (1975) *Punishing Criminals*, New York: Basic Books

Wilson, J.Q. (1968) *Varieties of Police Behavior*, Cambridge, MA: Harvard University Press

—— and Herrnstein, R. (1985) *Crime and Human Nature*, New York: Simon & Schuster

—— and Kelling, G. (1982) 'Broken windows', *Atlantic Monthly*, March, pp. 29–38

8 / Women and crime

This chapter explores the nature of female criminality, an area traditionally ignored by sociologists to date. For this reason, female crime has been described as the invisible area in sociology. The first task, therefore, is to explain why it has been ignored. We then need to examine the extent of female crime as revealed in the official statistics, and to see whether they reflect the true extent of female criminality. Finally, we will explore the explanations offered for female crime (or the lack of it).

Invisible women

Virtually every sociological theory of crime manages to exclude any serious discussion of women. Examine any of the key sociological texts from the main theoretical perspectives of Marxism (Chambliss, Hall), functionalism (Durkheim and Merton), subculture (the Chicago School, Cohen, Downes) and labelling (Becker): what they all have in common is the dismissal of women to footnotes, except for discussions of prostitution. Traditional (and contemporary) sociology of deviance is a 'sociology of the boys'.

Feminist critique of traditional criminology

How did this come about? Frances Heidensohn (1985) has suggested that there are four reasons:

Figure 8.1 Guidelines: Attitudes to women and crime

- vicarious identification

- male domination of sociology

- lower recorded levels of female crime

- the nature of sociological theories of deviance.

Figure 8.1 Guidelines: Attitudes to women and crime

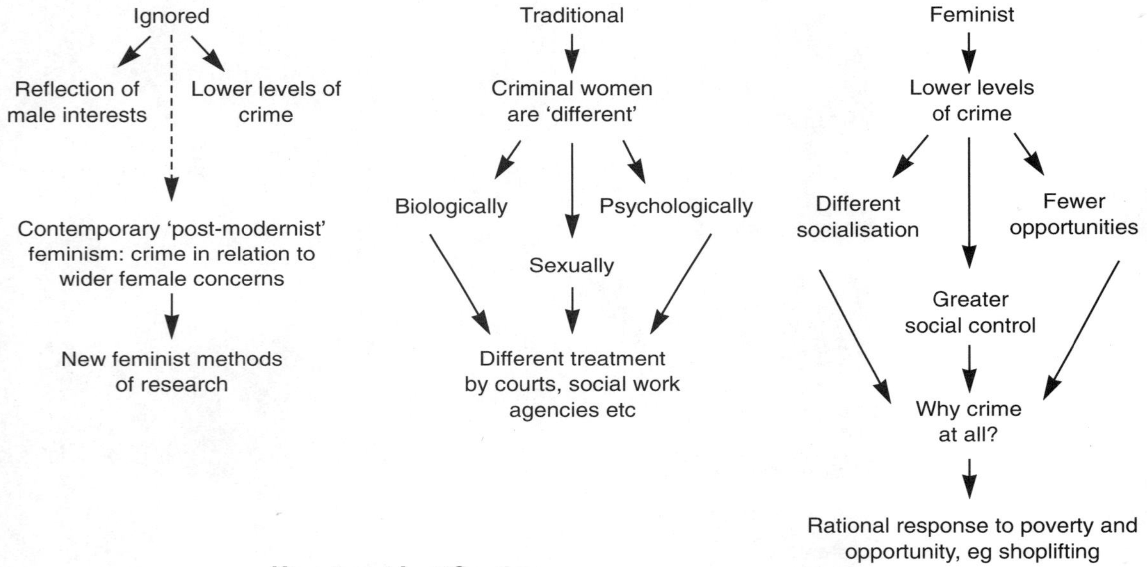

Vicarious identification

Male sociologists were attracted to the sort of life and subcultural activities that delinquents exhibited. It was thrilling to 'bring back news from the fringes of society, the lower depths, the mean streets'. These sorts of investigations were not traditionally possible for female sociologists. The 'mean streets' were 'off limits' to them. In addition, the male sociologists who did study the lives of working-class adolescents were generally precluded by their interests and their gender from studying the lives of working-class girls.

Male domination of sociology

Although the overwhelming majority of students of sociology are female, the teaching of the subject – particularly at Higher Education level – has been dominated by males. Male assumptions have therefore become rooted in the subject.

Lower recorded levels of female crime

Several male sociologists tried to study female crime but were unable to uncover anything. For example, in his classic study of 1,313 gangs in New York, Thrasher (1927) could find only one delinquent female 'gang'. We shall examine the statistics of female crime later in this chapter.

The nature of sociological theories of deviance

Heidensohn argues that the theories of deviance proposed by male sociologists simply accepted stereotyped ideas about females. She suggests that all the theories of crime already developed could be undermined by asking how they could incorporate an explanation for the rates of female crime.

For example, if Albert Cohen was right that the frustration experienced by young working-class boys leads them into delinquent behaviour, what about the girls? Merton's model of anomie was also implicitly based on potential male responses. Marxist theories were so concerned to analyse the effects of social class that they usually overlooked the divisions of gender in society. Before feminism developed, there were no available theoretical tools to develop models which could incorporate explanations of the female crime.

 Examine the extent to which the theoretical approaches to crime you have studied (for example, Merton's anomie theory, or Cohen's subcultural theory) can be used to explain female criminality.

Official criminal statistics

Figure 8.2 A comparison of male and female offenders, found guilty by the courts or cautioned

Source: Criminal Statistics (1991), quoted in Heidensohn (1994)

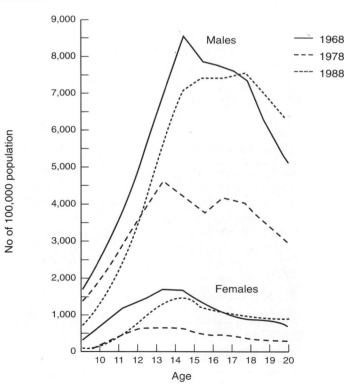

1 *Looking at Figure 8.2, work out (approximately) the difference in the ratio per 100,000 of the population betwen male and female offenders.*

2 *What is the figure in your own area? You are unlikely to be able to find out the ratio of serious offenders but you could do an analysis of the cases taking place in your magistrates courts locally. There are at least two ways in which you could design a piece of research to find out the ratio of male to female defendants. Work out how you could do this and then undertake the research. At the end of your research compare methodologies – which method was simpler and apparently more accurate when compared with national statistics?*

A number of writers have suggested that criminal statistics do not reflect the extent of female crime. The first person to claim this was Otto Pollak (1950), who argued that much of female crime was *masked*. He gave the examples of prostitution and shoplifting, which are commonly not reported to the police.

More contemporary research, particularly in the USA, has attempted to show that women's involvement in domestic violence against partners, children and older frail people in their care is significantly higher than is recorded, or found by self-report studies (see below).

In Britain, the NSPCC conducted a study from the mid to the late 1980s of over 8,000 children who were abused. They did find a much higher proportion of women involved in physical abuse than had been thought, but still overwhelmingly it was the fathers who were the (suspected) main perpetrators. Just taking the figures for natural mothers and fathers, as opposed to step-parents or lovers, where the children lived with that parent, fathers were suspected in 61 per cent and mothers in 36 per cent of cases.

Table 8.1 Offenders found guilty in all courts by sex and type of offence, England and Wales, 1993

Indictable offences	Males		Females	
	Nos (000)	%	Nos (000)	%
Violence against the person	35.5	91.3	3.4	8.7
Sexual offences	4.3	98.0	0.1	2.0
Burglary	39.2	97.5	1.0	2.5
Robbery	4.8	94.1	0.3	5.9
Theft and handling stolen goods	99.5	81.8	22.1	18.2
Fraud and forgery	13.6	77.7	3.9	22.3
Criminal damage	8.6	91.5	0.8	8.5
Drug offence	19.9	90.9	2.0	9.1
Other (excluding motoring)	34.2	90.5	3.6	9.5
Motoring	10.3	95.4	0.5	4.6
Total	269.9	87.7	37.7	12.3

Source: Social Trends (1995)

The official statistics of crime clearly show that overall males are five times more likely to commit crimes than females. By the age of 28, when the levels of offences falls to an extremely low level, 33 per cent of males and 6 per cent of females have been convicted of a 'serious' offence. However, it is important to note that in the last 20 years the increase in female crime has been threefold, while for males it has been twofold.

It is most notable that crime is an activity for the very young female. The peak age for offences is 13–15 for girls, whereas for males it is 14–18. However, the age spread for females committing crime has been widening rapidly, so that there has been a doubling of the rate for 10–12 year olds and a tripling for 14–17 year olds.

Apart from different *levels* of crime and slight differences in the *ages* of criminals, there are also some significant differences in the *types* of offences. Here are a few examples of the differences (the numbers represent the male:female ratio):

Serious motoring offences   30:1

Burglary   25:1

Robbery   20:1

Violence against the person   10:1

Theft and handling   3:1

Self-report studies

To find out the true crime level sociologists developed *self-report studies*. Basically, these involved asking samples of girls to read through a list of deviant acts and to tick those they had committed at some time. This technique was used by Anne Campbell (1981), who concluded that instead of a 5:1 male:female crime ratio the true figure was about 1.2:1, indicating that the levels of crime were more or less equal for males and females.

However, there appears to be some doubt about the validity of Campbell's research. When questions concerning trivial offences were excluded from the self-report studies for females, the official female crime ratios were much nearer the official ratio for male crimes.

Steven Box (1981) reviewed all the available evidence and concluded that overall the proportion of female to male offences may be underestimated by the official statistics, but that when it comes to *serious* offences the official statistics are a fairly accurate guide.

Differential treatment by the police and courts

A bitter debate has developed in sociology concerning the treatment of women by the police and courts. American studies by researchers such as Kalven and Zaesel (1966) suggest that there is a 'chivalry factor' which encourages juries and judges to be more lenient towards women.

In Britain, NACRO (the National Association for the Care and Resettlement of Offenders) has commented that a number of special factors influence magistrates and judges in their approach to the sentencing of women. In particular, factors such as the exclusive responsibility for running the home and caring for dependants, or the fact that an offender may be pregnant, are typical (see NACRO 1980). The result is that twice as many women are cautioned (rather than being prosecuted), and a higher proportion receive a discharge.

An extreme alternative position holds that courts are actually harsher with female defendants because the 'juvenile court functions as a management tool, equipped to correct … female behaviour which … flaunts normative expectations by challenging family authority and threatening truancy and sexual promiscuity' (Casburn, 1985).

In fact, the truth of the matter seems to be more complicated than either of these polarised positions would have us believe. Courts seem to operate a double standard when it comes to female criminals. Light sentences seem to be imposed on those who fulfil the traditional female role, while women who do not fit normal gender patterns, or whose behaviour has offended traditional 'moral codes', are more likely to receive harsh punishment.

A similar debate has taken place over the attitudes of police officers towards female offenders. Are they likely to treat them more leniently? We do know that far higher numbers of females are simply cautioned compared to males: 45 per cent of boys and 70 per cent of girls were let off with cautions in the early 1980s, according to Mott (1983). This may be because police officers hold stereotyped beliefs concerning young females – for example, that girls are likely to have been led astray by male companions, or that boys are more likely to be criminal types than females.

1 It has been found that female police officers have higher arrest rates of women. Can you suggest why, based on the information provided here and your knowledge of gender roles? The following quotation from a study of the Metropolitan Police conducted by the Policy Studies Institute (1984) may help: 'Ideas about sex, drinking and violence are linked together in a cult of masculinity which is thought to provide the key to the criminal world.'

2 It has been suggested that female crime is related to the ways that males and females are socialised into gender roles. Could you suggest an explanation along these lines for the increase in female crime?

3 Girls' most popular crimes are theft – usually shoplifting. Can you offer any explanation for this? It might be a useful exercise to interview local shop managers about this (especially in high street clothes shops).

Women in prisons

There are just over 2,000 women in prison in Britain, accounting for approximately 4 per cent of the total prison population. This represents a significant proportional increase over the last 20 years. For example, there were just under 1,000 women in prison in 1970, when the Home Office was predicting that 'as the end of the century draws nearer [there will be] fewer or no women at all being given prison sentences'. Interestingly, the increase in recent years in imprisoned women is greater in proportion than the increase in offences – particularly serious offences – committed by women.

The majority of women offenders have been convicted and imprisoned for non-violent crimes. In 1993, for example, 37 per cent of all female prisoners were jailed for non-payment of fines – and in the same year 300 women were jailed for non-payment of their TV licence.

According to a study by the National Association of Probation Officers(1996), 80 per cent of those jailed were either unemployed or on some form of state benefit. This included a large number who had not paid fines in order to provide for their children.

Figure 8.3 Adult females sent to prison in 1993

Source: 'Behind bars: women in prison', *Guardian*, Education section, 23 January 1996

Explanations for female crime

Biological theories

Early explanations for female crime were generally based on presumed biological differences between males and females. At the turn of the century the Italian criminologist Lombroso studied female criminals and found that they were abnormal because they lacked some of the 'natural' female traits, which included reserve, docility and sexual apathy. He found that female criminals were very like men in that they had 'exaggerated sexuality' – what today we would probably describe as normal sexual desire.

Lombroso's writing can be dismissed as a historic relic, but in the same way that male deviance is still explained by some 'experts' in biological terms, there have been recent explanations for female deviance using this framework.

Cowie, Cowie and Slater (1968) found that, in general, girls have a higher level of immunity than boys to 'environmental stress' (meaning such things as an unhappy home life), and it is only when 'constitutional predisposing factors' exist that they will turn to crime. In essence, therefore, crime is 'related to biological ... differences, including differences in hormonal balance; and these would at the ultimate remove be derived from chromosomal differences between the sexes'.

In the 1980s came the first mention of pre-menstrual tension in criminal cases, based on the theory that the stress caused by menstruation could cause women to act irrationally and in such instances they could not be held responsible for their actions.

Biological explanations have been criticised on a number of grounds. The strongest criticism is that they confuse gender roles with biological sexual differences. It is not that women are biologically docile and sexually passive – they are brought up to be that way through the processes of socialisation.

Moreover, biologically based theories ignore the fact that laws are *social constructions*. Laws are created by people and vary from society to society and over time.

Psychological theories

Biological and psychological explanations have become closely entwined in criminology. Hans Eysenck's psychological theory of the cause of crime is equally applicable to both males and females. Eysenck (1970) argued that there are two basic personality types – extroverts and introverts. He believed that extroverts are the people most likely to commit crime.

Eysenck tested his thesis on groups of married and unmarried mothers. According to Eysenck, being an unmarried mother is a sign that the person is more likely to be promiscuous, and therefore deviant. He found that the unmarried mothers were both more extroverted and also exhibited much higher degrees of emotionality and neuroticism than did the married mothers.

Talcott Parsons (Parsons and Bales 1955) also suggested a theory which links the disciplines of psychology and sociology. He claimed that in American society the male adult role model is work-centred, while the woman's is home-centred. He suggested that male delinquency is a result of identification with the mother. After the childhood or 'latency' years are over – during which time both males and females are 'home-centred' – culture demands that the male adopt a masculine or 'job-centred' role. In response to this, young men react strongly against all traits associated with femininity, and this initially excessive 'masculinity' can sometimes lead them into delinquency. For the majority of girls the move towards an adult female role model is not problematic and so does not lead to delinquency. Female crime can therefore be related to either the influence of the dominant male in adulthood or the result of some problem in socialisation in the latency period (perhaps being brought up by the father).

Contemporary sociological theories

Traditionally, the few studies of female crime that were undertaken concentrated on finding the differences between 'normal' women and deviant women. Because it was assumed that women were *naturally* less likely to commit crime than men, the most common explanation was to stress how criminal women showed 'manly' characteristics.

Recent approaches to female criminality have been directed less at explaining what special attributes female criminals have and more at examining why relatively few females commit crime compared to males. It is suggested that the answer to this can be found in four areas (see Figure 8.4):

- different socialisation
- stricter social control
- fewer opportunities for women to commit crime
- economic marginalisation.

The first three of these areas suggest constraints on female crime, the fourth suggests one area which generates crime.

Figure 8.4 Reasons why the female crime rate is lower than the male

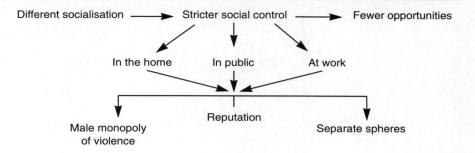

Different socialisation

It is a standard sociological argument that the expectations of behaviour associated with each of the sexes – in other words, gender roles – are created through the process of *socialisation*.

From infancy, children are taught that the sexes are different and that there are clusters of attributes which males and females ought to have. Female roles contain such elements as attractiveness, softness, caring, sweetness and domesticity. Male roles, on the other hand, stress elements such as toughness, aggressiveness and sexuality.

Gender differences include:

- *the games children play*
- *the language used to describe them*
- *their forms of dress*
- *the toys bought for them*
- *the books and magazines published*
- *the subjects considered suitable for study at school and after*
- *the types of employment they should aspire to.*

Give examples of each of these differences in socialisation. Refer to textbooks on the sociology of gender for help with this activity.

As a result of socialisation, girls could be said to be 'lacking' in the values which are generally associated with delinquency, particularly the elements of toughness and aggressiveness associated with masculinity in our society.

This approach is supported to some extent by the low levels of conviction of females for violent street crime. This is the area where there is the largest difference in the numbers of convictions of men and women. The offences for which females are more likely to be arrested than males are shoplifting and prostitution, and these can be tied in with the different sex role expectations for females. For example, shoplifting derives from the role of mother and family-provider and prostitution from the other element of the female role, that of sexual provider in exchange for economic benefits.

Offending against nature?

When the magistrates' magazine Justice of the Peace questioned a group of judges about the criteria they used in passing custodial sentences, one reply read: 'In the case of some children or girls, behaviour which was unchildlike or unfeminine …'

'Boys will be boys,' and boys are naughty. A son's overnight absence will probably earn him no more than a knowing wink from dad, just as his drunk and disorderly behaviour is 'all part of growing-up'. For failing to come home on time, hanging around in the wrong part of town, or adopting dubious friends, a girl is far more likely than a boy to be declared 'in moral danger': for which, at the instigation of her parents, school, social worker, or the police, she may be taken into the care of the local authority.

The criminal justice system sees girls as offending not only against society but against their true natures as well. Criminal girls are maladjusted: real women would not commit crime because real women would not jeopardise their domestic role – of caring wife and mother – and its rewards.

Source: Adapted from Ingram, 'Trials and errors', *Guardian*, 17 February 1987

Discuss the controversial issues raised by the above newspaper article.

Social control

Another concept, which cannot be clearly distinguished from socialisation, is *social control*. These terms overlap and strengthen one another. While reading this section, remember that the controls men place upon women's behaviour also become embedded in the consciousness of women.

It is the area of social control which has attracted most attention from feminists recently. Their point is that women are less likely to commit crime, not from any natural streak of goodness or kindness, but rather because they spend most of their lives being confined by men in law-abiding roles. Females are far more constrained in their lives than males are.

Some feminists compare the *nuclear family* to a prison in which women are trapped. Women are constrained in their nuclear families through ideological bonds, based on the belief that they ought to be the ones who look after children and that this should be done to the highest standards possible. Women who 'fail' in the role of mother and housewife are the butt of family and community disapproval, as the culture of British society stresses that the primary role for a woman is as wife and mother. The same constraints do not apply to males, since husbands are merely expected to 'help' their wives in the home. The effect of these ideological expectations is to lock women into a narrow, family-centred role, controlled to a large extent by men.

Heidensohn (1985) suggests that where women fail in the demands imposed upon them, control may take the form of physical violence against them. There are relatively few acceptable ways for women to escape the pressure of control in the family. One of these, according to the psychiatrist Procek, is through neurosis or depression, rather than crime: "Women's mental illness is the form taken by their power struggle within the personal space of the family"(*Psychiatry and the Social Control of Women*, 1981).

Sara Thornton (right), who had her conviction for 'murder' reduced to 'manslaughter' in 1996, is calling for a review of the way the legal system deals with women who kill after provocation. She is shown here with her daughter just after her release.

One important point, however, is that women go willingly into marriage and the domestic role associated with it, as a result of their earlier socialisation into gender roles.

The way male expectations of female behaviour in the home constrain the freedom of women extends to the wider public treatment of women. Three examples of the *constraints on women in public are*:

- *the male monopoly of violence*: Culturally and historically men have maintained a monopoly over the use of violence. Females are simply not socialised, as some men are, into the use of violence as an acceptable means of resolving problems. The Rambo figure is adored by both males and females alike, the army consists primarily of men, and war is a 'man's game'.

- *fear of a 'bad' reputation*: Females are expected to be far more passive than men in sexual matters, and girls who are 'forward' are likely to suffer through a 'bad reputation'. In an interesting study of how girls are labelled by boys into categories such as 'slag' or 'tight bitch', Lees has shown how this labelling can have major consequences on the way girls behave. No respectable boy would like to be seen going out regularly with a 'slag', for example. Conversely, the girls hated being labelled as a 'tight bitch'. The result was a cautious (and narrow) line between the two extremes. According to Lees, there are no equivalent expressions to describe boys. Nor is the behaviour of males as closely controlled in sexual matters as that of females.

● *the dominance of 'public' life by men*: Men and women inhabit different worlds. Women's sphere is the private world of home and the public areas connected with it, such as the supermarket. The male sphere is the public one – the workplace, the streets at night, pubs, which are all more male preserves than female ones. In pubs, for example, single women are made to feel uncomfortable and the general view (held by males) is that they must be there to 'look for a man'. Indeed the majority of places outside the home pose a threat to women. Quite simply, you usually have to go out to commit crime, and women do not go out alone as often as men do!

 Devise a number of different ways of examining how women are controlled by men (for instance, observing male responses to women in pubs or checking on Lees's argument by asking males how they categorise females). How do women see this control? Does it influence their daily lives?

Opportunities to commit crime

The result of socialisation and control is that women have less desire and less opportunity to engage in deviant, risk-taking or criminal acts. During adolescence, for example (the peak of crime for both sexes), they are far more likely to be confined to the home as the result of the parental social control mentioned earlier. This is different to the male adolescent culture in that it takes place indoors, not out on the streets, where opportunities for delinquent behaviour might arise.

In adulthood, females are constrained through the material demands of looking after their husbands and children, through housework and cooking for example, which take up all their time and energy. Free time for other activities is severely limited. Interestingly, the only serious crime in which women are represented in greater numbers than men is shoplifting; shopping represents one of the few areas where women actually have the opportunity to commit crime.

In employment, women are generally restricted to lower-level, routine employment and therefore rarely have the opportunity to engage in white-collar crime.

Women are also socialised against becoming involved in violent crime. The socially accepted female role does not include toughness or aggressiveness, and women who express these 'masculine' traits are not rewarded. It is therefore likely that they will not be drawn to this form of crime.

Finally, many women may not have the specific 'knowledge' to commit crime. The sort of technical knowledge required to steal a car, or even a car radio, is more readily available to the male reading motoring magazines (generally aimed at a male audience), whose casual conversation may well be about the 'masculine topic' of the relative merits of different motor cars.

'Oh, that's why men commit more crime than women!'

Source: Adapted from an advertisement in *Marxism Today*

Marginalisation

This refers to the idea that women are often pushed to the economic margins of society. According to Chapman (1980), part of the reason for the increase in the numbers of women stealing is that they form the bulk of the poor. Interestingly, the second most common offence for females is fraud, which is closely associated with prosecutions for false welfare benefit claims.

Pat Carlen, another writer who subscribes to this argument, claims that where women are suffering poverty and where they have lost faith in the justice of the welfare system they are more likely to commit crime (Carlen 1988).

As there is considerable evidence linking poverty to crime among males, what is surprising is the very low rates of crime committed by women given that they form the majority of the poor.

 The sociological explanation we have considered for differences in the rates of crime is rather complicated. It consists of four key areas:

- *different socialisation*
- *stricter social control*
- *fewer opportunities to commit crime*
- *economic marginalisation.*

Each of these has then been further subdivided. Make brief notes on each division and subdivision, using Figure 8.4 as your guide. Please note that the social control of women at work is included in the figure, but it is up to you to find out how women are repressed and controlled in the workplace.

Debates within feminism on crime

What surprises most students of the sociology of crime and deviance is that feminism seems to offer few new theories to explain why some women do commit crime. Generally, feminist sociologists have used the low levels of female crime as a starting point to explore wider issues of concern regarding the role of women in society; the explanations they do offer are in fact explanations for the *low* rates of female crime.

Nevertheless, the question remains: Why do those women who commit crimes do so?

The answers feminist theorists have provided are not straightforward; in essence they argue that this is the wrong question to ask, and that attempting to answer it in these terms cannot help move forward our understanding of the relationship between women and crime.

In order to explore this area we will look at the following issues:

● feminism and definitions of crime

● motives and meanings

● the role of gender in theory

● methodology.

We will then look at two examples of feminist research in action.

Feminism and definitions of crime

Smart (1990) and Cain (1990) have both argued that the very definition of crime and even of criminology effectively marginalises women and women's concerns. Their arguments are part of a growing critique of sociology by post-modernists who claim that the attempts of past sociologists to create grand theory is mistaken, and that even the traditional academic subjects such as criminology have to be challenged and deconstructed. In doing so the essentially sexist basis of the assumptions underpinning the subjects will emerge.

Criminological thinking has been developed by men and reflects their assumptions about the world, including their beliefs about women and women's roles in society. Cain has suggested that what is needed is a 'transgressive' criminology that derives from women talking and discussing their concerns. This must start *outside* conventional criminology because this excludes large areas of women's experience that are crucial to understanding criminal acts committed by women, and conversely the low levels of criminal acts by women.

Cain argues that we (or rather women, as this should be a women-only enterprise) should start with the wider issues of how gender differences are constructed and maintained and then move on to examine the particular role of criminal justice agencies in this process. In other words, criminality and criminal justice agencies are only part of a wider picture. The study of crime becomes part of the study of women in society.

Transgressive criminologists do ... share a set of social concerns and knowledge of a body of literature with 'regular' criminologists, whether conventional or radical. But our questions are about women not about crime. And should crime, law and criminal justice institutions ever turn out to be of little importance to our central questions, we would probably stop being criminologists.

Source: Cain (1990)

1 Why do you think Cain has termed her approach to criminology 'transgressive'?

2 *Explain in your own words what you think Cain means by the terms 'conventional' and 'radical' criminology.*

3 *Explain in your own words what sort of criminology Cain is arguing for.*

4 *Do you agree with Cain's comment concerning stopping being criminologists?*

Carlen (1992) argues against this approach, claiming instead that it is the role of feminists to develop theories which can help reconstruct the very definition of crime, and provide new insights. Feminist analysts should not dismiss the concept of crime and the project of criminology out of hand.

Motives and meanings

Developing from these arguments is an insistence that it is necessary to listen more carefully to the voices of women and their distinctive explanations for the crimes they commit (or the crimes they do not commit because of social control).

Carlen maintains that women who commit crime should be given a 'privileged audience' when they speak of their reasons for breaking the law. Murder is a good example because it is so rarely committed by women. For many feminists and an increasing number of legal professionals, the circumstances in which women murder must be very closely examined, using different criteria of judgement from those used by men. When women kill a violent partner, even though there was no specific and direct provocation at the time of the killing they may have been driven to violence by the long-term effects of the abuse they suffered; this is the so-called 'slow fuse' argument. The recent acquittal of three women for the 'murder' of violent and abusive partners has resulted from attempts to understand the acts of these women through their eyes rather than through the male-derived structures of the law.

Furthermore, feminists claim, there should be greater emphasis in academic research on letting women speak for themselves when attempting to understand the causes of their crimes. A different set of meanings and motives can be uncovered which may not fit the conventional explanations for crime.

Women's groups angrily condemned the actions of a judge who gave a suspended sentence yesterday to a man convicted of strangling his wife. The verdict came on the last day of the Home Office's first domestic violence awareness campaign, which was launched by David Maclean, the minister responsible for criminal justice. It cost £170,000 and was entitled 'Domestic Violence is a Crime – Don't Stand for It'.

Mr Hunt strangled his wife as they sat in the car quarrelling over his affair with a married colleague. The court heard that during the argument she tried to get out and began kicking. Mr Hunt said he tried to restrain his wife to stop her hurting himself.

In imposing an 18-month sentence, suspended for two years, Judge Kenneth Taylor said he was 'quite satisfied you were outrageously provoked'.

'This decision of the court is a licence for men to kill their wives,' said Sandra Horley, the chief executive of Refuge, the women's refuge organisation. Harriet Wistrich, spokesperson for the Justice for Women group, said: 'It just highlights the inequality in the treatment of men and women in the law.'

Source: Adapted from Christopher Elliott, 'Equality under law', *Guardian*, 29 October 1994

In July last year Emma Humphreys and Sara Thornton were released from jail, Humphreys as a result of a successful appeal and Thornton on bail pending a retrial [her conviction was eventually overturned]. Both women had been serving life sentences for killing partners who had repeatedly abused them.

Their release has been heralded as a landmark ruling for women, and could lead to appeals being lodged by an estimated 70 women in prison for the murder of their violent partners. The pressure group, Justice for Women, claims that judges are too willing to show sympathy to men. They say that women, who are 100 times more likely to be killed by their partners than men, receive heavier sentences if convicted of the murder of a partner than men charged with the same offence.

Source: 'Behind bars: women in prison', *Guardian*, Education section, 23 January 1996

1 According to the spokeswomen quoted in the first extract, the decision of the court provided a 'licence for men to kill their wives' and 'highlights the inequality in the treatment of men and women in the law'. What is your view of this case?

2 To throw more light on the subject of wife–husband murders and husband–wife murders, use a library CD-ROM to seek out newspaper reports of murders from 1992 onwards. A number of issues have emerged about the nature of 'provocation'. What examples can you find? What might they tell us about the nature of 'murder' and changing perceptions of the nature of male and female violence?

Carlen adds that letting people explain their own criminality, both in research and in court, is a good idea – but that the principle ought to apply to both males and females. Furthermore, in discussing the issue of research, she points out that the 'pure' voices of women are not heard: they are always edited and organised within a framework chosen by the researcher. It is therefore always the researcher, and perhaps in court the lawyer, who remains in control.

The role of gender in theory

Following the arguments of Cain and Smart, Frigon (1990) calls for a distinctive and separate criminology which will turn its back on all theoretical and conceptual ideas of traditional sociology ('malestream sociology', as she terms it).

A slightly different proposal is put forward by Cain herself, as we saw earlier, who suggests that the issue of gender should be the starting point for feminist research in criminology, and that other factors such as class and race should be secondary.

Carlen disagrees, arguing that while gender is crucial its importance may vary with the particular topic or area of study. Furthermore, she says that moving completely away from 'conventional' sociology means that many of the insights which could be developed and modified for feminist analysis will be lost.

The role of gender in methodology

The above arguments clearly have major implications for methodology, and feminist researchers have indeed insisted that traditional research methods tend to exclude or distort the voices of women.

Gelsthorpe (1990) suggests that there are four themes around which feminist research in criminology must distance itself from traditional criminology:

- *Topic*. Feminist researchers must concentrate on issues that are directly relevant to women, and which 'will contribute to ending the oppression of women'.

- *Process*. Sociologists have always debated the advantages and disadvantages of using qualitative versus qualitative methods. Although they accept that surveys are sometimes useful, feminists prefer qualitative studies which seek to uncover and understand the viewpoints of women through in-depth interviewing or ethnographic studies.

- *Power and control*. Oakley (1981) argued that the traditional form of interviewing in which the researcher directed questions at the interviewee in order to uncover answers to questions already formed and structured by the interviewer was a 'masculinist paradigm'. It demonstrated a clear division of power between interviewer and the person interviewed, which tended to reflect the masculine characteristic of imposing power on others. Feminists have tried to develop a more democratic form of research which allows its subjects a say in the content and process of the research project itself. This is a form of 'action research' which Gelsthorpe terms 'egalitarian research'.

- *Desire to record the subjective experience of doing research*. Feminist criminologists question the notion of 'objectivity', which they see as a smokescreen to hide the power of male hegemony. The research process, according to feminists, is a very subjective affair in which the views and feelings of the researcher are significant in forcing the direction of the research project. Feminist researchers therefore constantly seek to clarify their own motives and experiences in order to understand their subjects and to be aware of the direction of their research.

> 'Feminism forces us to locate our own autobiographies and our experience inside the questions we might ask' (McRobbie 1982). Explain this remark and its implications for feminist research.

Girls in the gang: an example of feminist research

In the early 1980s Anne Campbell studied a number of gangs in New York. Unlike earlier research on gangs, which had sidelined women, Campbell's work focused on the roles of female gang members, showing how important they were to the continuation of the gang.

Members of one of the 250 active gangs in San Antonio, Texas. 70 of these gangs are female or partially female.

The first point that Campbell noted was that the stereotype of the gang as being of composed solely of young males who tended to hang around street corners was inaccurate. The young men had to go somewhere when they were not 'hanging around', and this was where women were crucial.

Second, Campbell found that gangs were relatively organised. This did vary considerably, but there was usually a shape to the gang and a set of rules concerning behaviour.

Third, gang members were not always very young. There was a considerable range of ages, though at the time of study few members were over 30 years old.

Campbell found that women were full members of the gangs she studied, were usually treated with respect and often provided a range of support services which enabled the gangs to continue. For example, in one mainly Puerto Rican gang – the Sandman (Club) – the finances of the gang were largely dependent upon selling drugs. Buying the drugs was usually performed by the males, but dividing the drugs into units for sale was conducted by women and the actual sales of the drug were more likely to be undertaken by women than by men. Furthermore the money obtained by selling during the day was given into the safekeeping of Connie, the most senior female in the gang.

When it came to fights and acts of provocation, the women were expected to carry knives and to fight alongside the men. If necessary they would use guns, though guns were not used if possible because they tended to attract greater attention from the police.

Campbell explored the sexual values of the various gangs she studied and found that female gang members tended to have fairly traditional views on limiting their sexual activity to regular partners. Those women who did sleep with a number of gang members were looked down upon by other female members and were likely to be ostracised. Campbell found strong evidence of marriage and permanent relationships between gang members; children were looked after and raised within the gang culture.

Campbell's methodology was primarily ethnographic: she spent six months dropping in on the female members of the gangs so that she became a (relatively well) trusted outsider to them. However, she also engaged in relaxed but nevertheless focused interviews. Campbell points out that she never forced the research in any direction, but let it drift as the women talked about their lives and relationships, thereby constructing the actual structure of the research project much as described earlier when we examined the issues of process, power and control.

I kept as low a profile as possible. I tried to let conversations take their natural course and be an appreciative audience. They talked to me as individuals on rainy afternoons and as part of the group on humid summer nights in front of the projects [housing developments]. After a while they let me use the tape recorder so that I could get their story right and tell it in their own words rather than mine.

I understand more clearly now than I did when I began the research why both the girls themselves and I talked so much about relationships. Recent feminist writing in social science has identified the central role of expressive relationships in women's lives, compared with the instrumental relationships of males. Women's lives are intimately involved with others as daughters, wives and mothers. [Campbell 1981]

Campbell's work is clearly feminist in that she chooses females as her topic and she undertakes a form of methodology which gives power and expression to the views of the women concerned. The result is that she has uncovered overlooked aspects of gang life – the existence and importance of women, the relationships between the women (and the men) and the sense of continuity and stability.

Prostitution and heroin use

The point that emerges from undertaking explicitly feminist research is that models which are useful for explaining male actions may be inappropriate for females. Further evidence of this can be seen in research conducted in Holland by Blom and van den Berg (1989).

These researchers wanted to understand why women in Amsterdam and Rotterdam became prostitutes, and to investigate whether there was a relationship with heroin use. Initially they tried using a theoretical model developed a couple of years earlier to explain heroin use among young males. This model suggested that heroin use involved a career that could be described in terms of (i) a starting position (based upon social class and family background), (ii) a transitory position (based upon youth subcultures), and (iii) a final position within a 'heroin structure' (based upon relations within and outside the heroin world, self-image and future perspective). The methodology used with the males had been a series of interviews which concentrated on an 'ethnographic' account of life on heroin.

When Blom and van den Berg began their research, however, differences emerged almost immediately in terms of methodology and in the usefulness of the explanatory framework.

Methodology

Access to the prostitutes was controlled by males who were able to afford the researchers adequate 'protection'. In the interviews that the researchers conducted it became apparent that a female researcher was useful because the women felt comfortable talking to her and they said things that they may not have done to a male researcher.

The numbers of prostitutes willing to be interviewed and the depth of their replies meant that the original form of ethnographic account of life 'on the streets' began to limit the research. The researchers gradually moved to a 'biographical' approach as it became clear that the only way to understand the shift to heroin use and to prostitution was through an understanding of female–male relationships.

Theoretical explanation

The male model of heroin use was based very much on the significance of the subculture which the young men entered and which partially directed their activities. The model was similar in some ways to Cloward and Ohlin's illegitimate opportunity structure (page 51). However, it did not apply to females because the subculture was of less direct importance to them, according to the researchers. Their relationship to the same subculture was mediated through the males. Although the researchers found five quite distinct types of heroin user-prostitutes, with different attitudes and circumstances, entry into the world of heroin use and prostitution was in almost all circumstances linked to personal relationships, with a male or a female 'best friend', so the subcultural model was inappropriate.

The researchers concluded that had they simply applied 'masculine' research and theoretical models to the heroin user-prostitutes they would have missed the specifically female components which helped to explain the prostitutes' activities more clearly.

Summary

In this chapter we have been exploring the gender dimensions of crime and deviancy. Female crime has been ignored by (male) sociologists on the grounds that crime is far less likely to be committed by women than by men. But of course this may itself give us clues about the causes of criminal behaviour in men. What differences are there in social constructions of gender that makes men more likely to be criminal? The explanations for crime which sociologists have suggested tend to focus on the issues of control and marginalisation. Women are much less likely than men to commit crime because they are socialised differently and controlled more strictly. Also, because of their more marginal position in the employment market, they are less able to commit white-collar crime. The crimes which women do engage in – for example, theft and prostitution – are often rational responses to the problem of how to get money or goods when they are living in poverty.

However, more radical feminist analyses of the relationship between women and crime have pointed to a whole range of sexist assumptions that underlie the very academic field of criminology. They have attempted to link the subject to the wider sphere of women's oppression. They have also argued for the necessity of different methodological approaches.

Readings

The achievements of feminist research

Feminist (and non-feminist in recent years) writers alike have achieved a great deal. They have exposed criminology as the criminology of men. Theories of criminality have been developed from male subjects and validated on male subjects. Thus, they are man-made. Whilst there is nothing intrinsically wrong with this, the problem is that these theories have been extended generally to include all criminals, defendants and prisoners. It was assumed that the theories would apply to women; most do not ...

Feminist researchers have ... made female offenders and victims visible. They not only developed a critique of 'accumulated wisdom' about female offenders and victims, but illuminated institutionalised sexism within criminological theory, policy and practice. For example, they identified the way in which traditional gender-role expectations influenced the treatment of both female defendants and female victims (and hence indirectly of women generally). Thus, they showed that girls were penalised for behaviour which was condoned, if not encouraged, for boys; that being a good wife or mother governed courtroom decision-making and that women who alleged abuse found themselves suspect.

The importance of alternative modes of social control and their interconnections with criminal justice system controls has also been explored by feminist writers. They have made apparent the correspondences between the policing of everyday life and policing through more formal mechanisms.

Theories of crime must be able to take account of both men's and women's (criminal) behaviour. They must also be able to highlight factors which operate differently on men and women. The fact that most theories do not do this is now widely accepted. What is not yet widely realised is that criminology, despite the fact that its primary subject matter is male offenders, focuses hardly at all on men and masculinity. It deals with men without acknowledging this and hence creates theories about criminals without a conceptualisation of gender. For feminists this is a key construct.

Source: Gelsthorpe and Morris (1990)

1 *Overall, what aspect of criminology has been 'exposed' by feminist writers?*

2 *What examples of 'institutionalised sexism' have been uncovered?*

3 *Can you explain the meaning of the sentence, 'They have made apparent the correspondences between the policing of everyday life and policing through more formal mechanisms.'*

4 *What elements should a more complete theory of criminology contain?*

5 *The authors suggest that although criminology has mainly focused on male crime, it has not really focused on men and masculinity.*

What do you think this means, and what implications follow for criminology and criminological research?

Examination Question

"Many sociological approaches to deviance have ignored the extent to which females are involved in crime."
Discuss the evidence for and against this view.

AEB, Summer 1995

Bibliography

Box, S. (1981) *Power, Crime and Mystification*, London: Tavistock

Blom and van den Berg (1989) 'A typology of the work and life styles of heroin-prostitutes', in Cain, M. (ed.) *Growing Up Good: Policing the Behaviour of Girls in Europe*, London: Sage

Cain, M. (1990) 'Towards transgression: new directions in feminist criminology', *International Journal of the Sociology of Law*, Vol 18, No 1, pp 1–18

Campbell, A. (1981) *Delinquent Girls*, Oxford: Blackwell

Carlen, P. (1988) *Women, Crime and Property*, Milton Keynes: Open University Press

—— (1992) 'Criminal women and criminal justice: the limits to, and potential of, feminist and left realist perspectives', in Mathews, R. and Young, J. (eds) *Issues in Realist Criminology*, London: Sage

Casburn, A. (1985) *'Girls will be girls'*, in Heidensohn (1985)

Chapman, J. (1980) *Realities and the Female Offender*, Lexington, MA: Lexington Books

Cowie, J., Cowie, B. and Slater, E. (1968) *Delinquency in Girls*, London: Heinemann

Eysenck, H. (1970) *Crime and Personality*, London: Paladin

Frigon, S. (1990) 'Review of Carlen, P., *Women, Crime and Poverty*', *International Journal of the Sociology of Law*, Vol 18, No 2

Gelsthorpe, L. (1990) 'Feminist methodologies in criminology: a new approach or old wine in new bottles?', in Gelsthorpe and Morris (1990)

Gelsthorpe, L. and Morris, A. (1990) 'Transforming and transgressing criminology', in Gelsthorpe and Morris (eds) *Feminist Perspectives in Criminology*, Milton Keynes: Open University Press

Heidensohn, F. (1985) *Women and Crime*, London: Macmillan

Heidensohn, F. (1994) 'Gender and Crime' in Maguire, M., Morgan, R. and Reiner, R. (1994) *The Oxford Handbook of Criminology*, Oxford: Oxford University Press

Kalven H., Zaesel, H., Callahan, T. and Ennis, P. (1966) *The American Jury*, Boston: Little, Brown & Co

Lees, S. (1986) *Losing Out*, London: Hutchinson

Leonard, M. (1995) 'Masculinity, femininity and crime', *Sociology Review*, September

McRobbie, A. (1982) 'The politics of feminist research', *Feminist Review*, No 12, pp 46–57

Mott (1983) *Adult Prisons and Prisoners in England and Wales*, 1970-82, Home Office Research Study

National Association for the Care and Resettlement of Offenders (1980) *Women in the Penal System*, London: NACRO

Oakley, A. (1981) 'Interviewing women: a contradiction in terms', in Roberts, H. (ed.) *Doing Feminist Research*, London Routledge

Parsons, T. and Bales, R.F. (1955) *Socialization and Interaction Process*, New York: Free Press

Pollak, O. (1950) *The Criminality of Women*, Philadelphia: University of Philadelphia Press

Smart, C. (1990) 'Feminist approaches to criminology, or post-modern woman meets atavistic man', in Gelsthorpe and Morris (1990)

Thrasher, F. (1927) *The Gang*, Chicago: University of Chicago Press

The 1988 film, *The Accused*, where the Assistant District Attorney (Kelly McGillis) helps Sarah Tobien (Jodie Foster) bring to trial not only the men who raped her but also the witnesses who let it happen.

Traditionally sociology has concentrated on the criminal or the deviant, paying relatively little attention to the 'victim'. The first thought to strike anybody in discussing the idea of a victim is that this is a totally innocent person who happens, by chance or by bad luck, to have a crime committed against them. But, as in all sociology, this first, simple thought misrepresents the complexity of the matter.

The social construction of victims

The victim—perpetrator relationship

Let us start with crimes such as murder or child abuse. Here the victim is rarely random, as there is normally an identifiable relationship between perpetrator and victim. In the case of an adult murder the perpetrator is usually a partner or lover; in child abuse or child murder he or she is generally a relative, friend or neighbour.

The victims of burglary may be more randomly selected, but even here, despite a clear-up rate of only 10 per cent, we do know that the people most likely to be burgled are those living within a limited geographical distance of the perpetrator and that they are likely to be drawn from the poorer sections of society. So in burglary, too, there is a pattern behind the apparent randomness.

Defining the victim

People play a critical role in determining whether they are the "victims" of crime. In over 90 per cent of cases it is the victim who reports a crime to the police, so someone must make a decision that he or she is actually the object of crime. So victims are self-defined in most cases. Where people choose not to report matters to the police, it is possible that they do not define themselves as victims, even though in some objective way they may be the objects of a crime.

Take the example of two groups of youths who have consumed large amounts of alcohol or other drugs on a weekend evening. One group of youths attacks the other, and a fight ensues. The fight is broken up by onlookers, and the evening continues. No report is made to the police. Can we consider the group of youths who were the object of the attack as "victims" – especially if the following week they attack the other gang in revenge?

Similar problems of self-definition arise with child sexual abuse, rape and domestic violence.

Figure 9.1 Guidelines: Victimology

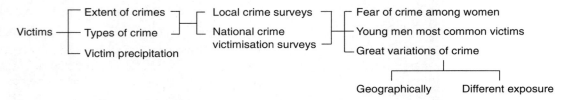

Sensitivity to crime

The process of defining oneself as a victim depends not just on knowing what is criminal, but also on changing sensitivities to crime and social disorder. Let us take the example of two areas of Liverpool covered in the Merseyside Crime Survey. One area, Granby, had much higher rates of 'objective' crime but, according to victim surveys, proportionately fewer crimes were reported to the police than in the much more affluent area of Ainsdale.

In Ainsdale people were less ready to accept behaviour that would have been regarded as normal in the inner-city area of Granby. Vandalism, and groups of youths congregating in the streets or causing a nuisance in local shops, were part of life in Granby, but they were perceived as threats in Ainsdale. The numbers of people defining themselves as victims are likely to increase when there is increasing sensitivity to crime.

Studying victims

The origins of 'victimology' are generally traced back to Von Hentig (1948), who suggested that the law

> makes a clear-cut distinction between the one who does and the one who suffers. Looking into the genesis of the situation, in a considerable number of cases, we meet a victim who consents tacitly, co-operates, conspires or provokes.

Using a series of psychological and social variables, Von Hentig drew up a classification of individuals who were 'victim prone'.

Mendelsohn (1956) went a step further than Von Hentig and drew up a list of personal characteristics which made some people more susceptible to victimisation than others. His work attempted to quantify the extent of the victim's 'guilt contribution to the crime' along a continuum ranging from 'completely innocent' (victim) to 'most guilty'.

Wolfgang (1958) attempted the first systematic empirical study. He examined 558 murders in Philadelphia, USA, and concluded that, based on his definition of victim precipitation, 26 per cent of all the 'homicides' were the result of a victim-initiated resort to violence.

Possibly the most controversial use of victim precipitation can be found in the work of Amir (1971). He studied 646 forcible rapes in Philadelphia and concluded that almost 20 per cent were victim precipitated. Amir's definition of victim precipitation included elements such as the following:

the victim actually – or so it was interpreted by the offender – agreed to sexual relations but retracted … or did not resist strongly enough when the suggestion was made by the offender …

Other researchers, particularly from a feminist perspective, reject the whole concept of victim precipitation when it comes to rape. Hall (1985) found in her study of women in London that as many as one-third of her respondents had been raped or sexually assaulted. Being raped is not something that happens to particular types of females, who are different from normal women, but rather it happens to a high proportion of 'ordinary' women.

The danger with the notion of victim precipitation is that it shifts responsibility for the committal of crime away from the offender and onto the 'victim'. In some cases this may be justifiable, as we saw in the illustration earlier where groups of youths engage in fighting, but it is far less acceptable when talking about sexual assault. Walklate (1989), among others, has strongly attacked victimisation studies, describing them as 'victim-blaming' studies.

The thin line between recognising the non-random nature of victim selection and shifting the blame onto victims for their own victimisation has been a constant difficulty for victimisation studies.

Victimisation surveys

Victimisation surveys have become one of the most common tools of criminological research, and have contributed greatly to the development of left realism, the theoretical approach we discussed in Chapter 5.

Victimisation surveys are usually of two types:

- *national surveys* of a whole country in which people are asked to provide information on crimes which have been perpetrated against them;
- *area or neighbourhood* surveys in which a specific, usually inner-city, neighbourhood is targeted, and sociologists engage in a more detailed study of the same issues.

National crime surveys

National studies were first developed in the USA in the late 1960s, but did not arrive in Britain until 1982 with the first British Crime Survey (BCS), carried out on behalf of the Home Office. This consisted of a study of 10,000 people over the age of 15. The main aim of the study was to examine the extent of crime in the UK in a completely independent way from the statistics provided by the police.

What had become apparent by the 1980s was that official statistics provided by the police significantly underestimated the number of offences. People were reluctant to report crime for a variety of reasons (which are discussed in Chapter 10, pp. 00), and were only really likely to report crime where there was a benefit of some kind to them – for example, when an insurance claim could be made. But the BCS gathered other information as well, such as the impact of crime on victims, fear of crime, and the victims' and the public's experiences of how the police dealt with them. There were six such surveys between 1982 and 1996.

The first BCS caused a sensation. It showed that only one in four crimes against property and one in five offences of violence were recorded in the official statistics. Interestingly, and perhaps alarmingly as well, between the first and the fourth survey the *actual number* of crimes reported to the police rose, but a smaller proportion of crimes (out of all those committed) were reported to the police.

The BCS found that the risk of being a victim of minor offences was high, but the chance of suffering a serious offence was very small. Theft was the most common crime, and particularly theft linked in some way to vehicles. A staggering 36 per cent of all recorded offences involved thefts from or of vehicles.

Burglaries made up 9 per cent of the crimes, violent offences such as wounding and robbery made up 5 per cent and 'common assaults' comprised a further 12 per cent.

Criticisms of national crime surveys

National crime surveys have been criticised for three main reasons:

- *Omissions*: The original crime surveys tended to under-represent a number of groups – particularly the young, the geographically mobile (including young 'drifters' and the homeless), and ethnic minorities. Victimisation studies also exclude fraud, shoplifting and a range of other crimes, so they only give a snapshot of a small range of crimes.

- *Awareness*: In order to reply to the victimisation study, the person needs to be aware that a crime has been committed against them and that they are a victim. As we have seen, this depends on the definitions made by the 'victim'. Furthermore, people forget what has happened to them if asked about the previous year.

- *Coverage*: Just as important, the first national surveys gave average figures for crime over the whole country. The result of averaging figures for crime victimisation was that the surveys very significantly underestimated the chances of being a victim of crime for the large sections of the population who were young, female or living in the inner cities. For instance, saying that the statistically average adult could expect to have his or her home burgled once every 37 years gave the impression that

Britain was largely a crime-free society; the problem is that there is no such thing as the 'statistically average adult'.

Under criticism from significant numbers of radical criminologists, the British Crime Surveys developed 'sweeps' which entailed taking proportionately larger samples from certain areas and among certain groups than others – in effect, looking more closely at inner-city areas and different types of housing.

Once BCS information was broken down, the differences in experiences of crime were quite dramatic. It emerged quite unambiguously that the risk of being a victim was closely related to geographical area, an individual's age, sex and pattern of routine activities such as drinking alcohol and going out in the evening. Examples of the striking differences include the following:

- Robbery is twice as likely to occur to those under 45 as it is to those over that age.

- Robbery is twice as likely to occur to men as to women.

- Eighty per cent of the victims of assault are men.

- The most common victim of an assault is a single male, under the age of 30, who goes out to pubs more than twice a week, drinks fairly heavily, and himself assaults others.

- The risk of being burgled is five times higher for those living in urban areas.

Some issues remained cloudy, and little light was shed on them by the BCS. Domestic violence in particular seems not to be reported to the BCS, even though it has emerged that victims know their assailant in over 30 per cent of assaults of all kinds, and that about 17 per cent of assailants (in all cases of assault) are relatives, partners or former partners.

Race issues did leap out at the researchers, however. In particular, it emerged that people of both Afro-Caribbean and Asian origin were more likely to be the victims of crimes than whites. Those of Asian origin were especially likely to suffer high levels of loss or damage, and experienced greater levels of violence against them. Over 24 per cent of Asian-origin victims believed that the offence was primarily racist in character, compared to 15 per cent of Afro-Caribbeans.

Local crime surveys

In an attempt to overcome the weaknesses apparent in the BCS, a number of local crime surveys have been carried out. The best known are the Merseyside and Islington crime surveys, conducted in the mid to late 1980s. The aim of these local surveys has been to work with local crime prevention agencies (such as the police, local authorities, housing departments and victim support organisations) to examine what really concerns people living in inner-city areas and to look at positive ways of tackling these worries. As we have indicated, these surveys have been closely connected with the emergence of left realism; they have also made a particular focus of domestic violence, which we examine in detail in the next section.

What has emerged most strongly from the local surveys has been the very uneven patterns of victimisation and the risk of repeat victimisation. In Merseyside the levels of burglary were more than three times the average for the country as a whole, and in Islington (North London) the figure was almost double the average.

The biggest differences between national and local statistics were in sexual and domestic assaults. The 1988 British Crime Survey, for example, found a level of 4.2 per cent of women experiencing domestic violence, while the North London Survey in 1992 claimed that 12 per cent of its female respondents had suffered domestic violence. The figures for sexual offences were as low as 0.3 per cent for the national survey and 6 per cent for the North London survey.

Fear of crime

It is important to distinguish between the reality of being a victim, and the fear of crime. The two are not necessarily linked. Young, working-class males are the most likely victims, but express least concern, whereas the elderly most frequently express fear, although they have among the lowest levels of victimisation.

The second Islington Crime Survey (Crawford et al. 1990) attempted to determine the factors affecting the fear (as opposed to the reality) of crime. The researchers asked questions about where people were most afraid – on the street, on public transport or at home – and how their behaviour was affected by this. The results of this and other surveys suggest that fear is mainly an urban phenomenon and linked to poor street lighting, urban blight, and groups of youths congregating on street corners. Individuals are also influenced by media images and by the perceived inability of the police to prevent crime.

In the second Islington Crime Survey over 60 per cent of respondents gave their fear of crime as a reason for not going out, and over 41 per cent rated it as an important reason for not going out. People developed strategies to allow them to go out at night. These included avoiding certain places and only going out when accompanied. The importance of the fear factor is demonstrated by the finding in the first Islington Crime Survey that 36 per cent of women never went out at night for fear of crime.

Consequences of crime for victims

Being a victim also entails consequences for the victims. Maguire (1994) asked the victims of burglaries about the worst aspect of their experience; only 32 per cent cited loss of belongings, yet 42 per cent mentioned concern and worry about a sense of 'intrusion' into their home and lives. Even more extreme are the responses of victims of assault and violence: Shapland (1984) found that 75 per cent of a survey of over 300 people were still expressing concerns over two and a half years after the incident. Perhaps the longest-lasting effects are felt by the victims of child abuse: Morris (1987) found that they suffer from feelings of shame and guilt even as adults, and as children they suffer from low levels of self-esteem and problems at school.

The Islington Crime Survey

It is sometimes suggested that crime, although frequent, is a minor irritant, given the range of problems the city dweller has to contend with. The public, on this view, suffer from hysteria about crime. Panics abound – particularly about mugging, sexual assault and violence – which are out of touch with reality. These arguments are backed up by evidence from sources like the British Crime Survey, which says that the 'average' person can expect 'a robbery every five centuries ... a burglary every 40 years ... and a very low rate for rape and other sexual offences'.

But the inner-city dweller is not the average citizen. Our study, with its ability to focus in on the highly victimised, indicates the realism of their fears.

It is scarcely odd that 46 per cent of people in Islington should admit to worrying 'a lot' about mugging, given that over 40 per cent of the borough's population actually know someone (including themselves and their family), who has been mugged in the last twelve months. Nor is it unrealistic to worry about burglary when its incidence in the borough runs at five times the national average.

Why are women more fearful about crime than men, when most studies show they have a far less chance of becoming victims? Our survey suggests that, in the inner city at least, their fears are perfectly rational. Women here are more likely to be victims of crime than men.

The reason for the shortfall in past findings is the nature of the crimes committed against women, and their reluctance to admit them to a stranger engaged in a social survey. Using carefully trained, sympathetic researchers, we found a considerably higher rate for female victims. The reason is threefold: sexual assaults are almost exclusively a female 'prerogative'; so is domestic violence; and street robbery against women is greater than against men.

In terms of non-sexual assault alone, women in the borough are 40 per cent more likely to be attacked than men. Sexual assault in Islington is 14 times the national average. A fifth of the women we interviewed knew someone sexually assaulted or molested in the previous twelve months. Over half had experienced sexual harassment of a non-criminal kind.

And all of this occurred even though the women took much greater precautions against crime than men. They were, for example, five times more likely never to go out after dark than men; three times more likely to always avoid certain types of people or streets; and, very significantly, six times more likely to always go out with someone else, instead of alone.

Source: Jones and Young (1986)

1 What significant differences occurred in the findings between the BCS and the Islington survey?

2 Why were the findings so different between the two surveys?

3 What does this tell us about the national statistics of crimes against women?

Multiple victimisation

It is one of the themes of this chapter that victims are not entirely random members of the population. One disturbing aspect of this is that whereas some groups or households are untouched by crime, other households are repeated victims – so although about one-third of those surveyed in the British Crime Surveys had been victims of crime, about half of those victimised reported more than one victimisation. Looking at the statistics another way, about 70 per cent of offences were perpetrated against respondents who experienced multiple victimisation.

In a detailed study of the BCS statistics Trickett (1992) showed that the areas of the country with the highest rates of crime also had the highest rates of multiple victimisation. Particularly interesting is Trickett's argument that the increase in crime in Britain over the last ten years did not generally occur across the country as a whole, but if an area already had a high crime rate it suffered an increase in crime, and this was largely due to an increase in multiple victimisation.

Why should a household be the subject of multiple victimisation? At the time of writing there is little published research on this, but a number of factors are possible:

● A particular property, premises or car might be especially vulnerable to theft. Therefore different thieves might independently select the same target.

● The particular household may be picked on for the specific characteristics of the household members – for example, victimisation on racial grounds.

● The same offenders repeat their crimes, having succeeded in the past.

Table 9.1 Examples of levels of multiple victimisation (%)

No. of times victimised	Domestic violence		Mugging		All violence	
	% of victims	% of all incidents	F	M	F	M
1	49	20	87	70	68	38
2	16	14	7	12	16	17
3	35	66	6	19	17	45

Source: Adapted from Mayhew et al (1993)

Table 9.1 summarises levels of multiple victimisation for violence in various settings and forms.

1 a. What percentage of victims of domestic violence are subject to more than one incident of violence?
b. Can you offer any explanation for this?

2 a. *What percentage of victims are 'mugged' more than once?*

    b. *What percentage of all incidents is this?*

    c. *Could you make any suggestions as to why this is?*

3 *What percentage of all violent incidents are incidents of repeat victimisation?*

Gender and victimisation

The majority of crimes committed against women occur in the home. 'Domestic violence' ranks as the second most common form of assault among all violent crimes, and rape is one of the most under-reported crimes. The British Crime Survey revealed that 46 per cent of all female victims of violence were assaulted in their own homes. In a study in North London, Mooney (1993) uncovered the fact that 10 per cent of all women had experienced violence from their partners in the previous 12 months.

Figure 9.2 Gender and victimisation

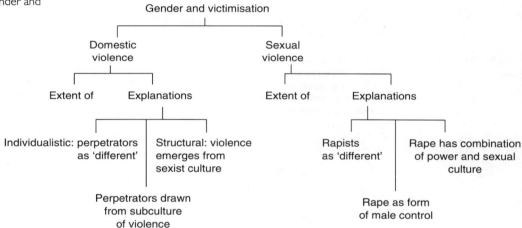

Although the home may be the place where most violence against women occurs, in surveys they express much greater fear when they are outside it. According to the first BCS, 35 per cent of women aged 30–60 felt 'very unsafe' after dark. The second Islington Crime Survey found that 43 per cent of women stayed in 'a lot or quite a bit' after dark because of fear of crime, including 27 per cent of women under 25, who might be expected to be most likely to want to go out at night for social reasons. Furthermore, over 90 per cent of all the young women who do go out alone after dark alter their behaviour to take some 'form of avoidance', which could involve carrying a weapon or avoiding certain streets. The survey also revealed that 20 per cent of women did not use public transport because of fear of crime.

The statistics for crime against women are somewhat confusing in that the national crime surveys indicate that women are less likely to be victims of crime than men, while local inner-city surveys point to rather different conclusions. This has led to a fairly heated debate about the 'myth' and the 'reality' of women as victims.

The myth of women as victims

Some sociologists, such as Clemente and Kleinman (1977), argue that women's fears are exaggerated and that the chances of sexual assault, for example, are minimal for the average woman. They point to the fact that there are only 16 sexual assaults for every 100,000 members of the population. Compare this, for example, to the proportion of 410 burglaries or 1,490 acts of vandalism for every 100,000 people.

From this observation has developed the theory that the media exaggerate the extent of sexual crimes. They do this because of the unfortunate fact that reports of crimes such as horrific rape cases are 'newsworthy' events that sell newspapers. Women themselves receive a distorted impression of the dangers of going out after dark and as a result fear going out and stay indoors. As so many women avoid walking in the streets at night or travelling by public transport, the streets become emptier, and the fewer people in the streets at night, the greater the chance of an assault going unseen. The result it that the minority of women who choose to go out at night are in greater danger than they otherwise have been. Figure 9.3 illustrates this process, as outlined by Clemente and Kleinman.

In effect, this argument dismisses women's fears as unrealistic. As Clemente and Kleinman argue, 'Fear of crime ... has become a problem as serious as crime itself.'

Figure 9.3 Media, fear and crime

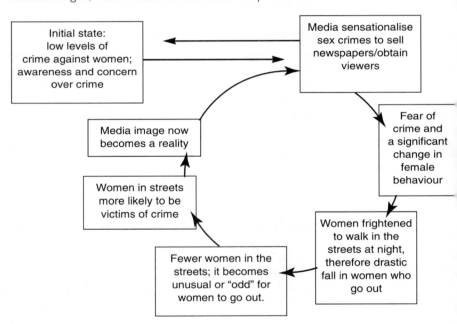

The differential exposure approach

According to this approach, certain groups of women really are more likely to be victims of crime than men. The argument has two parts:

● Female victims are highly *concentrated* among certain groups and in certain areas of cities. Overall rates may be low, but in inner cities they are very high indeed. Women's fears are therefore justified in these areas.

● The types of crimes specific to women, that is, sexual assault and marital violence, are those *least likely* to be reported and recorded in official statistics.

In the United States, where most of the research has been done, the relative rates of rape vary significantly between different groups. For example, a poor black woman is six times more likely to be raped than a rich white woman, and a woman aged 16–19 is seven times more likely to be raped than one aged 35–49.

In Britain the Merseyside Crime Survey showed that in some parts of the inner city *half* of all women under the age of 50 said that they had been 'upset' by some form of sexual harassment in the streets.

It is not just sexual harassment that is targeted primarily against women. The BCS suggests that the overwhelming number of victims of bag-snatching and mugging are women. Again, this form of crime is specific to inner-city areas.

These points led Lea and Young (1984) to maintain that certain categories of women living in inner-city areas really are more likely to be the victims of criminal attacks, and that theirs is not an irrational fear.

The fact that the crimes most commonly committed against women – rape and marital violence – are the ones least likely to enter the official statistics is explored in detail in the following two sections.

Table 9.2 Staying in very often or fairly often after dark, by age and gender (%)

Age			Gender	
16–24	25–44	45+	Men	Women
36	44	63	40.5	74

Table 9.3 Went out alone, fear of victimisation, a lot and quite a bit, by age and gender (%)

Age			Gender	
16–24	25–44	45+	Men	Women
34	40	37	34	57

Table 9.4 Staying in a lot or quite a bit after dark because of fear of victimisation, by age and gender (%)

Age			Gender	
16–24	25–44	45+	Men	Women
27	27	31	17	43

Table 9.5 How much is fear of being a victim of crime the reason for not going out alone after dark? Women, by age (%)

	16–24	25–44	45+
A lot/quite a bit	90	75	70
Not very much/not at all	10	25	30

Note: The table represents percentages of the sample – those who do not go out alone after dark.

Source: Crawford et al. (1990)

Tables 9.2 – 9.5, drawn from the second Islington Crime Survey, concern the relationship between staying in at night and fear of crime.

Look at Table 9.2.

1 Are men or women more likely to stay in at night because of fear of crime?

2 Which age group is most affected?

Look at Table 9.3, which refers to people who do go out alone in the evening, and concerns their fears of being victims.

3 Describe the information provided in this table, by age and sex.

4 What similarities and differences emerge between Tables 9.3 and 9.4? Can you offer any explanations?

Look at Tables 9.2 and 9.5. They refer to people who told the interviewers that they normally stay in after dark – those who are frightened for some reason, and also those who do not go out by habit or inclination, or because of domestic responsibilities.

Maxfield (1988) argued that 'The type of person you are (for instance, married, elderly, or with young children at home) is more important in determining how often you go out than fear of crime ... mobility appears to be more restricted by age, marital status, gender and having young children in the home than it is by fear.' The above tables do not precisely answer this criticism, but they do suggest a possible answer as to whether staying in at night is a personal choice or is forced on some people.

5 Do you agree with Maxfield, having examined these tables? Explain why you have come to your decision. (For me the crucial factor is the information provided about 16–24 year olds, whom I would expect to want to go out.)

6 I teach students between the ages of 18 and 30, and when I do a quick show of hands regarding fear of going out in the evening (in Cambridge), very few are concerned. Try a more scientific approach.

7 Interview a police spokesperson from the Victim Support Unit or a volunteer from the charity Victim Support. If possible, ask if you can also speak to two or more people who have been victims of crime (for research purposes 'multiple victims' of crime would be best). Ask the spokesperson the extent of multiple victimisation in your area. Find out the impact on the individual(s) concerned. What factors appear to make them more likely to be (multiple) victims of crime?

Sexual violence

The extent of sexual violence

In the early 1990s there were on average about 4,500 offences in England, Wales and Scotland each year which were defined as 'rape and attempted rape'. We know that this does not represent the true figure, as every survey ever done on the reporting of sexual crimes has indicated a huge under-reporting brought about by shame and the desire not to go through the humiliating process of a court case –

even though the woman is actually the victim. The true extent of rape and attempted rape, however, is open to debate, as victimisation studies have shown widely differing results. The first British Crime Survey found only one unreported rape out of 5,000 women interviewed, yet in a study by Hall (1985) only 8 per cent of women who stated they had been raped actually reported it.

The relationship of rapist to victim

The commonly held view is that rape occurs in a dark alley late at night and is committed by a stranger. The reality is rather different.

In a survey of over 1,000 married women, Painter (1991) found that approximately 14 per cent had been raped by their husband, and that in almost half of these cases violence had been used. Married women are twice as likely to be raped by husbands as by acquaintances or boyfriends, and seven times more likely by husbands than by strangers. Mooney (1993) uncovered the fact that 6 per cent of women had been raped (or forced to have sex) by partners in the previous 12 months, and again just under half of them had 'consented' as a result of violence.

Explanations for rape

Figure 9.4 Different explanations for rape

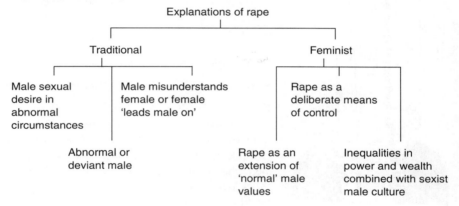

Traditional explanations

The traditional explanation offered for rape focuses on:

- the supposed natural sex drive of the rapist, and
- the precipitating actions of the victim.

The *rapist* is commonly regarded as a man who is unable to control his overwhelming sexual desires. Usually he is incompetent or frustrated in sex and as a result may turn to rape. Interestingly, this explanation is often linked to a defence of prostitution, which is seen as allowing a sexual outlet for men who would otherwise suffer from complete sexual frustration. This is in essence a *biologically based* explanation, as men are viewed as having powerful sexual drives which must be fulfilled. It also implies that women do not have the same degree of sexual desire.

The second element of the traditional approach to rape centres on the *victim*. Women are sometimes seen as encouraging the rape through their manner or style

of dress. One psychologist even suggested that some women are masochistic and may actually enjoy rape; this may cause them subconsciously to 'lead certain men on' whom they find attractive.

Another version of victim theory concerns the fact that, although women may enjoy sex, they are culturally expected to limit their sexual contacts, so the 'advantage' of rape is that it allows them to perform sexual intercourse but frees them of the associated guilt.

The consequences of these traditional beliefs concerning rape are profound. If the person who rapes the victim is known to her and is to all extent and purposes 'normal', was it really rape? Was she partly to blame because of some remark, style of dress or attitude? Allegations such as these may lead some women to decide not to report the rape to the police.

Most men (and, therefore, police and judges) perceive rapists as significantly different from 'normal' men. Those who rape are a distinctive category, suffering from certain biological, psychological or social problems. Therefore, if they are confronting a person accused of rape who is apparently normal and who may be known to the victim, they experience a contradiction with the stereotype of the rapist and may be inclined to distrust the accusation of rape. They may also harbour suspicions concerning the actions of the victim, which they may interpret as having led up to the rape.

The radical-feminist perspective: rape as control

A completely different interpretation of rape comes from the radical-feminist perspective. Susan Brownmiller (1975), for example, has argued as follows:

> from prehistoric times to the present … rape has played a critical function. It is nothing more or less than a conscious process of intimidation by which all men keep all women in a state of fear … men who commit rape have served in effect as frontline masculine shock troops, terrorist guerrillas in the longest sustained battle the world has ever known.

Note that Brownmiller claimed rape is a 'conscious' act by men to retain control over women, and although it is performed by relatively few men it serves the purposes of *all* males.

The feminist perspective: rape as 'normal' behaviour

Carol Smart (1976) argues that rape is to some extent 'normal' in a society in which the women are expected to engage in sexual bargaining. According to her view, the very basis of marriage has traditionally been the exchange of regular sexual favours by women for the security of the relationship. Smart points out that the images of women portrayed in the media and the attitudes socialised into both sexes from an early age stress the importance of sexuality and the attractiveness of females.

Furthermore, men are encouraged to seek sex, and women to put up an initial resistance before 'giving in'. Indeed, a woman who appears to encourage sex is regarded as 'loose' by many men. The men are therefore *encouraged* to be active (possibly even aggressive) and the women to appear reluctant.

The significance of Smart's argument is that rape is not a distinctive, deviant act which is *opposed* to the normal sexual relations in our society, rather it is an *extension* of normal sexual values and gender relations.

The passage from Brownmiller quoted above is shocking to many male students of sociology when they first read it. A rather less shocking version of a similar argument has been made by Jill Radford and Elizabeth Stanko (1991):

> As feminists we argue that sexual violence is used by men as a way of securing and maintaining the relations of male dominance and female subordination, which are central to the patriarchal social order. We recognise that patriarchy is crossed through and is in interaction with other power structures, namely those of race, class, age and status regarding disability. These shape women's experience of sexual violence and the response of the police and others. We firmly believe that it is through challenging the patriarchal order by ... autonomy that men's violence must be confronted.

1 *Traditional explanations of rape and violence against women tend to stress that men who commit these acts are 'abnormal'. What implications does this have for understanding the actions of all men?*

2 *What implications does Radford and Stanko's argument have for women?*

3 *How can their perspective alter our sociological theorising and research on the subject of violence against women?*

4 *Devise a method for finding out the attributes people regard as 'manly', then list them. Can this information be related to the argument over the different reasons for rape?*

The Marxist-feminist perspective

This approach has most clearly been proposed by Steven Box (1983), who has suggested that it is:

> the historical conjuncture of 'sexist male culture', coupled with gross inter- and intra-gender inequalities in wealth, power and privileges, and firmed up by techniques of neutralisation and a legal system in which institutionalised sexism is embedded, that forms the roots of rape.

This is rather a densely worded explanation, so it may be useful to break it up into smaller parts:

● *Sexist male culture.* Box argues that in British culture women are regarded as inferior and that their social worth is measured by their attractiveness. We examined this earlier, when we looked at Smart's argument.

● *Gross inter-gender inequalities*. Men hold most significant positions of power. For example, in employment males are more likely to hold the managerial and supervisory positions. Therefore, Box argues, various forms of sexual harassment may be tolerated by women in the workplace in order to keep in the boss's good books.

A question of promotion?

● *Techniques of neutralisation*. Matza originally suggested the idea of techniques of neutralisation in his explanation for juvenile crime (Matza and Sykes 1961; see chapter 3). Briefly, Matza suggested that there are cultural 'excuses' which we all use to justify ourselves when we commit deviant acts – for example, 'I didn't know what I was doing, I was drunk.' Delinquents merely carry these excuses a bit further to justify their behaviour. Box suggests that there are culturally acceptable excuses for rape, too, including the idea that women put themselves in situations where they are more likely to be raped (for instance, by hitch-hiking) so, according to the perpetrators, they are partly to blame for what happens to them.

● *Institutionalised sexism in the legal system*. The assumptions which the police and the judicial courts act upon when dealing with rape reflect, according to Box, the sexist attitudes of the wider society. The idea discussed above that rapists must be in some way 'abnormal', for example, means that judges (and possibly juries) and police officers find it hard to believe that ordinary men like themselves could possibly be guilty of rape. The fault must therefore lie somehow with the victim.

Most sociological analyses of rape have moved away from placing the stress on biological urges, or psychologically disturbed individuals, towards a depiction of rape as a normal outcome of our society. Box's approach is Marxist because it locates these elements within the framework of capitalism.

Examine the contents of daily tabloid newspapers. Do they support the feminist perspective on sexuality?

Domestic violence

The extent of domestic violence

Like most other forms of crime, the reported level and the unreported extent of domestic violence differ significantly. The British Crime Survey suggests that there has, however, been a significant increase in the proportion of domestic violence 'offences' reported to the police: in the original survey only one in five incidents were reported, but by the early 1990s this ratio had risen to one in two. Unfortunately, Mooney (1993) suggests that in Islington, at least, the figure remains at about one in five (22 per cent). In all Mooney found that 10 per cent of women had been the victims of violence by partners, and 5 per cent of respondent had at least one broken bone. Mooney also points out that over their lifetime up to 25 per cent of women had been victims of domestic violence, including assaults by parents, step-parents, siblings and other relatives.

 You may be able to interview victims of domestic violence if you approach your local police (or victim support group) and ask them to pass on your request to the local women's refuge (a 'safe house' for female victims of violence). Record an interview for your group to uncover the reality of the lives of women who have been subjected to violence.

The police response

Mooney noted a significant change in police practices regarding domestic violence since the late 1980s. After advice from the Home Office, most police forces have Domestic Violence Units, generally staffed by female officers. Police officers are expected to refer 'domestic assaults' to these units. This has led to an increase in prosecutions.

However, there is still considerable under-recording of domestic violence. Police officers view some degree of conflict between spouses as quite common and not necessarily to be regarded as 'serious'. The level at which a 'simple' marital dispute becomes an assault is left to police officers' discretion.

A second factor influencing the police decision to prosecute derives from a belief that wives are likely to withdraw their complaint after a short 'cooling-off' period. Interestingly, of the cases which do proceed, only about one in ten women withdraw their complaint.

A third and crucial factor influencing the perceptions of police officers is that of privacy. Pahl (1985) has stressed the importance to police officers (and the law in general) of the distinction between acts committed in a 'public place' and those committed in a private home or institution. In British culture the right of a person to the privacy of his or her own home is strongly emphasised; anything which takes place within its confines is regarded as the personal business of the family.

Female partners and wives are reluctant to report assaults against them for the following reasons:

● Many women fear that reporting violence to the police or social services will only lead to further violence against them.

● Many women regard the violence against them as a personal matter between themselves and their male partner and may be too embarrassed to report it.

● A victim may sometimes blame herself for her partner's violence. She feels she may in some way have 'deserved' the violence as a result of her inadequacy as a wife.

● Some women believe that the police are largely indifferent to their plight.

Table 9.6 The prevalence of domestic violence in a woman's lifetime, by type of violence

Violent behaviours	Per cent
Mental cruelty Including verbal abuse (e.g. the calling of names, being ridiculed in front of other people)	37
Threats of violence or force	27
Actual physical violence	
Grabbed or pushed or shaken	32
Punched or slapped	25
Kicked	14
Head butted	6
Attempted strangulation	9
Hit with a weapon/object	8
Injuries	
Injured	27
Bruising or black eye	26
Scratches	12
Cuts	11
Bones broken	6
Rape (def. = made to have sex without consent)	23
Rape with threats of violence	13
Rape with physical violence	9
Composite violence	30

Source: Mooney (1993)

Table 9.6 concerns the percentage of women who have experienced domestic violence in their lifetime, and what their injuries were.

1 What percentage had been the victims of mental cruelty?

2 Can you see any methodological difficulties in working out the extent of 'mental cruelty' and making objective/statistical statements?

3 What percentage had been threatened with force?

4 What was the most common form of violence, according to Mooney?

5 What evidence in the table suggests the seriousness of these forms of violence?

6 What percentage of women had been raped? Note that the majority of these assaults were committed by their partners.

7 Now, within the group of students you are studying with, be honest. Either write down the information anonymously or, if you feel confident with each other, openly discuss (a) if you have ever used violence (as defined here) against a female or male partner or ex-partner, and (b) if you have ever had violence used against you by a partner or ex-partner.

8 Devise a very simple questionnaire and ask students in your institution whether they have used violence or been the victims of it by a partner or ex-partner.

Table 9.7 Domestic violence by class*

Class	Violence at any time %	Violence in last 12 months %
Professional	25	7
Lower middle class	29	11
Working class	30	10

* Domestic violence refers to 'Composite Domestic Violence', i.e. actual physical violence minus 'grabbed, pushed and shaken'. 30 per cent of women at some time in their lives and 10 per cent in the last 12 months had experienced violent behaviour that fell into the Composite Domestic Violence category.

Source: Mooney (1993)

It is generally argued that violence against women is perpetrated by the less-educated, working-class male. What comment can you make, looking at Table 9.7? Who is most likely to commit violence against a woman?

Table 9.8 Reporting of the violence

Of those experiencing domestic violence,* the following people and agencies were informed:

	Violence at any time %	Violence in last 12 months %
Friend	46	36
Relative	31	29
General Practitioner	22	17
Police	22	14
Solicitor	21	12
Social Services	9	7
Women's Refuge	5	3
Victim Support	2	1
Citizen's Advice Bureaux	2	1

* Domestic violence refers to 'Composite Domestic Violence'. 10 per cent experiencing violence at any time and 6 per cent in the last 12 months said they had told another agency not specified on the questionnaire: these included the Housing Department, hospital doctor, therapist or a Court official.

Source: Mooney (1993)

1 Who are women most likely to contact concerning violence?

2 What percentage report the violence to the police?

3 *Request an interview with your local police Domestic Violence Unit. Ask them why women do not contact them.*

Explanations for domestic violence

Explanations for domestic violence fall into three general categories. The first of these stresses the *individual* and looks for defects in his personality or background. Broadly speaking, this falls in with the *positivistic* approach to the explanation of crime. Here the argument is that, as 'normal' men do not assault their partners, violent husbands or male partners are abnormal in some way. This approach then looks for the differences between the normal male partners and the violent ones.

The second approach stresses the distinct *subcultural values* held by men who assault their partners.

The third approach stresses the *structural* context in which the violence takes place. The behaviour of the violent male is not seen solely as a result of his defects, but also as a result of a society which allows, or even promotes, violence against women partners.

The individual

M. Faulk (1980) studied men who had been convicted of assaulting their wives. He concluded that the majority of them could be classified as mentally ill. Wife assault therefore represented the actions of a few disturbed individuals.

It should be noted that Faulk's sample was not at all typical, as it consisted of men who had been *convicted* of violence against their wives. If the extent of under-reporting marital violence is a great as suggested earlier, these men could not be assumed to be typical.

Alcohol has also commonly been associated with domestic violence. Pahl (1980), for example, found that 52 per cent of husbands in her sample 'often drank to excess' according to their wives, and this has been supported by a majority of other studies. However, a study of violence in Scotland conducted by Dobash and Dobash (1979) found that only 1 per cent of attacks were precipitated by heavy drinking. The question of why the men drink heavily in the first place also needs to be considered.

Violence in the childhood home was blamed by Gelles, Straus and Steinmetz (1980) as the cause of adult violence. People who grew up in violent homes were more likely to use violence than those who had not. One in ten husbands who grew up in violent families used serious violence against their wives. The problem with this as an explanation for domestic violence is that the other nine who grew up in violent homes did not appear to use violence.

Other psychologically based approaches have followed the line of investigation into childhood experiences. For example, it has been suggested that those who assault their partners are likely to have had 'domineering, rejecting mother relationships'.

Finally, one group of researchers has stressed the deviant nature of the husband–wife relationship, suggesting, for example, that where a wife is 'aggressive' and tries to 'control the relationship' the husband may turn to violence. We seem here to be returning to an approach which 'blames the victim', as we examined earlier in our discussion on the causes of rape.

The subculture of violence

The second explanation for domestic violence moves the spotlight away from the individual specifically, and instead focuses on the subcultural values of the violent individual. Wolfgang and Ferracuti (1967), for example, examine the way in which certain working-class groups are brought up to regard violence as acceptable behaviour. This, they claim, helps to explain why the bulk of reported marital violence occurs among the working class.

There are some major problems with this approach, however. They centre around the fact that we cannot be sure domestic violence really does occur mainly among the working class. Middle-class women may be less likely to report it. According to the 1993 House of Commons Select Committee on Domestic Violence, violence in the home crosses all social barriers and is not limited to the working class. If we accept the argument that domestic violence is spread throughout society, the claim that there is a specific subculture of violence, restricted to the working class, must be wrong.

1 *Look back at the reasons given for the under-reporting of domestic violence and suggest why there may be differences in reporting levels between working-class and middle-class women.*

2 *If you were to conduct a study of marital violence, what methods would you use?*

Structural explanations

This final type of explanation, generally associated with the feminist position, is based on the argument that marital violence is not isolated, deviant behaviour which runs against the generally accepted values. Instead, it is argued that domestic violence happens due to the low status of women in society (and in the family in particular) and the belief that the male ought to be the dominant member of the family.

This approach was put forward most forcibly by the Dobashes (1979) in their study of 109 wives who were the subjects of assaults by their husbands. There are three strands to the argument:

- *Historical.* Throughout history, the use of violence by husbands has been culturally acceptable and even the law has seemed to accept that a certain level of violence is justifiable for a husband to maintain discipline within the family.

- *Cultural.* In contemporary British society the family is an unequal institution in which the male receives most benefit and where he is expected to be dominant. The use of coercion is acceptable if the wife fails to perform her 'duties' adequately. Women are socialised throughout childhood into the correct behaviour expected of them in marriage, as good mothers and wives. Men, too, are raised with high expectations of the wife/mother role. There is far less stress in our culture on the domestic duties of the husband.

- *Specific factors.* The Dobashes, and also Pahl, argue that specific factors may spark off violence, including disputes over money, jealousy on the part of the husband, and drunkenness. However, these can only lead to violence when there is a cultural 'context' which says that one way to resolve these problems for the male is to assault the female.

Explanations for domestic violence, therefore, have moved away from the individualistic idea that violence is the action of a man 'abnormal' in some way. Instead much more structurally based explanations suggest that violence against women is both widespread and, perhaps, alarmingly 'normal'.

Summary

Traditionally, victims have been the poor relations in the study of crime, not important enough to hold the investigative gaze of the sociologist. However, when researchers did begin to examine the role of the victim, they found that victims are not picked totally at random – certain groups of people in certain situations are more likely to become victims than others. A series of national and local surveys established that the least powerful are the most likely to be victims of crime and, furthermore, that those who are victims once are more likely than average to become the victims of further crimes.

Sexual violence and domestic violence are crimes generally perpetrated by men on women. Some of the arguments put forward in the general discussion on victims emerged in this more specific context as well, notably the suggestion that the victim's behaviour in some way leads to the crime being committed against her.

When the spotlight was turned on the men who engage in these acts, the first explanations tended to suggest that these perpetrators were somehow abnormal, biologically or psychologically. However, gradually, under the influence of feminist analyses, the debate has shifted to the ways in which our society permits, or possibly even encourages, sexual abuse and violence against women. Current feminist analyses therefore seek to understand the origins of these acts in terms of the concept of masculinity.

Readings

I was very tired that night and I went to bed early. Then he came to bed, and my little girl woke up, because she'd wet the bed. Anyway, I went to see to her and I took the sheet and I moved it round so that I moved her off the wet part. And I went back to bed. Anyway, she cried again and he went out to see to her. And I didn't know what had hit me. He came in and he ripped the clothes off me and grabbed me by the feet, and dragged me out of bed. And he kicked me out into the hall and he called me all these names, and he said, 'How dare you leave that child with a wet sheet on the bed.' And he threw me into her bedroom. So I did the little girl, changed the bed all right round again, and then I went into the bathroom and locked the door, because I was so upset. He came in and knocked the bolt off and he dragged me back into our bedroom to make the bed. And I remember I had my dressing gown on and he threw me all the way down the hall and he ripped my dressing gown and then he threw me on the floor and he was kicking me and I was sitting there screaming. And then he said he'd give me half an hour and then I was to go back into the bedroom and I was to apologise and he meant apologise properly. He put one arm round my throat and he slapped me and punched me and he said, 'How dare you look at me as if I'm repulsive to you. You're my wife and I'll do what the bloody hell I like to you.'

Source: Pahl (1985)

1 This extract suggests that the husband's motivation was closely related to his definition of:

    (a) his role

    (b) a wife and mother's role.

Could you explain this?

2 Which explanation(s) for marital violence does this extract support?

Examination Question

Evaluate the contribution of sociological studies to an understanding of victims of crime.

AEB, Specimen Paper

Bibliography

Amir, M. (1971) *Patterns of Forcible Rape*, Chicago, IL: University of Chicago Press

Box, S. (1983) *Power, Crime and Mystification*, London: Tavistock

Brownmiller, S. (1975) *Against Our Will*, London: Secker & Warburg

Clemente, F. and Kleinman, M. (1977) 'Fear of crime in the United States', *Social Forces*

Crawford, A., Jones, T., Woodhouse, T. and Young, J. (1990) *The Second Islington Crime Survey*, London: Middlesex Polytechnic

Dobash, R. and Dobash, R. (1979) *Violence Against Wives*, Wells: Open Books

Faulk, M. (1980) 'Men who assault women', in Gelles, R., Straus, M. and Steinmetz, S. (eds) *Behind Closed Doors: Violence in the American Family*, New York: Anchor

Hall, R. (1985) *Ask Any Woman*, Bristol: Falling Wall Press

Jones, T., Maclean, B. and Young, J. (1986) *The Islington Crime Survey*, Aldershot: Gower

Jones, T. and Young, J. (1986) 'Crime, police and people', *New Society*, 24 January

Lea, J. and Young, J. (1984) *What is to be Done about Law and Order?*, Harmondsworth: Penguin

Maguire, M. (1994) 'Crime statistics, patterns and trends', in Maguire, M., Morgan, R. and Reiner, R. (eds) *The Oxford Handbook of Criminology*, Oxford: Oxford University Press

Matza, D. and Sykes, G. 'Juvenile delinquency and subterranean values', *American Sociological Review*, October

Maxfield, M. (1988) *Explaining Fear of Crime*, Home Office Research Unit Study No. 43, London: HMSO

Mayhew, P., Aye Maung, N. and Mirrlees-Black, C. (1993) 1992 *British Crime Survey*, Home Office Research Study 132, London: HMSO

Mendelsohn, B. (1956) 'Victimology, a new branch of bio-psycho-social sciences', *Revue Internationale de Criminology and Police Techniques*, Vol. 10, No. 31

Mooney, J. (1993) *The North London Domestic Violence Survey*, Centre for Criminology, Middlesex University: Islington Council

Morris, A. (1987) *Women, Crime and Criminal Justice*, Oxford: Oxford University Press

Pahl, J. (1985) *Marital Violence and Public Policy*, London: Routledge

Painter, K. (1991) *Wife Rape, Marriage and the Law*, Manchester: Manchester University Press

Radford, J. and Stanko, E. (1991) 'Violence against women and children: the contradictions of crime control under patriarchy', in Stenson, K. and Cowell, D. (eds) *The Politics of Crime Control*, London: Sage

Shapland, J. (1984) 'Victims, The Criminal Justice System and Compensation', *British Journal of Criminology*, 24/2, 131-149

Smart, C. (1976) *Women, Crime and Criminology: A Feminist Critique*, London: Routledge

Trickett, T.A., Ellingworth, D., Farrell, G. and Pease, K. (1992) 'What is different about high crime areas?' *British Journal of Criminology*

Von Hentig, H. (1948) *The Criminal and His Victim*, New York

Walklate, S. (1989) *Victimology*, London: Unwin Hyman

Wolfgang, M. and Ferracuti, F. (1967) *The Subculture of Violence*, London: Tavistock

Figure 10.1 Guidelines

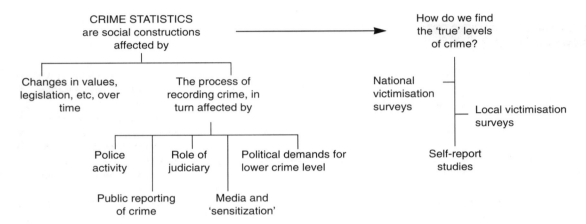

CRIME STATISTICS
are social constructions
affected by

How do we find
the 'true' levels
of crime?

Changes in values,
legislation, etc, over
time

The process of
recording crime, in
turn affected by

National
victimisation
surveys

Local victimisation
surveys

Police
activity

Role of
judiciary

Political demands for
lower crime level

Self-report
studies

Public reporting
of crime

Media and
'sensitization'

Official statistics seem to indicate that crime levels varied only slightly from 1876 until the 1930s. There was then a gradual increase until the mid-1950s, followed by a sharp rise, and the crime rate stabilised again in the mid-1990s.

One point worth noting is that the rise in crime was not limited to the UK, but also occurred in most other democratic societies – although not in Switzerland or Japan.

1   Look at Figure 10.2 and describe the overall pattern of burglary and theft from 1945.

2   What comments could you make about the relationship between burglary and theft, as illustrated in Figure 10.2?

3   What has happened since 1989? List as many possible explanations for the changes in the statistics as you can think of. When you have finished this chapter, go back and see if there are any changes you would like to make.

Figure 10.2 Recorded crimes of burglary and theft in England and Wales, 1946–83, in thousands

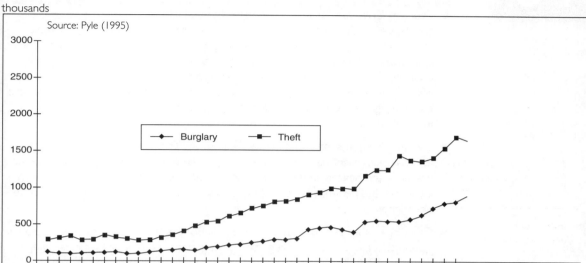

Source: Pyle (1995)

Figure 10.3 Crimes recorded by the police, 1987–92

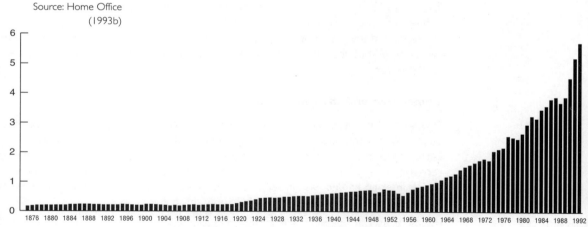

Source: Home Office (1993b)

1 At what period did crime start to rise steeply?

2 Could you suggest any reasons why we might be wary of accepting the picture provided by Figure 10.3?

3 Statistics are generally believed to provide factual evidence upon which we can base theories and explanations. Do you agree with this?

4 What implications does your answer to question 3 have for research methods in sociology?

Measuring trends in crime

There are a number of problems in comparing statistics over time. These include:

- *Changing legislation.* Legislation can alter the definitions of criminal acts, and can criminalise activities which had previously been regarded as legal. For example, there was an increase in legislation dealing with crimes of fraud during the 1980s in a response to the changes in the organisation of share dealing in the City of London. The 1990s have seen legislation against trespassing and public order offences. On the other hand, some acts have recently been legalised; for example, the legal age for homosexual acts between consenting males has been lowered from 21 to 18.

- *Changing interpretation of the law by the judiciary.* The increasing influence of the feminist movement has slowly widened what is regarded as unacceptable sexual practices and has led judges to view sexual offences more seriously. This in turn influences the possibility of arrest for certain offences which may previously have been ignored.

- *Changing moral values and greater sensitivity.* Both of the above reflect and help to influence changes in what is regarded as acceptable behaviour as values change over time. Racially motivated attacks, sexual abuse of children and domestic violence are examples of activities which have become increasingly unacceptable and for which there is general agreement that greater law enforcement ought to be encouraged.

Linked to these changes are shifts in the acceptability of 'deviant' activities in general. There may have been a decrease in the degree of latitude given to other people's behaviour: noise is considered more intrusive as the perceived value of privacy increases, and the gathering of groups of young people – which may in the past have been disliked but accepted as 'horseplay' – is now more likely to be seen as a threat to civil order.

Crime levels and changing values

Changing moral values are a major factor affecting crime rates. Increases or decreases over time in crime rates may well be a reflection of changes in the acceptance of particular forms of behaviour. Increases in crime statistics might result from increasing sensitivity to any form of deviation although there has actually been an increase in social order and a decrease in serious crime. More reporting of crime might 'in reality' mean less 'real' crime! Figure 10.4 shows how this might happen.

Figure 10.4

Source: Derived from Young (1994)

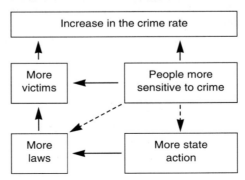

208

- *More state action*: Because there are increasing numbers of police, more people are being arrested, and since a considerable amount of crime will always be unknown to the police, the official statistics can rise without there being a rise in 'real' crime.

- *More laws*: Because there is more legislation on the statute book, there are more possible crimes.

- *More sensitivity*: People have become more sensitive to crimes such as violence, therefore more are being reported to the police.

- *More victims*: Because of the increased affluence there are more things to steal and people go out more, living more exposed lifestyles. As opportunities have risen, so have crimes.

1 Can you give two examples of crimes that were regarded as less serious 30 years ago than they are today? (If you cannot think of any, refer back to Chapter 8.)

2 Could you suggest any reasons why people have become more sensitive to crime?

3 Can you relate your suggestions to any particular theoretical approaches?

4 Look back at Figure 10.3. How might the comments above on 'more victims' help us to understand the figure?

5 Sensitivity to crime may vary by age (among other things). Conduct a small-scale survey. Construct a list of 'common-sense' offences – for example, assault, 'mugging' (though of course there is no specific criminal offence known as mugging), burglary, rape or sexual assault. Include also other possible concerns, such as loud noise from neighbours, danger from traffic or drug use. Take a cross-section of ages. Ask your respondents to rank your list of crimes and concerns in order of importance. Can you find different sensitivities in the different age groups?

Collecting and recording of statistics

These issues are examined in more detail later in the chapter, but it is worth noting here that about 40 per cent of 'crimes' reported to the police do not actually appear in the official statistics. The police may regard certain reported 'offences' as too trivial, or not to be law violations, or simply to be false accusations.

The significance of the term 'trivial' can be illustrated by the change in the guidelines issued by the Home Office before and after 1977 regarding criminal damage of less than £20 in value. Before 1977 these cases were regarded as trivial and excluded from the statistics, but after 1977 they were included. The result was a 7 per cent rise in crime.

One crime or lots of crimes?

A thief breaks into a house shared by 12 students and steals from each of them: as far as the police are concerned one crime has been committed. The following day the same thief breaks into a block of flats and then steals from all 12 apartments in the block: the police will record 12 crimes. As can be seen by these examples, the 'unitary' nature of a crime is difficult to define, since similar acts may be counted as a single crime or as a number of crimes.

Defining crime

We will look at this subject in more detail later when examining the activities of the police and the judicial system. For the moment we should recall that a criminal act is a *social construction* which involves the police and judiciary defining and then categorising acts according to their own organisational needs.

Official crime statistics are classified by the Home Office into 71 groups and then reassigned into eight categories. The categories are useful guides to crimes but they are of course very broad classifications of a series of *previous* classifications. The result is a table such as Table 10.1, which is published in *Social Trends*. This is more an indicator of the way the police, the judiciary and the Home Office engage in the complex process of categorising information than an indication of what 'actually' happened. The table seems to be giving us 'hard facts', but really it is a social construction based on previous social constructions.

Table 10.1 Notifiable offences[a] recorded by the police: by type of offence

thousands

	England and Wales			Scotland			Northern Ireland		
	1981	1991	1993	1981	1991	1993	1981	1991b	1993
Violence against the person	100.2	190.3	205.1	8.0	15.5	13.8	2.9	4.0	4.8?
Sexual offences	19.4	29.4	31.3	2.1	3.1	3.7	0.3	0.9	1.2?
of which: rape	1.1	4.0	4.6	0.3	0.5	0.5	–	0.1	0.2?
Burglary	718.4	1,219.5	1,369.6	95.7	116.1	97.8	20.5	16.6	15.7?
Robbery	20.3	45.3	57.8	4.2	6.2	5.6	2.7	1.8	1.3?
Drug trafficking	–	11.4	14.8	1.6	3.3	5.2	–	–	–
Theft and handling stolen goods	1,603.2	2,761.1	2,751.9	201.1	284.3	250.4	25.4	32.0	33.2?
of which:									
theft of vehicles	332.6	581.9	597.5	32.5	44.3	42.8	5.1	8.4	9.0?
theft from vehiclesc	379.6	913.3	925.8	..	..	89.4	6.5	7.2	6.7?
Fraud and forgery	106.7	174.7	162.8	21.4	26.4	23.7	2.6	4.8	5.5
Criminal damaged	386.7	821.1	906.7	61.7	89.7	84.2	5.2	2.4	2.9
Other notifiable offences	8.9	23.2	26.1	12.4	48.1	58.6	2.8	1.0	1.1
All notifiable offences	2,963.8	5,276.2	5,526.3	408.2	592.8	543.0	62.5	63.5	66.2

[a]Includes attempted offences. Scottish figures of 'crime' have been grouped in an attempt to approximate to the classification of notifiable offences in England and Wales and Northern Ireland. However, differences in the legal systems, recording and counting practices and classification problems mean that Scottish figures should not be compared with those for England and Wales and Northern Ireland.
[b]No longer includes assault on police and communicating false information regarding a bomb hoax. These offences have been removed from the categories 'Violence against the person' and 'Other notifiable offences'.
[c]In Scotland, data have only been collected from January 1992. The figures include theft by opening lockfast places, from motor vehicles and other theft from motor vehicles.
[d]In Northern Ireland the figures exclude criminal damage valued at £200 or less.

Source: Social Trends 25 (1995)

Factors affecting the reporting and recording of criminal statistics

In this section we will examine why the rate of reporting and recording of crime is so low. The reasons are complex and intertwined, so we will consider them under the following headings:

- the public's reporting of crime
- the police
- the judiciary
- political pressures
- the media
- invisible crime
- corporate crime.

The public's reporting of crime

Less than 10 per cent of crime is directly observed or uncovered by the police. The remaining 90 per cent comes from complaints from the public.

The main findings of the British Crime Surveys concerning the reporting of crime to the police were as follows:

- People do not report crimes which they define as too petty, or which they believe the police will define as trivial.

- People report crimes when there is an advantage in it for them. Thus 98 per cent of thefts of motor cars were reported to the police, presumably because the victims were insured.

- Some crimes are regarded as private matters to be settled between individuals.

- The victim may not want to harm the offender. This is particularly important in intra-family crime, such as the theft of money by a brother.

- Victims may be too embarrassed to complain to the police. This seems particularly important in the case of sexual offences, where the police are perceived as uncaring and the procedures for dealing with rape victims appear humiliating. Estimates of the true extent of rape are unreliable, but even the British Crime Surveys, which certainly under-represent the true level of rape, suggest that the real level is two and a half times the official estimate.

- The victim may be unable to inform; at the very worst he or she may be dead.

Kinsey, Lea and Young (1986) have developed a model of the relationship between the local communities and the police, which they claim explains why inner-city communities are unwilling to report crimes to the police or to assist police officers. They argue, firstly, that inner-city communities have little faith in the police, believing that they are biased against them. For instance, in the Merseyside Crime Survey (a large- scale study of the police and crime patterns around Liverpool), overall 30 per cent of respondents expressed a lack of belief in police fairness. This inhibits them from informing the police if there is no direct benefit to them from doing so.

Secondly, according to Kinsey, Lea and Young, respondents in inner-city areas are reluctant to report cases of street crime to the police for fear of reprisals by the criminals. This can equally be seen to illustrate a lack of faith in the police.

Thirdly, the Merseyside Crime Survey found that there was an inverse relationship between levels of crime and willingness to report crime. Where there was least crime – in the middle-class suburbs around Liverpool – there was the greatest willingness to report crime to the police, but in areas of highest crime there was the least willingness to report it. This has an important effect on the crime statistics. For instance, in Granby (a working-class district), 21 per cent of the locals had witnessed a theft from a motor car, whereas in Ainsdale (an affluent suburb) only 4 per cent had done so. Yet while the people of Ainsdale would report it, a significant proportion of the people of Granby would not.

Through your local library, the courts and local authority you can track down the crime statistics for your town.

1 *Find out what categories for crimes and criminals are used. Why are these categories used?*

2 *Are there any particular areas of your town which have higher rates of crime than others? Could you offer any explanations for this?*

3 *Are there any types of crime which are particularly high? Can you offer any explanations?*

4 *Devise a questionnaire which asks people which areas in town and what groups of people are most connected with crime, and what sort of crime is committed in your town. Do their replies match the 'facts' you have uncovered? Ask the same questions of the police. Do their replies match the 'facts'?*

The police

The police play a crucial role in deciding which complaints by the public should be categorised as crime, and the acts that should be defined as illegal.

The police response to the reporting of crime

The overwhelming majority of complaints to the police consist of petty crimes. Police officers are likely to categorise these acts as crimes as much on the basis of the social status of the person complaining as on the nature of the act itself. Interestingly, the PSI survey of the Metropolitan Police (1983) found that they were more likely to respond to a complaint if made by a member of an ethnic minority.

Categorisation of crimes

One of the major influences on the crime statistics is the way acts are *categorised*. Exactly what distinguishes one crime from another (for instance, assault with intent to rob versus plain assault) is unclear. It is up to the police officers themselves to decide the most appropriate category. On that decision rests the fate of the individual (as one category of crime may be far more serious than another) and the construction of the official statistics. The eventual decision by the police officer is usually a result of *police discretion*, which we examined in Chapter 9.

Dispersal

The police operate with clear ideas about the areas where trouble is most likely to occur, usually in certain inner-city areas and large-scale council estates, and they allocate their officers accordingly. This means that there is a greater likelihood of police officers being aware of offences in these areas than elsewhere.

Routine 'stop and search' may also uncover more crime. However, according to the PSI study, there were 1.5 million Metropolitan Police 'stops' in 1981, but only 8 per cent of those stopped were found to have committed an offence, and only 3 per cent of the total were actually prosecuted. It could be argued that the purpose of 'stops' is to establish a police presence and to ease police officers' boredom.

Variations in the numbers and type of policing occur between the affluent suburbs and rural areas and the inner cities. Fewer police are sent to suburbs and the countryside, and the style of policing here is likely to be 'consensual', with the officers seeing their role as supporting the community. In inner-city areas there are more police officers, and they see their role as *controlling* the local population in what Lea and Young (1984) term a 'military policing' role.

 Police forces are usually very helpful when asked to assist in research. Arrange a day or evening with your local police station. Are the points made in this section borne out by the reality of policing?

Differential enforcement

Police officers in different 'forces' often have different attitudes to crimes. These reflect the priorities of the senior police officers in the various forces. The significance of this variation for the official crime statistics is that concentration by one force on a particular area may generate apparent high levels of 'crime' for a particular offence. Certain forces, for example, are known to be stricter on drink-driving offences, others on prostitution, etc.

The police are noticeably more concerned with 'street crime' than other forms of crime, particularly white-collar or corporate crime. This is partly a result of the police definition of 'real policing', which consists of dealing with street crime and the more serious 'physical' forms of crime such as bank and post office robberies.

Discretion

The most important police influence on the official statistics comes through their use of discretion, a subject we examined in Chapter 9. According to several studies, including the PSI one mentioned earlier, the most important factor when youths are stopped by police is their *demeanour*. If they are cooperative and show respect for police officers they are less likely to be arrested than those who show inadequate respect. In a US study by Piliavin and Briar only 4 per cent of 'cooperative' youths were arrested, compared to 66 per cent of those deemed 'uncooperative'.

Reported, recorded and unrecorded crime

Figure 10.5 Recorded and
unrecorded crime, 1993

Source: Home Office,
Research Findings 14

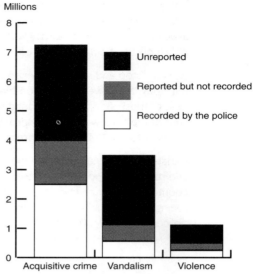

1 *What is the overall relationship between the three elements of the statistics –
reported, recorded and unrecorded – shown in Figure 10.5?*

2 *Are there any differences between the three elements when comparing
acquisitive crime, vandalism, and violence?*

3 *Explain in your own words why people choose not to report offences.*

4 *Explain in your own words why police officers choose not to record offences.*

Police culture

Understandably enough, most police officers seek promotion. In order to achieve this
they must show their superiors adequate arrest rates, yet not too many to show up
their colleagues or they will be left out of the close-knit police camaraderie. The
resulting balance of arrest rates will influence the total and types of arrests.

Furthermore, it has been found, for instance by the PSI study, that police officers
show considerable evidence of racist attitudes. It is claimed that this could affect their
decision to arrest, although the PSI study found no specific evidence of this.

*When discussions take place over how effective the police are, the debate
usually centres around the 'clear-up rate'. This is generally taken to mean the
number of crimes which the police solve compared to the numbers committed.
Figure 10.6 shows that the 'reality' of the situation is more complex than this.*

1 *Explain in your own words why 'crimes known to the public' may not be
reported to the police.*

2 *Why would the police not record certain crimes ('crimes unrecorded')?*

3 *Explain the meanings of 'taken into consideration' and 'written off'. (This
may take a phone call to your local police station!)*

4 *What factors could affect the size of the category 'Crimes directly detected'?*

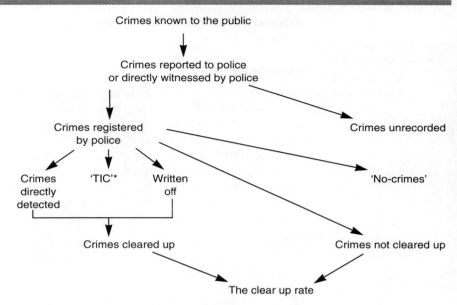

Figure 10.6 The construction of the clear-up rate and crimes 'taken into consideration' at the request of the offender

Source: Kinsey, Lea and Young (1986)

* Crimes 'taken into consideration' at the request of an offender

The judiciary

The role of the police is to act as 'gatekeepers', deciding which acts will be classified as crimes. It is from the police figures that the criminal statistics are derived. The influence of the courts is in deciding, not what criminal acts have been committed, but whether the persons accused are guilty. Nevertheless, it is worth briefly glancing at the work of the courts, as they throw light on how the statistics on convictions may also be 'manufactured'.

There have been many studies of the relationship between racial and social class backgrounds, appearance in court and conviction. Steven Box (1983) suggested that the variety of conclusions drawn by these studies indicated that there was 'thin evidence' to suggest that blacks and working-class people are more likely than others to be found guilty in court. These studies overlooked the fact that the overwhelming majority of people who appear in the courts are drawn from lower working-class backgrounds (with blacks appearing in much greater numbers than their proportions in the population), and that eight out of ten people who appear in court plead guilty. This point is worth looking at in detail.

The British judicial system could not work without the huge majority of the accused pleading guilty. The fact that they do so might be an enormous compliment to the British police, but it might also be evidence of *plea bargaining*, which is the practice of offering a person the possibility of a reduction in sentence if they plead guilty.

Most studies of this practice have been conducted in the USA. Sudnow (1972) found that it was routine to charge an offender with a more serious charge than was warranted and then 'negotiate' so that he or she pleaded guilty to the offence the prosecutor really wanted to pursue. In Britain few studies have been done, but according to Baldwin and McConville (1977), who studied 121 Crown Court defendants in Birmingham, plea bargaining is routine here too. Even defendants who are resolved to plead not guilty are generally pressured by the *defending* counsel into pleading guilty in the hope of securing a light sentence.

Political pressures

The role of the state is of particular importance to Marxist writers such as Hall and Gilroy (see Chapter 4), who argue that laws are created and enforced to selectively benefit or control particular sections of the population. The entire edifice of the police and judiciary exists to repress the working class; it is no accident, therefore, that young working-class males, both black and white, are heavily over-represented in the prison population. Furthermore, the types of offence on which the police concentrate, and which form the vast majority of recorded crimes, are those associated with the working class. The absence of corporate and white-collar crime in the statistics also reflects the political structure.

Writers who take a labelling perspective have examined the role of politicians in altering the laws, influenced by 'moral entrepreneurs' or simply public opinion. These issues were considered in Chapter 6.

Rivals vie over crime policies
Howard and Straw on guard to show who's toughest

Convicted paedophiles will be monitored for up to 10 years after leaving prison, even if they take jobs which do not bring them near children, Home Secretary Michael Howard will tell the Commons tomorrow. His announcement will open what civil servants have nicknamed 'crime week' – during which Tory Ministers and their Labour Shadows will vie with each other to prove who is toughest on crime.

Shadow Home Secretary Jack Straw plans pre-emptive action with a press launch aimed at showing that the Tories are soft on crime, deliberately mimicking tactics that the Tories have frequently used in the past.

Government plans to allow employers to see criminal records are scheduled to be released on Tuesday, although the scheme has caused serious rifts in Whitehall. Civil servants were conducting a 'national audit of offender employment policies'. The inter-department committee was due to recommend that ex-offenders should be kept out of trouble by giving them work. But its efforts were scuppered when the head of the Home Office's probation division warned committee members that managers would not want to employ former offenders when they saw their criminal records.

Ministers were also worried that the tabloid newspapers would attack the Government if criminals were seen to be getting jobs at the expense of the unemployed.

Source: Adapted from *Observer*, 16 June 1996

1 *Refer back to Chapters 4 and 6, and construct a chart comparing the Marxist and labelling perspectives on the media and politics. Separately, examine the nature of deviance amplification and the process of police 'sensitising'.*

2 *Take any one example of this process and construct a diagram to illustrate it.*

The media

The role of the media is discussed fully in Chapter 6. The two main approaches again stem from the Marxist and labelling perspectives, both of which stress the deviance-amplifying nature of the media through the sensitising effects of newspaper and television reports on the activities of various groups.

Invisible crime

Invisible crimes are those of which the victims are generally unaware. These are usually white-collar crimes, for example, where an employee regularly embezzles his or her employer, which could range from fiddling travel expenses through to major alterations of the accounting system.

Indeed, Ditton (1979) and Mars (1983) discovered that in many jobs theft is seen as a normal way of increasing a wage. Ditton describes how bread salesmen actually gained status from their colleagues for their ability to cheat the shops they delivered to. Salesmen would overcharge, or would maintain the normal price but reduce the numbers of loaves delivered. They would justify their actions using *techniques of neutralisation* (see Matza, 1964). For example, large stores would claim that they allowed for wastage anyway, so why should the workers not keep a few loaves back for themselves to sell elsewhere?

Mars describes how waiters would routinely steal food and overcharge customers, regarding these practices not as illegal (or even immoral) but as perks of the job to compensate for low wages. Mars also researched the regular overcharging of customers by garages: these charged the full price for a service, yet did only as much work as they needed to remain undetected.

There were two things that all these 'fiddles' had in common. First, the customers were rarely aware that they were the victims of crime – hence the term 'invisible crime'. Second, even when the perpetrators were caught, punishment was extremely lenient and hardly ever involved calling the police. In the case of a garage or restaurant, for example, the customer might get angry or even refuse to pay, but that was the end of the matter.

Fiddles have a long history, Elmsley describes a number of eighteenth-century fiddles; for instance:

> Journeymen hatters indulged in 'buggin' by which they substituted cheaper materials for those which master hatters had put out to them. Shoemakers acted similarly, buying cheap leather from carriers and substituting it for the more valuable material received from the master; the more valuable leather was then converted to their own use.

Prosecutions were rare, and many of these fiddles were considered a 'right' by the workers. An example was a six-month-long strike of weavers in Essex in 1757 when the employers attempted to stop them keeping left-over material, even though legally this was theft.

1 *List some examples of 'fiddles' or 'perks' with which you are acquainted.*

2 *Are these considered illegal? What justifications are used for them?*

3 *Are fiddles normal? Is there any way you can find out? Discuss the alternatives available. Do you think it would be possible for you to research the area of fiddles? If you think so, do it! (For example, you might want to interview retired workers to discover the 'truth' about how widespread fiddles and perks are.) If you cannot think of examples, or are unable or unwilling to do some research, then have a look at the books by the authors mentioned above or Hobbs (1988).*

4 *What does this tell us about the extent of 'crime' and about the difference between 'thieves' and 'ordinary people'? Can you see any implications for traditional positivistic explanations of crime?*

Corporate crime

We examined the issue of corporate crime in detail in Chapter 4. Here we are concerned with its relevance to the criminal statistics.

Corporate crime consists of illegal acts performed by large companies which directly profit the company rather than individuals. A major problem is that companies are so powerful that they may be able to persuade governments and the public that their actions are not illegal, even if the harm is far greater than all the losses caused by 'street crime' put together.

Even where large companies do break the law in pursuit of profits, they are rarely subject to police investigation; it is likely that they will be dealt with through other government agencies or commissions. W.G. Carson's classic study of the enforcement of factory safety legislation (Carson 1971) is a useful example here. When factories were found guilty of breaking the law concerning safety at work, they were usually written to, pointing out that a particular issue 'required attention'. In only 1.5 per cent of all cases where an 'enforcement notice' had been sent (that is, where the company had broken the law) was the company prosecuted.

Of course, the problem of law enforcement becomes even more difficult when the criminals are the government!

Related comments can be made about fraud. First, the counting rules cause a great number of repetitive fraudulent acts, especially those involving cheque cards and false entries in accounts, to be recorded as only one or two 'sample' offences. Second, many fraudulent tax or benefit offences are dealt with administratively by the Inland Revenue, Customs and Excise, or Social Security Department. Third, if one measures the importance of property offences in terms of the value of goods stolen rather than the quantity of incidents,

fraud comes out as of enormously greater significance than other categories. For example, Levi (1993) points out that the *minimum* value threshold for a case to be accepted for investigation by the Serious Fraud Office is a fraud of £5 million and that in April 1992, the Frauds Divisions of the Crown Prosecution Service were supervising cases involving nearly £4 billion. By contrast, the combined costs of the common offences of 'auto crime' and burglary for 1990 were estimated by the Association of British Insurers at under £1.3 billion. (Levi also points out that the alleged fraud in any one of several major cases – Barlow Clowes, Guinness, Maxwell, BCCI, Polly Peck – alone exceeded the total amount stolen in thefts and burglaries recorded by the police.)

Source: Maguire (1994)

1 Explain the significance for the statistics on fraud of:
(a) sample offences
(b) being dealt with 'administratively'
(c) minimum value thresholds.

2. Maguire compares the costs of fraud with the costs of burglary. All surveys have found fraud to be relatively low among most people's concerns regarding crime, especially when compared with auto crime and burglary.
(a) Can you suggest reasons for this?
(b) The police place much greater resources into combating auto theft and auto crime than they do against fraud. Should they do so, in your opinion, given the differences in the financial costs to society?

Victimisation surveys

As we saw in Chapter 8, in an attempt to overcome the difficulties and defects associated with the police recording of crime statistics an alternative approach was suggested which involved asking a cross-section of the population what crimes had been committed against them. The advantages, it was argued, included that people would be more likely to report crimes to an anonymous survey than to the police, and that direct reporting would eliminate the organisational processing carried out by the police.

The results of the first surveys of this kind, carried out in the USA in the early 1970s, were quite staggering For example, 'personal injury' crime appeared to be occurring at twice the official rate, and property crime, excluding burglary, at three times the official rate. Victimisation surveys have since become so successful a tool that there are now regular international surveys coordinated by the United Nations.

The methodology used in UK victimisation surveys

The British Crime Survey (BCS) uses a sample of 14,500 people aged 16 and over (before 1994 it was 10,000) and covers a range of crimes, but excludes (by its very nature, because it covers individuals in households) such things as fraud, drug use and crimes against businesses.

Respondents are asked if they or anyone else in their household have been the victim of a list of crimes in a particular year. The crimes are described in normal, everyday language rather than in their legal terms. They are then asked if they 'personally' have been a victim of any of another list of offences. If they say yes, they are asked to give more detail on up to five of them. The figures are then collated in terms of 'household offences' and 'personal offences'.

In the survey published in 1994 about 18 million crimes were counted, the vast majority against property, broken down into the following categories:

● 20 per cent of offences were of vandalism.

● 30 per cent were incidents of theft.

● 9 per cent were burglaries.

● 24 per cent were incidents involving motor vehicles.

● 5 per cent were more serious violent crime (wounding and robbery).

● 12 per cent were assaults involving little or no injury.

(The figures are approximate.)

Similarities and differences between BCS and police statistics

About two thirds of the crimes reported through the BCS can be compared with the police figures; of those that could be compared, the BCS uncovered 11.6 million offences compared to the police recording of 3.1 million.

According to the replies of the respondents in the BCS, 41 per cent of offences were not reported to the police. Different types are crime vary in the likelihood of being reported. Car theft and burglaries are usually reported, whereas theft from the person and attempted motor vehicle theft are not.

As we saw earlier, the police do not record all the crime reported to them as they may consider it too trivial or inaccurate to warrant recording and taking action over. Approximately 27–30 per cent of crimes reported to the BCS were fully recorded by the police.

Between 1981 (when the BCS started recording statistics) and 1991 the number of recorded crimes rose by 111 per cent, but the BCS statistics indicate a growth of 77 per cent, about 33 per cent less than the police figures. Yet between 1991 and 1993 (the latest figures available at the time of writing) the BCS figures increased more rapidly than the police statistics. This can be explained by balancing the increased willingness of people to report crime on the one hand with fewer reported crimes being recorded by the police in the 1990s on the other.

An interesting fact that emerges when comparing the two sets of statistics is that there is not a constant difference between them for every type of crime. Crimes of violence have increased *much less* than police statistics suggest, as has vandalism. On the other hand, burglary and theft have increased *more rapidly* than police statistics suggest. These points are illustrated in Figure 10.7 and Table 10.2.

Figure 10.7 Indexed trends
in different offence groups,
1981–93 (1981 figures =
100)

Source: Home Office,
Research Findings 14

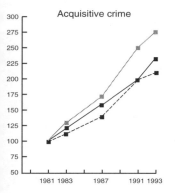

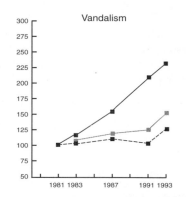

Table 10.2 Percentage of crimes reported to the police					
	1981	1983	1987	1991	1993
All BCS offences	31	34	37	43	41

Source: Home Office, Research Findings 14

Figure 10.7 and Table 10.2 show the overall relationship between the numbers of crimes reported to the police and the numbers reported to the BCS researchers.

1 What do they tell you about the likelihood of people reporting offences to the police?

2 If you were a critic of the BCS methodology – or just a cynic about statistics – are there other comments you could make about the percentages in the table?

Criticisms of the BCS

At first sight the use of the BCS appeared to solve many of the problems faced by sociologists in gathering adequate and accurate data on the extent of crime. However, there are a number of problems that have prompted criticism.

Exclusion

The first and obvious criticism, fully accepted by those conducting the BCS surveys, is that it massively undercounts certain types of crime – most obviously fraud and corporate crime. When one considers that the amount of money lost through these crimes is greater than the total losses through all other forms of theft and robbery, this is clearly an enormous hole in the information net.

Another example of excluded or undercounted crime is sexual violence. Indeed, the 1983 BCS only uncovered one case of unreported rape and 17 cases of sexual assault (18 in the 1985 survey). These figures were below any possible reasonable estimates. In a later survey in London by Hall (1985) only 8 per cent of those claiming to have been raped actually reported the offence to the police.

The fallacy of the average place

The second criticism was that the BCS seemed to give the impression that all individuals shared similar risks of being victims of crime. One famous quote from the first BCS (Hough and Mayhew 1983) states that a statistically average person aged 16 and over can expect:

- a robbery once every five centuries (not including attempts)
- an assault resulting in injury (even if slight) once every century
- a family car to be stolen or taken by joyriders once every 60 years
- a burglary in the home once every 40 years.

What concerned a number of sociologists was their belief that crime rates are significantly different, depending on the types of communities or geographical areas in which people live. These overall averages seemed to suggest that the fear of crime in inner cities was exaggerated whereas (according to the radicals) crime rates were much higher and a very real threat to people in certain areas. The stress on the statistical average therefore distorted the picture.

The fallacy of the average person

This follows from the fallacy of place. The BCS suggested that victims of crime were most likely to be male and young, and that the likelihood of becoming a victim was closely related to lifestyle. So young men who go out drinking to clubs at weekends are most likely to be victims of crime. They are also most likely to be the offenders. Offenders and victims are mirror images, according to the earlier BCS publications. Critics argued that the experiences of young women or the elderly, and of members of racial minorities, were not being sufficiently explored.

Table 10.3 shows the differences between various groups in their tendency to be victims of crime, according to the BCS.

 Go through each category listed in Table 10.3 and compare risks of crime, then summarise the social/geographical characteristics of those most likely to be at risk of:

1 contact crime

2 burglary attempts

3 vehicle thefts.

Table 10.3 Percentage of respondents victimised once or more during 1993

	Contact crime[1]	Burglary & attempts	All vehicle thefts[2]		Contact crime	Burglary & attempts	All vehicle thefts
Inner city	6	11	25	Household head over 60	1	4	10
Non-inner city	4	6	19	Household head under 60			
				– single adult + child(ren)	12	15	26
N. regions	5	9	24	– adults + child(ren)	5	5	23
W. Midlands	5	7	20	– no children	6	8	23
E. Mids/Anglia	5	5	16				
S. (not London)	4	4	17	White 4	6	20	
Greater London	5	8	21	Afro-Caribbean	8	13	26
Wales	3	6	21	Asian 5	8	23	
Home owner	4	5	19	Male 5	–	–	
Council tenant	6	9	25	Female 4	–	–	
Other rental	7	10	17				
				Aged 16-29	11	–	–
House	4	6	10	Aged 30-59	4	–	–
Flat/room	7	9	14	Aged 60 or over	1	–	–

Source: Research Findings 14

Notes:

1. Contact crime comprises woundings, common assaults, robberies and snatch thefts.

2. Actual and attempted theft of and from vehicles. Based on owners only. Risks for houses/flats are of incidents occurring in the immediate vicinity.

Local crime surveys

Criticism of the BCS stimulated the development of local victimisation surveys which sought to detail the experiences of people living in particular localities. The first and most famous study was the Islington Crime Survey (Jones, Maclean and Young 1986), followed by a large number of others including studies of Merseyside (Kinsey 1985) and a follow-up study of Islington (Crawford *et al.* 1990). These studies have largely been associated with the left realist school of criminology (discussed in Chapter 5).

The findings of these local surveys tended to 'flesh out' the national BCS and at the same time to contradict, if not the facts of the BCS, then at least the interpretations previously made.

The first point that emerged was that people living in inner-city areas were far more likely than the average person to be subjected to most forms of crime. In Islington, for example, over 30 per cent of all households in the borough would report at least one burglary, robbery or sexual assault within the previous year. Secondly, younger white females in Islington were almost 30 times more likely to be assaulted than those over 45. These examples show that neither place nor victim can be properly interpreted in 'average' terms.

The Islington studies and later ones by, for example, Mooney (1993) also concentrated on crimes which were not reported – in particular domestic violence and sexual assaults. Mooney found that about a third of women had suffered some form of injury as a result of domestic violence. This compares to less than 5 per cent in the British Crime Survey. Twice the BCS level of domestic violence was uncovered in the first Islington Crime Survey, and when the definition of sexual assault is widened to include sexual harassment, over 67 per cent of women under 24 had been 'upset' by this in the previous year.

It was clear that crime had a much stronger effect on the lives of people living in inner-city areas than on the statistical average of the BCS. Local surveys also showed that those of African, Afro-Caribbean or Asian descent were more likely than whites to be victims of crime.

Finally, local crime surveys began to move away from the strict definitions of crime towards a greater awareness and understanding of the behaviour and activities that disrupted people's lives. Thus they included (perceived) racial abuse, sexual harassment, and disputes between neighbours.

One of the most radical uses of the local survey was the work of H. Genn (1988), who followed up female respondents involved in a pilot study of crime in London. She uncovered a far greater concentration of crime against these women than any previous researchers had detected. She pointed out that the BCS had a limit of five incidents of crime, based on the assumption that this is likely to be the maximum number of incidents, yet for her respondents this way of conceptualising crime was wrong. Their lives consisted a long series of victimisations, generally involving violence (or threats of it) from a current or past male partner. It was difficult to identify specific incidents, and even where this could be done the result was an enormous 'undercounting' of the reality of the crime they suffered.

Self-report studies

An alternative, but perhaps less sociologically fashionable, method of determining the extent and patterns of crime is the self-report method. This involves asking individuals to complete a questionnaire which lists a range of legal or deviant activities. The respondent ticks off the activities he or she has performed.

The argument in support of self-report studies is that, as they are anonymous and usually administered to a cross-section of the population, it is likely that a more accurate figure can be obtained of the real number of crimes and who performs them than is given by the official statistics, based on caught offenders, or victimisation studies, which tell us nothing about the perpetrators of crime.

Self-report studies have provided an interesting challenge to official statistics, which present an image of crime as being performed by young working-class males, disproportionately of Afro-Caribbean origin.

Early self-report studies concentrated on the sex and class ratios of official statistics. Short and Nye (1958) and Campbell (1981) found that both middle-class youths and females in general were far more likely to commit crime than the official statistics suggested. There have been few or no self-report studies on youth of Afro-Caribbean and Asian origin, so that no conclusions can be drawn here (however, refer to the detailed discussion of the issue in Chapter 11).

In an overview of more than 40 self-report studies, Braithwaite (1979) concluded that, although there was a distinct bias in the official statistics, it was clear that young working-class males did commit more criminal acts than young middle-class males, and that adult working-class males were more likely to commit the types of crime which are 'handled by the police' than middle-class adult males.

As for issues of gender, according to a review of studies by Heidensohn (1989) the official statistics of crime may distort the picture to some extent but generally the statement that crime is overwhelmingly a male phenomenon is supported.

Methodological issues

Before we accept these conclusions, we should be aware that there are a number of severe criticisms of self-report studies. According to Box (1983) these can be centred around the issues of *validity*, *relevance* and *representativeness*.

Validity

To what extent are the replies given in the self-report tests true to reality? Self-report studies have most often been used with adolescents, because it is they who commit most crime (and, I suspect, it is easy for researchers to administer their questionnaires to students!). It has been argued that working-class youths may be particularly wary of admitting crime to middle-class representatives of authority, such as university researchers; on the other hand, middle-class youths may feel relaxed and cheerfully own up to everything. Of course, we could also suggest that both middle-class and working-class youths may feel the wish to exaggerate in order to impress their peer group (remembering that these questionnaires are often given out in school).

An attempt to entangle all these was made by Gold (1966), who used a combination of self-report studies and intensive interviewing. Gold's conclusion was that about 80 pre cent of those being interviewed were telling the truth.

Relevance

The second criticism of self-report studies has been that they list so many trivial items it is no wonder the differences between the various social classes are minimised; after all, everybody commits some tiny infraction of the law at some time. Furthermore, some studies have included acts of deviance which are not even illegal, such as 'defying parents' authority'. The outcome is that the studies are not really measuring significant infractions of the law, but trivial acts that are widespread among the population.

Representativeness

We noted earlier that the majority of self-report studies were given to adolescents in schools. This is useful for delinquency, but tells us little about serious adult infractions of the law – in particular, the extent of white-collar crime.

Self Report Study

1 I have ridden a bicycle without lights after dark.

2 I have driven a car or motor bike/scooter under 16.

3 I have been with a group who go round together making a row and sometimes getting into fights and causing a disturbance.

4 I have played truant from school.

5 I have travelled on a train or bus without a ticket or deliberately paid the wrong fare.

6 I have let off fireworks in the street.

7 I have taken money from home without returning it.

8 I have taken someone else's car or motor bike for a joy ride then taken it back afterwards.

9 I have broken or smashed things in public places like on the streets, cinemas, dance halls, trains or buses.

10 I have insulted people on the street or got them angry and fought with them.

11 I have broken into a big store or garage or warehouse.

12 I have broken into a little shop even though I may not have taken anything.

13 I have taken something out of a car.

14 I have taken a weapon (like a knife) out with me in case I needed it in a fight.

15 I have fought with someone in a public place like in the street or a dance.

16 I have broken the window of an empty house.

17 I have used a weapon in a fight, like a knife or a razor or a broken bottle.

18 I have drunk alcoholic drinks in a pub under 16.

19 I have been in a pub when I was under 16.

20 I have taken things from big stores or supermarkets when the shop was open.

21 I have taken things from little shops when the shop was open.

22 I have dropped things in the street like litter or broken bottles.

23 I have bought something cheap or accepted as a present something I knew was stolen.

24 I have planned well in advance to get into a house to take things.

25 I have got into a house and taken things even though I didn't plan it in advance.

26 I have taken a bicycle belonging to someone else and kept it.

27 I have struggled or fought to get away from a policeman.

28 I have struggled or fought with a policeman who was trying to arrest someone.

29 I have stolen school property worth more than about 5p.

30 I have stolen goods from someone I worked for worth more than about 5p.

31 I have had sex with a boy when I was under 16.

32 I have trespassed somewhere I was not supposed to go, like empty houses, railway lines or private gardens

33 I have been to an 'X' film under age.

34 I have spent money on gambling under 16.

35 I have smoked cigarettes under 15.

36 I have had sex with someone for money.

37 I have taken money from slot machines or telephones.

38 I have taken money from someone's clothes hanging up somewhere.

39 I have got money from someone by pretending to be someone else or lying about why I needed it.

40 I have taken someone's clothing hanging up somewhere.

41 I have smoked dope or taken pills (LSD, mandies, sleepers).

42 I have got money/drink/ cigarettes by saying I would have sex with someone, even though I didn't.

43 I have run away from home.

Source: Campbell (1981)

The questions above are taken from three self-report studies and show typical questions used in studying young people.

   1 Examine the questions. Do you think they accurately measure deviance?

   2 If you think the questions could be bettered, alter or replace them.

   Conduct a self-report study. Make sure you organise it so that people can take part anonymously.

The distinction between the serious and the 'one-off'

Taken together, the criticisms of self-report studies seem to be rather dismissive, but a particularly famous longitudinal study has used self-report techniques as one element of its methodology. This is the Cambridge Study in Delinquent Development, which has studied over 400 males aged between eight and the mid-thirties. The results help to untangle some of the confusing evidence so far reviewed.

In essence, the Cambridge study has found that most young males commit one or possibly two delinquent acts which could lead them to go to court, but very few young males engage in a large number of serious crimes; the majority of those who do have convictions for crime. This would suggest that the official statistics may well give a rather distorted count of who commits criminal acts, but it does reflect the general 'true' picture of who has a criminal career.

In 1993 Graham and Bowling conducted a national survey of 1,721 people aged 14–25, plus a further 'booster sample' of 808 young people chosen from the ethnic minorities. Interviews were conducted to find out about backgrounds, family life, school experiences and current lifestyles, but respondents' 'offending behaviour' and drug use were studied using self-report methods. The response rate was over 69 per cent. The self-report part of the study included 23 offences including arson, vandalism, shoplifting, assaults and even credit card fraud. Information was also requested on the use and selling of illegal drugs. Those admitting an offence were asked at what age they first committed the offence and how many offences they had committed within the previous year.

The conclusions were that half of all males and one-third of all females admitted they had committed an offence at one time – although the majority commit no more than one or two minor offences. Of those admitting an offence in the previous year, about a quarter of males and a tenth of females admitted to committing more than five offences. Of particular interest is the tiny proportion of offenders who account for a significant element of all crimes. The researchers uncovered the fact that about 3 per cent of offenders accounted for 25 per cent of offences.

Half of the males and a third of the females had used drugs. The most common used is cannabis; a third of the males and a fifth of the females used this weekly. Other drugs are used less often, though 20 per cent of males and about 13 per cent of females used other drugs weekly.

The self-report study showed its value in contradicting two 'facts' which official statistics tend to support. First, there was hardly any relationship between social class and offending, and once other factors such as family breakdown were taken into account there was no relationship whatsoever. Second, the rates of offending were almost identical for whites and those from Afro-Caribbean backgrounds.

Furthermore, those from Indian, Pakistani and Bangladeshi backgrounds have significantly lower rates of crime than the other two groups.

Figure 10.8 Percentage of males and females who said they had offended at some time

Source: Graham and Bowling (1995)

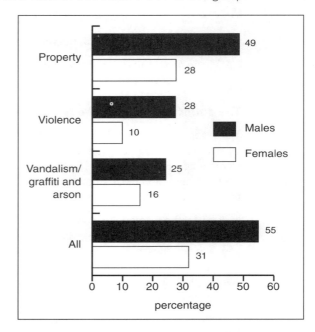

1 *Figure 10.8 illustrates some of the findings which emerged from Graham and Bowling's study of 14–25 year olds. Turn to pp. 163–4, which gives the official figures for female offending. How do the two sets of data compare?*

2 *Approximately one in three males under 30 have been cautioned or prosecuted for an indictable offence, according to the official statistics. What does the self-report study suggest?*

3 *What light do self-report studies throw on the idea that offenders are in some way different from non-offenders?*

4 *What comments could you make on 'positivistic' explanations for crime? Which sociological approach to crime and deviance do you think best 'fits' or explains the results of self-report studies like this one?*

Summary

In this chapter we have explored the nature of criminal statistics. We have found that, far from being a useful tool to provide us with information we need, they themselves are equally the object of our studies. Criminal statistics compose a bewildering series of social constructions, and the figures we are provided with by government are seriously open to question.

Nevertheless, the objective of gaining an overview of criminal activity cannot be abandoned, so alternatives to police statistics have been developed. The best known and probably the most accurate is the British Crime Survey, which is conducted every two years. It is a national study which paints a broad picture of what is happening.

However, there are enormous variations in the experience of crime across the nation, so researchers have turned to local victim studies. These have uncovered issues of great interest concerning the fears and experiences of inner-city residents in particular. The results of these surveys have been useful in policy making and have influenced contemporary sociological theorising.

Readings

Other kinds of official statistics are less simple, and criminal statistics are, for three main reasons, among the most misleading. Firstly, most crime is a secret activity inaccessible to conventional forms of social enquiry. Secondly, variations in criminal statistics are variably, unpredictably and sometimes only incidentally related to changes in the behaviour of criminals. Equally, if not more, significant are changes in the processes which transform invisible criminality into visible crime; indeed it is these processes which the statistics measure. And thirdly, the essentially political nature of criminal statistics makes them, alongside other 'social problem statistics' such as health and employment figures, especially vulnerable to political manipulation.

Source: Harris (1992)

1 *The author suggests three issues concerning the reliability of criminal statistics. Explain them in your own words.*

2 *The author mentions 'political manipulation'. Using a CD ROM, search the newspapers for debates on crime and criminal statistics. Can you find examples of political manipulation?*

Examination Question

Evaluate the usefulness of official statistics to a sociological understanding of crime.

AEB, June 1993

Bibliography

Baldwin, J. and McConville, M. (1977) Negotiated Justice, London: Martin Robertson

Box, S. (1983) Deviance, Reality and Society, London: Tavistock

Braithwaite, J. (1979) Inequality, Crime and Public Policy, London: Routledge

Campbell, J. (1981) Girl Delinquents, Oxford: Blackwell

Carson, W.G. (1971) 'White collar crime and the enforcement of factory legislation' in Carson, W.G. and Wiles, P. (eds) (1971) Crime and Delinquency in Britain, London: Martin Robertson

Crawford, A., Jones, T., Woodhouse, T. and Young, J. (1990) Second Islington Crime Survey, London: Middlesex Polytechnic

Ditton, J. (1979) Part-time Crime, London: Macmillan

Genn, H. (1988) 'Multiple victimisation', in Maguire, M. and Ponting, J. (eds) Victims of Crime: A New Deal, Milton Keynes: Open University Press

Gold, M. (1966) 'Undetected delinquency behaviour', Crime and Delinquency Journal, Vol. 3, pp. 27–46

Hall, R. (1985) Ask Any Woman: A London Enquiry into Rape and Sexual Assault, Bristol: Falling Wall Press

Harris, R. (1992) Criminal Justice and the Probation Service, London: Routledge

Heidensohn, F. (1989) Crime and Society, London: Macmillan

Home Office (1993) Information on the Criminal Justice System in England and Wales, London: Home Office Research and Statistics Department

Hough, J.M. and Mayhew, P. (1983) The British Crime Survey, London: HMSO

Jones, T., Maclean, B. and Young, J. (1986) The Islington Crime Survey, Aldershot: Gower

Kinsey, R. (1985) Merseyside Crime and Police Surveys: Final Report, Liverpool: Merseyside Metropolitan County Council

Kinsey, R., Lea, J. and Young, J. (1986) Losing the Fight against Crime, Oxford: Blackwell

Lea, J. and Young, J. (1984) What is to be Done about Law and Order? Harmondsworth: Penguin

Maguire, M. (1994) 'Crime statistics', in Maguire et al. (1994)

Maguire, M., Morgan, R. and Reiner, R. (1994) The Oxford Handbook of Criminology, Oxford: Oxford University Press

Mars, G. (1983) Cheats at Work, London: Allen & Unwin

Matza, D. (1964) Delinquency and Drift, New York: Wiley

Mayhew, P., Mirrlees-Black, C. and Aye Maung, N. (1994) The 1994 British Crime Survey, London: HMSO

Mooney, J. (1993) The North London Domestic Violence Survey, London: Middlesex University

Policy Studies Institute (1983) Police and People in London, London: PSI

Pyle, D. (1995) Cutting the Costs of Crime, London: IEA

Short, J.F. and Nye, F.L. (1958) 'Extent of unrecorded juvenile delinquency', Journal of Criminal Law, Criminology and Political Science, Vol. 49, pp. 296–302

Sudnow, D. (1972) 'Normal crimes', in Worsley, P. (ed.) Problems of Modern Society, Harmondsworth: Penguin

Young, J. (1994) 'Incessant chatter: recent paradigms in criminology', in Maguire et al. (1994)

Issues of control, policing and race

Control or conflict? Riot police halt anti-racist protestors on a race march in South London

In this chapter we will explore several distinctive but related issues. We start by looking at the nature of social control – that is, why and how people are coerced or persuaded to act in predictable, orderly ways. Then we move on to explore the way in which social control has changed over the last 200 years. In particular we will be interested in the way that control has expanded in terms of the numbers of people involved and the extent of its penetration into all aspects of life.

The extent of conformity in contemporary society would shock someone living in the seventeenth century: contrary to popular belief, most sociologists would argue that, rather than our enjoying an increase in freedom of expression and activity, there has never been a period in democratic societies where conformity has been so successfully pursued.

Social control is imposed by a very wide range of agencies, including the medical and psychiatric professions, social workers, educationalists, journalists, probation officers and not least the police. After our initial exploration of the wider issues we will concentrate our attention on the police.

Social control is applied in different ways to different groups of people, and one group who feel the full force of social control as applied by the police is young black youth. The final section will explore the imposition of social control on ethnic minority communities and the racialisation of criminality.

Figure 11.1 Guidelines: defining social control

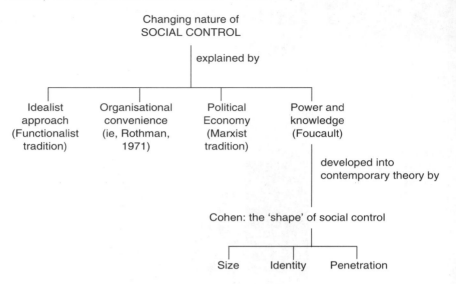

Social control

All societies have some form of social control through which the conformity of its members is maintained – or at least the belief that there is conformity is maintained. Social control is achieved in two ways – informally and formally. Informal social control typically takes place through a range of techniques of persuasion, threats and ridicule, usually (though not exclusively) expressed by family, friends and colleagues. Formal social control is generally regarded as being performed by the specific organisations with the power to coerce deviants if necessary, such as the police force, social work departments and medical authorities.

The changing nature of social control

Criminologists have been interested in how the form of social control has changed over time. Stanley Cohen (1985) has identified four *master patterns* that have been put forward to describe the changing nature of social control. By amending these slightly we can get an overview of the changes that have occurred over the last 200 years.

Increasing involvement of the state

This has involved the development of a rational and bureaucratic set of apparatuses for the control and punishment of criminals and for the care or cure of other deviants. Prominent among these institutions are the criminal justice system and the institutions concerned with mental health. In the latter part of the twentieth century the state has maintained control, but has increasingly handed over the operation of these institutions to private organisations: for instance, there are now private prisons, private security organisations and for-profit psychiatric institutions.

Increasing differentiation and classification of deviants.

Social control agencies are looking for the 'causes' of the various types of deviance. In order to explain one needs to classify and to provide specific explanations for each group or type of deviance. We have developed detailed classifications and explanations (including a range of competing ones) for crime – by age, cause, activity, sex, motivation – upon which we then base treatment or punishment. Similar classifications apply to other deviant groups, with each group's activities studied and explained by experts.

Increasing segregation of deviants

During the first half of the twentieth century deviants were increasingly separated from the public and moved into institutions. Subsequently there has been an increasing use of other forms of control as deviants are released back into the community. Control today increasingly takes the form of surveillance (community care or probation), electronic tagging or the administration of drugs. The people being controlled are supervised by experts – community psychiatric nurses, social workers or probation officers – all of whom believe that they are somehow doing the deviant good.

A shift of punishment

Punishment has changed from physical pain performed in public (for example, public executions and floggings) to greater control over the mind.

Explanations for the changing nature of social control

Sociologists have offered four types of explanations for the changing nature of social control.

Idealist

This approach has been linked with the functionalist tradition in sociology. Quite simply, it claims that the changes in the forms of social control have been a reflection of reforms intended to improve the state of humanity. As with all conservative explanations, there is an acceptance that mistakes are inevitable so, as in most reforms, some initiatives have failed or have been hijacked by professionals for their own benefits. This partially accounts for the failure of social control.

Organisational convenience

Rothman (1971) suggests that most reforms come about through moral crusades but that, when the reforms fail to provide the expected benefits, they continue to be perpetuated by the organisations charged with implementing them because this is convenient in terms of power, influence and employment.

Political economy

This approach is derived from Marxism, and writers in this tradition such as Melossi (Melossi and Pavarini 1981) argue that the type of discipline reflects the needs of capitalism. Prisons, for example, punish (and reform) the most difficult members of the working class and deter others from breaking the law. The increasing involvement of the state in the arena of social control reflects the need of capitalism for a more controlled and disciplined workforce, necessary for the division of labour in factories and offices. The development of other, more indirect forms of social control in the later periods of capitalism reflects the move away from factories to more flexible offices and work routines.

Foucault: power and knowledge

The most ambitious attempt to account for the history of social control was made by Michel Foucault. Foucault (1977) argued that power and knowledge are inseparable, so that although knowledge emerges from power, it in turn alters and shapes power.

The shift towards the development of institutions in the nineteenth century – that is, putting people into different types of asylums, children into schools, conscripted soldiers into barracks, criminals into prisons and the destitute into workhouses – were part of a grand design, according to Foucault.

Before capitalism the control exercised by royalty was direct, arbitrary and violent. But in line with rational capitalist society, new forms of control emerged which were more effective, widely distributed and exercised at the lowest political and economic costs. Power was conferred by knowledge, and this was accepted by those upon whom it was imposed. Punishment by public torture was replaced by a much more effective and insidious interest in the mind. The new forms of power were more forceful not because of the intensity of pain, but because it seemed inevitable. The developing form of power inflicted punishment more deeply in the 'social body', rather than the individual one. A new army of experts, including doctors, criminologists, social workers, lawyers and prison officers, took over the role of the punishers. Punishments or 'treatments' were codified and shown to be fair.

Foucault used the analogy of a type of prison that was invented at the time, but never actually used – a *panoptic* prison, wherein the prisoner could be seen at all times – to suggest that constant surveillance has become the hallmark of contemporary society. Deviants and criminals of all types are surveyed and their actions explained and controlled. For Foucault, the control of deviants has taken on a life of its own, as the experts accrue more knowledge which helps to explain ever finer gradations of deviance.

A bemused reader might wonder where all this takes us in a chapter on policing. But Foucault helps us to see that the role of the police is not unique, natural or inevitable, and that it has developed in a particular way as just one aspect of modern control techniques, sharing control with doctors and social workers among others. Furthermore, the idea advanced by modern reformers that the police ought to have some form of community role would, according to Foucault, simply be another way, perhaps more subtle, than the military-style policing which uses harsh methods (discussed below) to control inner-city populations.

The shape of social control

Developing Foucault's analysis, Stanley Cohen (1985) has suggested that the following three issues concerning the 'shape' of contemporary organisations of social control are crucial to an understanding of their increasing significance in society:

Size and density

According to Cohen, an ever-increasing number of people have been caught in the net of the deviance control. The numbers of people processed by the psychiatric institutions, by the criminal justice system and by the health service continue to grow every year. More and more people come to be labelled as deviant.

Changes in policing practice such as cautioning people instead of arresting and charging them have extended the network of control. In the past marginal deviants would have simply been told off by an individual police officer, but with the introduction of cautioning, police officers will follow this route rather than the informal telling off. Similarly, with the move away from psychiatric hospitals towards the use of drugs, counselling and community care, those who would have previously been labelled as merely eccentric might now be designated as candidates for care in the community.

In short, the newer, liberal forms of social control which are ostensibly meant to keep people out of institutions have actually extended the reach of social control.

Identity and visibility

The introduction of prisons and mental institutions created clear divisions between those outside and inside. Those inside were physically removed from society, and were also stigmatised by being made to wear special forms of dress, among other things. However, with the decline in mental institutions and the increase in forms of punishment for offenders in the community, the division between 'in' and 'out' is becoming blurred. The greater the attempts to retain offenders as full members of the community, the muddier is the difference is between offenders/deviants and normal people.

In the mid-1990s there were a number of trials in which offenders were electronically tagged to monitor their movements. In all other respects the offenders' lives were normal, so the distinction between in and out, deviant and normal, became blurred. This is an example of the state controlling people directly in the community, but Cohen also notes that we are encouraged to spy on each other through neighbourhood watch and other similar schemes. Ultimately all of us, and not just the deviants, come under observation.

Penetration

Cohen's last point concerns the way conformity and control are increasingly viewed as the responsibility of a broad range of non-state organisations, such as families, local communities and schools. These are expected to help ensure conformity on behalf of the state. Furthermore, Cohen points to the increasing use of surveillance cameras in both public and private spaces. Private spaces such as shopping arcades and theme parks have proliferated, and here particular patterns of behaviour are expected and certain sections of society (the poor, the young) are excluded – usually by private security guards.

Cohen's work shifts our awareness of social control. He demonstrates its all-pervasive nature and shows how it is on the increase while at the same time we are given the impression that it is being curtailed. What is more, the matter of who is being controlled and why is becoming less clear.

Visions of control

Imagine that the entrance to the deviancy control system is something like a gigantic fishing net. Society is the ocean – vast, troubled and full of uncharted currents, rocks and other hazards. Deviants are the fish.

Our interest is in the operation of this net and the parent recycling industry which controls it: the whole process, system, machine, apparatus or, as Foucault prefers, the 'capillary network' or 'carceral archipelago'. The whole business can be studied in a number of quite different ways. The fishermen themselves, their production-line colleagues and their managers profess to be interested in only one matter: how to make the whole process *work better*. They want to be sure, they say, that they are catching 'enough' fish and the 'right' fish (whatever those words might mean); that they are processing them in the 'best' way (that the same fish should not keep coming back?); that the whole operation is being carried out as cheaply and (perhaps) as humanely as possible. Other observers, though, especially those given the privileged positions of intellectuals, might want to ask some altogether different questions.

Source: Adapted from Cohen (1995)

 This extract is trying to describe metaphorically what deviancy control agencies actually do, rather than what they claim to do.

1 Apart from criminals, what other 'fish' are there?

2 Who might 'the fishermen, their production-line colleagues and their managers' represent, other than the police?

3 Explain the term 'carceral archipelago'.

4 What might be the 'altogether different questions' Cohen suggests we should ask?

The role of the police

Styles of policing

The role of the police in a democratic society can to some extent be illustrated by the actual nature of policing in Britain. A consensual society would be reflected in a police force which mirrored the wishes of the population, and the conflict model would suggest a police force which imposed itself upon the population. Evidence for both explanations can be found in the outcomes of studies into the styles of policing in Britain.

Figure 11.2 The police as an example of a control agency

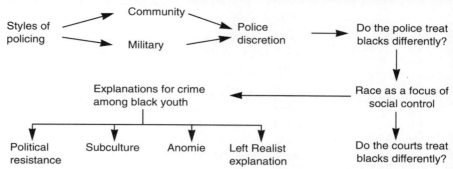

All police forces must make decisions about the most effective way to impose the rule of law and maintain order. The outcomes of these decisions are the styles of policing. If we look at policing styles as a continuum, at one end is *community* or *consensus policing* (which basically reflects the arguments of consensual writers) and at the other end is *military policing* (reflecting the conflict approach).

The consensual model

This is the model of policing that the police force themselves prefer to encourage. Essentially it supports the idea of the police officer or 'bobby on the beat' as an active citizen representing the interests of the majority of the population against the forces of crime and disorder. Police officers are close to the community and are trusted and supported by the community whom they serve.

This model relies upon large-scale support of the police by the public, who provide relevant information to patrol officers, usually on the beat. Police officers see themselves as part of the community, and the social characteristics of police officers (particularly racial) largely reflect those of the community. Information supplied by the community allows officers to target specific, individualised offenders. This model is of course an idealised one, but British police forces claim to aspire to it.

Traditionally, histories of the police have offered this as the traditional British style of policing. Supporters of this model accept that there has been a move away from community-style policing in the inner cities, but argue this is a reasonable response to high crime rates and high levels of violence.

A more positive image of inner-city police control, taken in Harlem, US. Police block off a number of streets in the summer and make them available as playgrounds for the neighbourhood children.

The conflict model

The consensual model of the police has been criticised by a number of writers, most notably Scraton (1985), who argues that the police were always an occupying force, imposed upon the working class and later the ethnic minorities.

According to Scraton, the modern police movement was gradually formed and imposed upon the working class over the last 200 years. The police targeted the political activities of the working class and the more informal street practices of the poorer working classes, which were regarded as a threat to the activities of the middle classes and the 'respectable working class'.

> Explanations of and proposed remedies for the 'dangerous poor' had little to do with the causes of inequality and the creation of a reserve of casual workers necessary for the expansion of industrial capitalism. Nevertheless, street crime and theft obviously threatened all neigh-bourhoods and households which were relatively better off. If 'respectable' people were to be protected, then it was the poor who would have to be punished, corrected, or, at least, saved. [Scraton 1985]

In essence, Scraton is arguing that the idea of community policing is a myth, and the reality in the UK has always been the 'military policing' style in the working-class districts.

In the military-style model the police are seen to be distinct and separate from the public. Because of the gap between the two groups the information required to make arrests is not forthcoming. In order to gather information much use is made of technology such as surveillance cameras and computerised files on suspects or suspected groups. Instead of patrols by individual officers, the police use vehicles and will have specialist groups trained in specialist functions. Under suspicion are not simply individuals but entire groups, who are harassed, controlled and segregated from the innocent public. An extreme variant of this model of policing has been used in colonial situations and in Northern Ireland, but critics of the police claim it is also applied in the inner cities and especially against young black males.

1   Explain in your own words, and using examples, the two 'ideal type' models of policing.

2   What experience have you had with the police? Which model does it seem to support?

3   Arrange an interview with local police officers. Show them these models and ask them which, in their opinion, is now more common.

Police discretion

Styles of policing may be changing and moving towards a more confrontational, military style, especially in the inner cities, but within policing styles a large element of discretion is always accorded to police officers. It is in the nature of policing that the law cannot provide a clear, unambiguous guide for police officers in every situation; police officers must therefore use their discretion. This is recognised by the authorities, and the sign of a good officer is his or her sensible use of discretion. Indeed, writers such as James Q Wilson (see Chapter 7) argue that it is more

Table 11.1 A comparison of consensus and conflict policing

Subject	Consensus policing	Military policing
The public	Supports the police	Fears/is in conflict with the police
Information from the public	Large amount, relevant to crime detection and specific	Small amount, low-grade and general
Mode of gathering information	Public-initiated, low use of police surveillance technology	Police-initiated, extensive use of surveillance technology
Police profile	Low profile, integrated with community, police officers as citizens	High profile, police as outsiders, marginalized, use of force and special militarised units
Targeting by police	Of specific offenders	Of social groups/stereotyped populations
Style of police intervention	Individual, consensual, reactive	Generalised, coercive, proactive
Ideal–typical example	English village	Northern Ireland

Source: Lea and Young (1984)

important for police officers to use their discretion wisely to maintain public order than it is to actually enforce the law.

However, if police officers are encouraged to use discretion in their interpretation of the law, we need to know about the assumptions on which they base their discretion. Reiner (1994) has suggested that there are three ways of approaching and explaining police discretion:

● individualistic

● cultural

● structural.

Individualistic explanations

This approach suggests that a particular 'personality type' (the authoritarian type) is drawn to policing, and that the sorts of decisions police officers make when they exercise their discretion are explained by this fact.

Colman and Gorman (1982) conducted a study of police officers after a series of serious public disorders in Brixton in the early 1980s. They concluded that certain individual police officers were racist, and that their policing methods against black people were strongly affected by their racism. The important point to underline here is that racism was said to be an outcome of individuals acting on their own. It was therefore possible to root out racism by tackling the relatively few individuals with racist opinions.

Cultural explanations

A second way of explaining police discretion places much greater emphasis on police culture. Skolnick (1966) argues that the common problems faced by police officers and the nature of the job they are doing draw them together in a distinctive subculture which in turn provides patrol officers with a particular way of perceiving the world and a particular 'vocabulary of motives'.

Skolnick suggests that there are three core characteristics of police culture (often termed in the UK as 'canteen culture'):

● *Suspiciousness*. This is taught to police officers as part of their training, and it also becomes an element in the way they treat others in their daily lives. Police officers need to evaluate individuals they encounter rapidly, in order to ascertain whether they have committed an illegal act. As a short cut they employ a number of stereotyped categories of 'typical offender'. One such category is often young, male and black.

● *Internal solidarity and social isolation*. Policing is potentially a dangerous job and officers need to rely upon their colleagues. The lower ranks of the police also have to be wary of the senior officers (particularly where complaints have been made and there is a formal investigation). This results in a strong sense of solidarity, particularly among the lower ranks of the police.

Police officers also have some difficulty interacting with the public because they are authority figures and most people keep a social distance from them. The result of this, combined with the sense of solidarity induced by the job, leads to social isolation from the public.

Most police officers are male, white and drawn from working-class backgrounds. Often they reflect values that are common in these groups – in particular racist and sexist values. The twin elements of solidarity and isolation amplify these values, encouraging stereotyping and helping to shield the officers from value changes in the wider society.

● *Conservatism*. According to Reiner (1994) the function of the police is to symbolise and safeguard authority, and this both reflects and creates a sense of moral conservatism among police officers. Politically, too, police officers have tended to be more supportive of the Conservative Party than a typical cross-section of the public. It has been suggested that, although the police are drawn from the working class, the effect of police culture is to 'deradicalise' them by pulling them away from their working-class backgrounds and sympathies. (This also fits with the concepts of solidarity and social isolation.)

It is, however, important not to stereotype police behaviour. Firstly, there are significant divisions within the police in terms of politics, moral values, career aspirations and openness to change. Secondly, there are regulations and laws which police officers must observe, and which the overwhelming majority do actually follow. It is not true to say that because a police officer has racist sympathies he or she will necessarily ignore the rule of law.

One example of the divisions within the police has been suggested by Reiner, who claims that there are four variations on the police subculture:

● *The peace keeper*. These are officers who seek to maintain order, but not to maximise arrests.

● *The law enforcer*. These officers perceive their job in terms of combating crime – this is defined as 'real' police work, as opposed to maintaining order or performing more routine tasks.

● *The alienated cynic.* Some police officers are either personally disillusioned with the job or they have failed to obtain promotion. They carry out the tasks required of them but have no wider purpose of controlling crime or maintaining the peace.

● *The managerially inclined professional.* These are police officers who want promotion and are prepared to be excluded from the lower ranks' police culture in order to obtain the desired post.

> The racism, sexism, impatience with legal formality, and other characteristics of police culture which have alarmed liberal critics are not simply manifestations of pathological authoritarian personalities, imported societal prejudices, excessive exposure to the Sun, or a self-sustaining canteen cowboy ethos. Such factors may over-determine the character of police culture; but the basic determinant is the role the police are assigned, which is moral street-sweeping. Their control powers are primarily directed against the young, male, disproportionately black, economically marginal street population who threaten the tranquillity of public space as defined by dominant groups. Police prejudices are more a product than a cause of the differential use of police powers, which is itself a result of the socially structured nature of the police mandate.
>
> *Source*: Reiner (1994)

1 The main text of this book suggests that there is a clear police culture. According to the extract, where does police culture (a) not derive from, and (b) derive from?

2 What, according to the extract, is the role of the police?

Structural explanations

These explanations refer to the wider pressures placed upon police officers to do their jobs. Firstly there are the formal requirements of the law, which provide the framework within which discretion operates. For example, in 1984 a major review of the powers and procedures of the police was introduced with the Police and Criminal Evidence Act (PACE). This extended the powers of the police while at the same time clarifying the rights of suspects. Perhaps the best known result of the Act is the recording of police interviews with suspects to prevent the fabrication of evidence. Whether police officers liked the changes or not, they were required to alter their practices to conform to them. Similarly, the 1994 Public Order and Criminal Justice Act considerably increased police powers to intervene in a range of activities which they had previously been allowed to ignore – for example, the disruption of blood sports.

Taking a step back from this, Marxist writers would suggest that one needs to explore the wider implications of the differences in power. Thus changes in the law are likely to be a reflection of the will of the more powerful sectors of society, so changes in policing largely benefit the more powerful. As a result, the 'neutral' policing activities which uphold the law are in fact heavily biased towards the powerful and against the poorer sections of society.

Stop and search

We have seen that there is a police culture, but we need to find out just how the culture and the structural factors actually affect the way the police operate.

Smith and Gray (1983) found that police officers had considerable difficulty explaining why they stopped certain people and not others. However, they tended to choose the stereotypical groups who looked unconventional in one way or another, especially perceived homosexuals and very significant numbers of young black males. Willis (1983) found that the police usually gave as grounds for stopping someone 'suspicious movements', yet the arrest rates following these stops were very low – typically about 10 per cent. To underline the point, 90 per cent of all those stopped were found to have committed no offence. An example of the disproportionate stop rate for black youth was that, although blacks comprised only 5 per cent of the population of the Metropolitan Police District, a Home Office study in the late 1980s found that stop and searches of black males comprised 16 per cent of all stops.

Arrest

McConville and Shepherd (1992) suggested that there are five working rules which police officers use to guide them in their decisions to stop or to arrest someone. These are:

- *Previous.* If the individual is known to the police, they are more likely to be stopped and more likely to be arrested.

- *Police authority.* If an individual challenges the authority of the police officer then he or she is more likely to be arrested.

- *Type of victim.* Some victims are more likely to be responded to than others. In general, the higher the social standing, the more serious the offence or the more 'deserving' the victim, the greater the chance of the suspect being arrested.

- *Workload.* The busier the police officer or the police station, the less likely that minor infringements will be acted upon.

- *Degree of suspicion.* This is a catch-all category based usually upon instinct or a belief that the person is out of place. A study by Jefferson and Walker (1992) found that people were likely to be stopped and searched if they were not in 'their own' areas.

Race and the criminal justice system

There has been vigorous debate within sociology on the relationship of young blacks with the criminal justice system. This debate illustrates some of the major issues of social control and policing.

Policing and ethnic minorities

Since the late 1970s there seems to have been an attempt by the police (and the Metropolitan Police in particular) to associate young black males with street crime. In their report to the 1972 House of Commons Select Committee on Race Relations the Metropolitan Police stated that the crime rate among black people was approximately the same as, and possibly even lower than, the crime rate for the population as a whole. By 1977, however, the police evidence to the Select Committee was very different – that 12 per cent of those arrested were of 'West Indian or African origin' (35 per cent of those for robbery and violent theft) although they only formed 4.3 per cent of London's population.

The police were aware that the arrest rate was not necessarily an objective measure of blacks' involvement in crime because it could be seen more as a measure of police bias against young black males than a true reflection of criminal activities. They therefore supported their evidence by pointing out that, for robbery and violent theft, victims identified approximately 36 per cent of assailants as 'coloured'. This identification of the racial characteristics of assailants by victims of street crime is a particularly important piece of evidence, according to the police, as it reflects an 'objective' account of incidents before police officers are involved.

At the time of writing this book, the percentage of assailants carrying out street robberies in London who were identified as 'non-white' had risen to over 60 per cent. The association of blacks with street crime has been used to justify large-scale police stop and search activities against young black males.

Criticisms

The police statistics have been criticised on a number of grounds, including the following:

- *Age.* Most crime is committed by the young. The ethnic minorities have higher proportions of young people than the population as a whole. Therefore a higher crime rate could be expected on these grounds alone.

- *Victim bias.* Morris (1984) argues that white victims are more likely to report crimes against them committed by blacks than those committed by whites. Morris suggests that this is the result of racial prejudice. It should be noted, however, that the bulk of crime is committed within ethnic groups.

- *Policing patterns.* Morris also suggests that as there are more police in inner-city areas, where the bulk of black people live, they are more likely to uncover higher rates of crime.

- *Police racism.* According to Gilroy (1982), when there was no report by a victim of crime, but where the police were directly involved (that is, where a victim has not reported the crime but the police 'uncovered' one), there were high arrest rates of blacks.

- *Type of crime.* Critics have also pointed out police emphasis on one particular category of crime, that of 'mugging' (which actually has no status in law). This may be associated with young blacks, but equally fraud may be associated with middle-aged white males, armed robbery predominantly with white males, and theft from shops with women. By concentrating on one category of crime the police are effectively associating blacks with crime in general. We should note, though, that victimisation studies have identified fear of street robbery as one of the highest concerns of people, both white and black, in inner cities.

> Police monitoring organisations in London have revealed an 'alarming and dramatic increase' in the number of young, black men being stopped and searched in the last four weeks.
>
> The increase follows the launch this month of Operation Eagle Eye, a police initiative to tackle muggings and street theft, after claims by Metropolitan Police Commissioner Sir Paul Condon that most muggers were young black males.
>
> Statistically, young black men are already 10 times more likely to be stopped and searched as their white counterparts. Sajda Malik of the Newham Monitoring Project, said: 'In Forest Gate, the levels for stop and search are so high for young black men that it's accepted as a part of life and never usually reported.'
>
> Scotland Yard said yesterday: 'Operation Eagle Eye is not based on stop and search, but on more surveillance. We can't respond with our own statistics because we don't have them.
>
> 'The operation has been warmly welcomed by the public, who have given widespread support of our efforts to make the streets unsafe to muggers. We confidently expect the operation will reduce incidents of mugging.'
>
> *Source*: Adapted from E. Mills, 'Police "hassling" enrages blacks', *Observer*, 27 August 1995

1 From the information you have on policing styles, police discretion and patterns of crime, what reasons could you suggest for the higher levels of stop and search for young blacks?

2 What style of policing does Operation Eagle Eye represent? Does this clash with the police officer's comments in the final paragraph? What other piece of evidence is contained in the extract to support your answer about the style of policing?

3 Ask if officers in your local police force will agree to discuss the issue of discretion. Would they agree that young black males are more likely to be stopped? Why do they stop some people and not others? Look back to the section on police discretion.

4 We have looked at the increasing level of control in our society. Apart from the stop and search levels, what relatively new technique of control has been introduced? Do you have this form of control in your local town centre? What are the implications for personal freedom?

'Race' and criminality: the debate

Discussion of this area is a minefield; indeed, some writers have argued that raising the issue and discussing it is itself racist. However, given the position of the police on the matter and the significantly higher rates of imprisonment of blacks than their proportion in the population, the issue is important.

Analysis of the propensity to offend can help us to understand whether the rates of imprisonment reflect the reality of offending or the reality of racism in the wider society which is, in turn, reflected in the criminal justice system. We should also be aware that all the statistical indicators point to significantly higher levels of deprivation and unemployment among those of Afro-Caribbean origin, and therefore the debate about race and crime is just as much one about deprivation and crime.

Police stops

Only about 2–3 per cent of all those stopped by the police in 'stop and search' operations are actually arrested. In 1994/95 over 690,000 people were stopped by the police – a rise of 20 per cent over the previous year.

There would appear, however, to be higher rates of stop and search among black and Asian youth than among white youth. The Metropolitan Police, for example, reported that 37 per cent of those stopped were from 'ethnic minorities', whereas they form 20 per cent of London's population. Further details which emerge from the British Crime Surveys show that Afro-Caribbean origin youths are more likely than any other group to be stopped.

When stopped, Afro-Caribbeans were more likely to consider police behaviour impolite than either white people or Asian people. Interestingly, though, according to the Policy Studies Institute (1983), those Afro-Caribbeans who were arrested were less likely to complain about their treatment than white people who were arrested.

Arrests

Although there are no national figures for arrests by ethnic origin, the figures for London do suggest a correlation between the proportion of offenders' ethnic origins as described by the victims and the breakdown of the origins of those arrested.

Arrest rates of alleged offenders were significantly higher for those of Afro-Caribbean origins than for whites. A study by Walker (1987) suggests that, although there may well be police bias in stops and arrests, statistically the difference in arrest rates is so high that the only way this could explain the discrepancy in the figures would be 'to arrest black people more or less at random and charge them falsely. Unless the courts are completely corrupt this would result in a radical difference in acquittal rates between black and white defendants in burglary cases, but there is no such difference.'

Prosecution

A series of studies, most notably by Landau and Nathan (1983), have demonstrated that for similar offences there is a higher rate of prosecution (rather than cautioning) for young Afro-Caribbean offenders than for white offenders. However, the figures for London indicate that for similar offences adult black and white offenders have very similar levels of prosecution. The figures show, for example, that 18 per cent of persons arrested, and 19 per cent of those persons prosecuted, were black.

The courts

Blom-Cooper and Drabble (1982) argued that black defendants are likely to be charged with more serious crimes than white defendants when the actual offences committed are similar. For example, black people are more likely to be charged with robbery than with theft. Furthermore, black defendants are more likely than other groups to be remanded in custody. Black defendants are almost twice as likely to plead not guilty as white defendants. However, there are minimal differences in acquittal rates between the various ethnic groups.

Sentencing

Judges have a range of penalties that they can impose, ranging from fines through various forms of probation and community-based punishment to prison. A large number of studies have attempted to find the differences between the various ethnic groups. Of these, Hood's study (1992) is probably the most statistically sophisticated, and this suggests that there is a greater likelihood of black defendants being given custodial sentences. Hood estimated that about 7 per cent of the higher number of black defendants being given custodial sentences was the direct result of discrimination. Referring back to the earlier point about black defendants being much more likely to plead not guilty, about 13 per cent of the difference in imprisonment rates was explained by this, as defendants who plead guilty tend to receive lesser sentences.

Prisons

Official statistics on the prison population show that Afro-Caribbeans and black Africans are over-represented (the two groups are combined in the official statistics) by about a factor of 7 in relation to their proportion of the population. However, although they are over-represented for all categories of offences, the figure rises to 27 times higher than their proportion in the general population for drugs offences, and just over 9 times for rape and robbery.

In reviewing all this evidence, Smith (1994) suggests that it is very unsatisfactory and inconclusive about the treatment of black people in the criminal justice system. However, it is clear that at each level in the criminal justice system there is an element of racial bias – in particular in the course of daily encounters with the police. But he continues that, despite this, there do appear to be higher rates of offending by Afro-Caribbean males.

Table 11.2 Rate of imprisonment of males by ethnic group (England and Wales, 1991): adults, rates per 10,000 population aged 20–39; young offenders, rates per 10,000 population aged 17–19

| | Ethnic origin | | |
| | A | B | |
	White	Black[d]	S. Asian[e]
Adult males			
All prisoners[a]	43.7	294.0	47.3
On remand[b]	8.5	61.3	7.7
Sentenced	35.0	223.3	36.4
Offence[c]			
Violence against the person	7.5	39.0	9.0
Rape	1.6	13.9	2.4
Other sexual offences	2.2	3.3	0.9
Burglary	5.1	14.7	1.0
Robbery	3.8	31.1	2.4
Theft and handling	3.0	13.5	2.1
Fraud and forgery	0.9	5.7	2.3
Drugs offences	2.0	53.0	8.5
Other offences	3.4	14.4	2.9
Young males			
All prisoners	54.0	292.8	34.1
On remand	13.6	79.5	8.3
Sentenced	40.4	213.4	25.8
Offence[c]			
Violence against the person	5.8	35.6	5.4
Rape	0.8	9.4	1.8
Other sexual offences	0.4	1.1	0.7
Burglary	10.2	18.3	1.8
Robbery	4.9	63.3	4.5
Theft and handling	4.7	20.0	1.4
Fraud and forgery	0.2	1.1	0.7
Drugs offences	0.7	7.8	1.3
Other offences	4.7	10.0	2.0

[a]Includes young convicted unsentenced prisoners and young non-criminal prisoners.
[b]Includes young convicted unsentenced prisoners.
[c]Covers offences with immediate custodial sentence only (this is the great majority).
[d]West Indian, Guyanese, black African (prison statistics); black Caribbean, black African (population statistics).
[e]Indian, Pakistani, Bangladeshi.

Source: Adapted from Smith (1994)

Look at Table 11.2.

1 *What differences are there in (a) rates of imprisonment, and (b) rates of remand between the ethnic groups, according to the table? Compare the figures for adult males first and then young males.*

2 *Which are the three most common categories of offence committed by young black prisoners?*

3 *Are these at approximately the same rate as for young white prisoners?*

4 *Which are the three most common offences for young white males?*

5 *Can you see any differences in offences between young males and adult males, either by ethnic origin or simply on the basis of age?*

Explaining differential arrest rates

In order to find out whether the Metropolitan Police claims were justified or not, the Home Office financed a study by Stevens and Willis (published as *Race, Crime and Arrests*, 1979). This two part research consisted firstly of a study of the relationship between recorded serious crimes and ethnic minorities in major British cities; and secondly, a study of the arrest data of the Metropolitan Police.

In the first part of their study Stevens and Willis concluded that there was absolutely no relationship between the proportions of ethnic minorities and the amount of crime: 'there is no tendency for areas with high West Indian or Asian populations to have high recorded indictable crime rates'.

The second part of the study examined the *arrest rates* in the Metropolitan Police District. The authors began by distinguishing between *intrinsic* factors which affect the arrest rate, and *extrinsic* factors.

Intrinsic factors

These consist of the variables of age and socioeconomic status.

● *Age* is important because, as we saw earlier, the vast bulk of crime is committed by young people and the age profile of the ethnic minorities differs from the overall British population, since they have a greater proportion of young people. However, when Stevens and Willis conducted a statistical test which isolated the age variable, they concluded that the higher arrest rates for blacks in the Metropolitan Police District could not be explained by the age profile, while for Asians the arrest rates should actually have been higher.

● *Socioeconomic status*: Stevens and Willis compared crime rates and ethnic groups for all 22 Metropolitan Police Districts against such factors as unemployment, household tenure and membership of 'socio-economic groups' (social class). Black, white and Asian arrest rates were all directly associated with social deprivation, but different factors seemed to affect the various ethic groups differently.

Extrinsic factors

By extrinsic factors Stevens and Willis meant differential law enforcement by the police.

First, they found little difference in the amount of crime being *reported* to the police between the ethnic groups, and most of these crimes according to the victims were intra-racial, that is white on white and black on black. When it came to arrest rates, they found that although there might very well be racial prejudice in the activities of the police, this alone could not explain the police arrest rates. For example, if all the differences in the arrest rates were a result of police activity alone, it would have meant that 66 per cent of all black offenders would have been arrested and only 21 per cent of white offenders. (These figures are obtained by comparing the ethnic origin of the offender according to the victim with the arrest rates of the police.) This seems too great a disparity to be true.

Further support for the argument that the higher crime rate of blacks cannot be explained by differential policing comes from the finding that 92 per cent of all recorded serious crimes were reported directly by victims – only 8 per cent were initiated by the police. This means that the police could only influence a very small proportion of recorded crimes.

While the study by Stevens and Willis seemed to suggest that there may be greater involvement of young males of Afro-Caribbean origins in a limited range of crimes, there is little or no evidence to suggest that overall those of Afro-Caribbean origin are any more involved in crime than are white youth. Evidence to support the similarity in levels of offending comes from a 1993 study for the Home Office conducted by Graham and Bowling. This study, which mixed interviewing and self-report methodologies, concluded that 'Asians – those of Indian, Pakistani and Bangladeshi origin – have significantly lower rates of offending than whites and Afro-Caribbeans, who have similar rates of offending.'

Figure 11.3 Percentage of ethnic minorities who said they had offended/used drugs at some time

Source: Young People and Crime, London: Home Office Research and Statistics Office, 1995

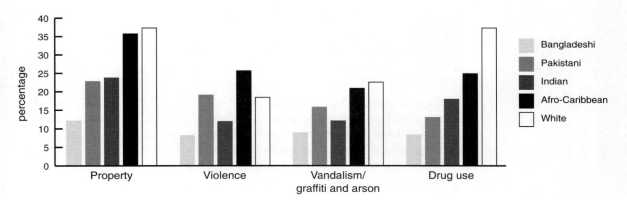

Figure 11.3 is drawn from a self-report study on crime and drug use conducted by Home Office researchers.

1 Overall, are there differences by ethnic group in offending and drug use?

2 Does the figure provide any evidence for a belief in higher levels of crime among those of Afro-Caribbean origin?

The role of the police in creating crime statistics – critical approaches

A number of sociologists have continued to be critical of the police, and argue that the criminal statistics are partly a result of police activity. However, these critics vary widely in their approaches.

The racist state

Since the publication in 1979 of Hall *et al's Policing the Crisis*, one influential strand of Marxist sociology has argued that the high arrest rate for blacks in inner cities is the result of deliberate police activity. This argument was taken up by sociologists from the Centre for Contemporary Cultural Studies who claimed that the police and the British state are racist and are pursuing a deliberate policy of oppression against blacks (CCCS 1983).

According to these sociologists it was in the early 1970s that the press began to concentrate on a new type of street crime termed 'mugging'. Intense political and media pressure led to a much stricter style of policing in the Brixton area of London, where most of the mugging was reputed to take place. The media, fed by police reports, focused the blame for the muggings on black youths. The new style policing consisted of aggressive 'stop and search' operations, conducted by groups of police officers who were especially brought in for these operations. The result, according to Hall, was that arrests rose not because the muggers were being caught, but because the police were arresting large numbers of black youths as a result of their prejudiced stereotypes.

Hall went on to claim that the police presence was not really an attempt to control mugging, but rather a response by the state to the threat to its authority posed by young blacks in general. The issue of mugging was merely a justification for the introduction of much more repressive, aggressive policing policies in inner-city areas.

For example, in 1981, during operation 'Swamp 81' in which Brixton was the target of a huge police operation, over 1,000 people were stopped and searched, yet less than 100 people were charged with any offence. The majority of these offences (for instance, obstruction) were directly the result of the police presence and would not have occurred without it.

This general approach has been followed by many Marxist writers. For example, A. Sivanandan (1981) described the police as 'a threat, a foreign force, an army of occupation – the thin end of the authoritarian wedge, and in themselves so authoritarian as to make no difference between wedge and state'.

Criticisms

The model of the state presented by this approach has been criticised because it is portrayed as too organised and clear-cut in the way it behaves in defence of capitalism. The idea that the police and top politicians connived to create a 'moral panic' over mugging in order to justify a repression of blacks is difficult to accept.

Second, there is little evidence that the police force as an *organisation* is based on racist lines – although some sociologists argue that racism is endemic in the lower ranks of the police, which is a different matter entirely. Since the mid-1980s police forces in the UK have undertaken a series of anti-discrimination and race awareness programmes in an attempt to eradicate racism in their ranks. At the institutional level they claim to have been relatively successful. On the other hand, there appears to be clear evidence that serving police officers – particularly those in the lower ranks – demonstrate racist attitudes and behaviour in their dealings with the public.

Institutionalised racism in the police: the PSI survey

In 1983 the Policy Studies Institute (PSI) conducted a study of the Metropolitan Police at the latter's request. The study's conclusions were a powerful critique of racism within the lower ranks of the police force. The PSI researchers went on to state that there was a proportion of racist police officers, and that racism was a normal part of policing in London. They found that racist language and assumptions underlay all police work, so that terms like 'coon' and 'nigger' were used routinely to describe blacks.

The PSI explanation of police behaviour is that racist attitudes derive from the population in general, and as the police are drawn from the wider white population it is to be expected that they will mirror their attitudes. They also point to a 'working culture' which lays heavy emphasis on the criminal nature of blacks.

The PSI research contrasts with the Marxist approach, described earlier, which stresses that the racism of police (which was already present) was directed towards blacks *by the state* as a deliberate part of the battle to control them, rather than an unplanned result of the police officers' working culture.

> The police take pride in being a disciplined service, so that many policemen obey rules they consider obsolete and suppress their private sentiments. One area car driver told a research worker, 'I freely admit that I hate, loathe and despise niggers. I can't stand them. I don't let it affect my job, though.' The research workers give reasons for believing that people like him succeed in preventing their private feelings from affecting their work. Others, though, may have less self-discipline. According to the study, the degree of tension between the police and black people 'was much less than might have been expected either from their own conversation or from accounts in the newspapers and on television'.
>
> Despite the use of racial epithets, where the victim was a West Indian the police were more likely to take some action, to make a full investigation, to move quickly and to catch the offender, than where the victim was white or Asian. A similar proportion of West Indians as of white people report victim accidents to the police; a majority of those who do so are satisfied with the service they get, although the level of satisfaction is a little lower than that among white respondents. As regards their willingness to call upon police services and the assessment of the service they receive when they do so, say the PSI, there is no crisis of confidence in the police among older West Indians. With the young blacks, though, it is a different story.
>
> *Source*: M. Banton, 'Keeping the force in check', *The Times Higher Educational Supplement*, 13 January 1984

1 *Can private values and work behaviour be separated, in your opinion? You could test this on other occupations (for instance, teachers, social workers).*

2 *What does the extract suggest concerning:*
(a) the attitude of blacks to the police
(b) the police response to complaints by the ethnic minorities?

Police tactics and the wider community

A third approach to the police, crime and the ethnic minorities argues that police tactics have actually worsened the crime situation.

In evidence to the Scarman Commission, the National Council for Civil Liberties criticised the use of stop and search methods by the police:

> Even if police officers behaved with impeccable courtesy towards every person stopped and searched and apologised to those found not to be carrying suspect items, many people would resent being treated as suspects when innocently walking to the tube or home. [Quoted in Scarman 1982]

According to Lea and Young (1984) the police do not always behave with 'impeccable politeness', with the result that the black community rejects their authority and refuses to cooperate with them.

In Britain the vast bulk of arrests by the police occur as a result of information provided by the public. If there is little or no information forthcoming from the public, the police are forced into a very different style of policing than has been traditional in Britain. In effect, they are forced into behaving like an 'army of occupation', or as Lea and Young term it, 'military policing'. This further alienates the local community, in particular the older, law-abiding generation. The result is a weakening of the sort of informal social restraints that operate to limit crime in most communities. Indeed, the whole of the black community unites, in certain circumstances, in dislike of the police – so much so that an arrest can easily turn into a confrontation of blacks against the police. Lea and Young term this 'mobilisation of bystanders'.

This explanation differs from the view that there is a racist state. Lea and Young accept that there really are higher levels of crime committed by blacks. This fuels police racism, which is already present, and gives another twist to the 'vicious circle' described above. The process is illustrated in Figure 11.2.

Criticisms

Central to the Lea and Young model are the arguments that (a) the police are actually discriminatory in their dealings with young blacks, and (b) the black community is aware of this.

However, the PSI study indicated that the police were trying to distinguish between their own racism and their duty as police officers (how far they are successful in that was not researched in the study) and noted that police officers were *more likely* to take seriously a report of a criminal offence against blacks than against whites.

Lea and Young's arguments were partially supported by a study of the attitudes of blacks to the police conducted by Gaskill and Smith (1983). These researchers found

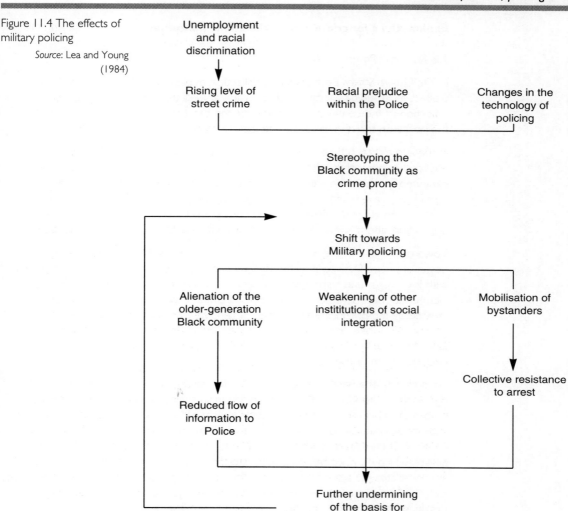

Figure 11.4 The effects of military policing

Source: Lea and Young (1984)

that only 30 per cent of young blacks were likely to hold the view that the police were 'good' or 'very good', compared to 60 per cent of young whites. They also found that the black community's negative views of the police were held irrespective of individuals' own experience of the police (that is, even if the police had been polite to the person questioned, he or she still viewed them with distrust). However, Gaskill and Smith found that the stop and search rates were virtually equal for young blacks and young whites in inner-city areas.

Finally, even if blacks have less faith in the police than whites, all available research indicates that they have similar rates of reporting crime to the police as the rest of the community. This would not fit into any of the above models of police–ethnic minority relations.

Explanations for crime among the ethnic minorities

The Race and Politics Collective

In *The Empire Strikes Back* (1983), a collection of papers by the Race and Politics Collective, including Gilroy and Bridges, it is argued that crime among blacks is a reflection of the continuing struggle between the 'colonial' powers represented by the police on the one hand and the local black communities on the other.

In the late eighteenth century, and throughout the nineteenth century, Britain acquired colonies through the exercise of military might. The colonies were then exploited for their mineral and agricultural wealth, while the population was initially forced into slavery and later into (starvation-level) wage labour. There was a continual need for the British to keep control over a conquered local colonial population, and this was done through a mixture of brute force and 'education'.

Towards the end of the British Empire, after the Second World War, there was a desperate need for labour as the British economy was being rebuilt. This coincided with low wages and high unemployment in the West Indies. There was nothing 'natural' about this, rather it was the result of the economic and social structure created by the British. Immigration to Britain was encouraged and became, therefore, a direct result of colonialism. Once they arrived in Britain, black immigrants were faced by racial hostility and suffered in terms of poor housing, low-paid jobs and exclusion from British social life.

According to the Race and Politics Collective, black people developed quite distinctive, oppositional subcultures to the main society, which derived from their history of oppression. Crime represents a form of 'organised resistance' to the authorities, drawing upon the traditions of the anti-colonial struggle. The key point here is that the blacks' 'criminality' is viewed from this perspective as a form of *politics*, which may not be recognisable to the outsider, but is nevertheless essentially a political struggle against oppression. The unusual political form also derives from the fact that black people have been excluded from organised political structures in Britain, such as the main political parties and the trade unions.

There are a number of difficulties with this approach. The first is that until recently there appear to have been particularly low rates of crime among those of West Indian origin in Britain. The high crime rate only appeared in the second (and third) generations. If crime is part of the anti-colonial struggle, why was (and still is) the first generation so law-abiding?

The second problem concerns the way in which the authors argue that black people commit crime as a form of political struggle. There is simply no evidence to support a widespread awareness of this among black youth. Indeed, the evidence suggests that black youth by and large subscribe to the general values and aspirations of the wider society. Rather than being in opposition, they appear conformist (apart from their view of the police). One must be suspicious when 'experts' can read meaning into behaviour of which the participants themselves may be totally unaware.

Subculture: resistance through rituals

A related approach stresses the development of youth subcultures as a form of resistance to capitalism. This general approach has been discussed; here it will be applied to the responses of black people.

You will recall that, according to the Marxist subcultural approach, youth form the weakest link in the control of the working class by the rich, as they are not yet locked into the system by mortgages, families and fixed employment. In response to the situation in which they find themselves, they develop 'magical' solutions via youth subcultures.

Black youth are no exception to this and have developed a number of different responses, reflecting their particular position in the British social structure. One early example was the adoption of Rastafarian beliefs by many young blacks which was a clear attempt to promote a distinctive African-derived form of culture in place of the dominant white one. Since then, the music, clothing styles and argot of US-based black culture have become enormously influential in the UK and, in fact, often lead white youth culture. The recurrent attacks on the content and style of black music suggest that it really has become a powerful alternative to mainstream values.

Of course, black music, language and dress styles are not illegal but, to sociologists who subscribe to the Marxist subcultural school, the development of alternative subcultures showed how the young blacks were 'resisting' the dominant hegemony (set of values) of capitalism and were indeed fighting back.

Other forms of potentially deviant and illegal resistance, however, have emerged. Friend and Metcalfe (1981), for example, commented that:

> black neighbourhoods opened up the possibility of surviving by alternative means, by a process of hustling involving activities such as gambling, undeclared part-time work, ganja (marijuana) selling, shoplifting, street crime, housebreaking and distributing stolen goods.

This explanation has also been criticised for focusing on the few deviant and illegal subcultures of black youth. There are a much wider variety of responses than the 'oppositional' ones cited by the Marxist subcultural school. Ken Pryce describes in detail both conformist and deviant responses in *Endless Pressure* (1979), a study of blacks in Bristol. Pryce argues that there are a wide variety of responses which blacks (and, by implication, Asians) make to British culture. He rejects the idea that all the responses are necesarily negative, deviant or illegal. Pryce found extensive religious networks amongst young blacks, as well as politically active groups and those who wished to follow a 'normal' career.

A further question, as we mentioned earlier, is whether sociologists can justify their explanations when the participants themselves may not agree with them. Rastafarians do not see themselves as 'resisting capitalism'.

Anomie and marginalisation

A third approach stresses the way blacks have been effectively marginalised from white society and, in response, have turned to crime. This approach uses a modified version of Merton's concept of anomie, ie that when a society stresses the importance of achieving financial success and the possession of consumer items, yet fails to provide people with any realistic chance of obtaining these goals legally, some people will turn to crime. This argument was put forward most noticeably by Cashmore in *No Future* (1984). He gave a portrayal of young blacks in Britain trapped in a situation where their aspirations and the reality of their economic situation do not match.

In contemporary British society status is partially measured in terms of material possessions, and young black people are as likely as any other young people to want cars, stereos, smart clothes, etc. The desire for possessions is fuelled by advertising and by a culture that seems to say, 'You are what you own.' Since there are particularly high levels of youth unemployment among blacks – up to 50 per cent in inner-city areas – they will spend large parts of each day simply congregating in city centre areas. Here they are surrounded by the consumer goods they want – a constant temptation. The outcome is that they are drawn into crime.

This model differs from Merton's use of anomie in that there is no attempt to look at the different responses to a situation of anomie (see Table 2.1, p. 27), and Cashmore specifically comments on the young blacks' awareness that much of their marginality is a result of being black and living in a 'world of Babylon', which exploits and degrades them. Their criminal activities are justified on the grounds that Babylon (the white society) has given them nothing, so why should they follow its laws?

Can the concept of anomie be applied to young blacks? Find evidence to prove or disprove the argument that blacks experience greater obstacles to success in British society. You should examine in particular the evidence relating to education, type of employment, unemployment, housing, experience of discrimination, and policing. The information can be found in most of the major textbooks on race, as well as in back copies of New Statesman and Society and in the journal New Community. For detailed project work you should write to the Commission for Racial Equality.

The modified version of anomie fails to account for the variety of responses found among young blacks. Why is it that only a small proportion of young blacks engage in crime, if they are all faced by similar 'blocks' against success?

The left realist approach

Lea and Young (1984) suggest that there are three elements to an understanding of crime and the ethnic minorities: marginality, relative deprivation and subculture.

● *Marginality.* Young blacks tend to be less successful in the education system; to have particularly high levels of unemployment; when they are employed, to be in lower-paid jobs; and to have few means of political expression. Lea and Young claim that, as a result of this, young blacks occupy a position on the edges of British society.

● *Relative deprivation.* Whereas most other explanations of black crime stress the differences in the values of white and black youth, Lea and Young argue that it is precisely the similarities between black youth and the rest of the society that cause the trouble. They claim that the culture of young blacks is distinct from that of the older generation and derives more from the expectations and aspirations of British society than from any hangover from West Indian society. It is precisely this similarity which can stimulate crime. Black youth have particularly high aspirations compared with their parents, for material goods and styles of life – yet the reality of their life in Britain is that they are unlikely to achieve these aspirations legally.

● *Subculture*. Lea and Young suggest that young blacks respond differently to the mismatch between aspirations and the constraints of reality, and that there is no automatic move towards crime, as Cashmore seems to suggest. They argue that the drift to petty crime by some blacks has been one of a number of responses.

Crime among other ethnic minorities

What is particularly noticeable in any discussion of crime rates is the absence of detailed discussions of Indians, Pakistanis and Chinese.

The case of the Chinese reflects a blind spot in British society in general. Suffice it to say that the conviction rates for Chinese are extremely low. This could be partially explained by the 'closed' nature of Chinese society in Britain and the fact that few crimes are reported to the police by the community, which prefers to sort out its own problems. It is interesting that where Chinese are convicted of violent crimes, it tends to be the result of a fight between Chinese and non-Chinese, where the police are subsequently called in by outsiders.

In the case of Indians and Pakistanis, the levels of convictions are also low. Various explanations have been suggested, some of which could also be applied to the Chinese.

Greater economic success

A survey for the Office for National Statistics in 1996 demonstrated the high levels of success amongst Indian families. However, the picture of economic success for Asians in Britain is not completely accurate. Indians still have higher unemployment levels that whites, with a level of 12% compared to the whites' 8%. People who are Pakistani or Bangladeshi in origin may exhibit particularly low crime rates, yet they have unemployment levels of 24% and 27% respectively. It would seem then that economic success cannot be the only reason for the lower crime levels.

Stronger family and community

Asian families are particularly strong and impose strict controls over family members. As in the situation of white females, the strict socialisation and control of social activities for Asian youth may limit their opportunities to commit (and possibly their interest in) deviant activities.

Distinct culture

One of the key points made by Lea and Young was that black crime rates are high because young blacks embrace British culture and are therefore more likely to be bitter when they fail. Asian cultures are more distinct, providing a clear alternative to the mainstream British culture. Asians are therefore less likely to feel marginalised or to suffer from relative deprivation.

However, as the numbers of Asian origin youth increase there is likely to be a limited increase in crime in much the same way as occurred among second-generation Afro-Caribbean origin youth.

An upsurge in criminality among young Pakistanis and Bangladeshis is likely, according to Home Office research. The prediction is based on the fact that the Pakistani and Bangladeshi populations in Britain have a young age profile and many are reaching their early teenage years and the peak age of offending.

'In 1991, 19 per cent of whites were aged under 15, compared with 22 per cent of black Caribbeans, 29 per cent of Indians, 43 per cent of Pakistanis and 47 per cent of Bangladeshis,' Marian FitzGerald, principal researcher at the Home Office Research and Planning unit, told the British Criminology Conference at Loughborough University yesterday. She said the research countered stereotypes that the Asian community was 'more law abiding', or was also deprived but less involved in crime than the black or white populations.

However, the Home Office researchers said the fact was likely to be masked as long as the official figures only had one 'Asian' category which included the larger population of Indians, who are sometimes more affluent. 'Once this becomes apparent and it reaches the public agenda, there is an obvious danger that we shall witness a new moral panic,' said Ms Fitzgerald.

She added that the stereotype of the black criminal and the 'Asian' victim was becoming unsustainable and, indeed, Asian groups had begun to allege discrimination by the police against them.

Source: Alan Travis, 'Increase in crime', *Guardian*

1 What main reason is given in the article for the likely rise in crime among young Asians?

2 In what way is the figure likely to be masked?

3 What stereotypes are changing?

Summary

In this chapter we have been exploring the issue of social control, meaning the ways a society keeps the activities of its members within certain boundaries, enforcing particular patterns of behaviour. The three issues of social control, crime and deviance are intimately connected, and social control is the underpinning issue.

The nature of social control and the way in which it has been enforced has changed over time, with (it is claimed) an ever-increasing shift towards more intensive and widespread forms of control. The ways in which people are guided and coerced into the 'correct' forms of behaviour have changed over time; there has been a move away from corporal punishment towards other forms of control, specifically control over the mind.

The social control agencies have in their different guises grown in size, changed in identity and penetrated a wide variety of spheres of our lives. These agencies include the health and social services as well as the police. In this chapter we focused on the police as an example of a control agency. We saw that there is a variety of forms of policing ranging from community policing at one extreme to 'military' styles at the other.

These forms of policing are not used randomly, but are applied to different populations. We looked at the issue of the policing of black youth as an example of how military policing occurs in practice. It would seem that there are two levels on which to understand this – the official one, which argues that there is a need to police black youth because of their high crime rate, and the unofficial, informal one which arises from the claimed racism of police culture.

Finally, to complete our examination of race, policing and crime, we looked at the various sociological explanations that have been offered for the pattern of offending ascribed to black youth.

Readings

Racialisation of statistics

'The available statistics have limited value as measures of ethnic minority criminality.'

That caveat was written six years ago by the Home Office, the last time it published a set of Metropolitan Police crime figures broken down by race.

Criminologists were united yesterday in applying the same stricture to the latest set which emerged from Sir Paul Condon, the Metropolitan Police Commissioner, in advance of a crackdown on street crime in August – only more so.

Most thought Sir Paul's figures – 80 per cent of those robbed in London identifying young black males as responsible – were either misleading or irrelevant.

Professor Jock Young, of Middlesex University, said: 'It's terribly easy to get the wrong end of the stick. This is a poverty issue, not a race issue.

'Mugging is carried out by young alienated inner-city males, poor males. Therefore, where you have a large black population which is poor and yet youthful you are bound to have a disproportion occurring.

'So in London it would be blacks and in Glasgow it would be whites. The racial thing is a red herring.'

Professor David Smith, of Edinburgh University, said: 'I think it's very dangerous. The question will be asked "What's the reason for giving a priority to this kind of crime, given that it's not such a high proportion of crime in London?" There are many other offences that could be targeted other than street crime.'

Prof. Smith said one of his concerns is that a headline figure of 80 per cent of muggings committed by young black men will be read too loosely.

'People will come to the conclusion that a high population of young, black men are involved in street crime.

'But the people who are involved in this in a big way are doing an enormous number of these crimes, so that it only takes a fairly small number of people to work up to all the street crimes, especially when you bear in mind the numbers of these crimes are not so enormous.'

While commentators recognise that Sir Paul might be trying to pull the teeth out of any controversy that would inevitably surround an attempted police crackdown on street crime involving saturation policing, his methods leave them puzzled.

Source: C. Elliot, 'Irrelevant figures questioned by criminologists', *Guardian*, 8 July 1995

1 What percentage of victims robbed in streets identified young black males as the perpetrators?

2 *According to Young, why is this a form of distortion of the facts?*

3 *Why, according to Smith, is the proportion of total crimes formed by street robbery a factor?*

4 *Explain how, if a relatively small number of people are engaged in this crime, this can also distort the 'race' figures.*

5 *This chapter has several times referred to scapegoating. Can you find evidence in this extract to support the view that young blacks are being scapegoated by the police?*

Examination Question

Examine sociological accounts of the relationship between crime and ethnicity.

AEB, June 1993

Bibliography

Blom-Cooper, L. and Drabble, R. (1982) 'Police perception of crime: Brixton and the operational response', *British Journal of Criminology*, Vol. 22, pp. 184–187

Cashmore, E. (1984) *No Future*, London: Heinemann

Centre for Contemporary Cultural Studies (1983) *The Empire Strikes Back*, London: Hutchinson

Cohen, S. (1985) *Visions of Social Control*, Oxford: Polity

Colman A. and Gorman, L. (1982) *Conservatism, Dogmatism and Authoritarianism amongst British Police Officers*, Sociology 16/1, 1-11

Foucault, M. (1977) *Discipline and Punish*, London: Allen Lane

Friend, A. and Metcalfe, A. (1981) *Slump City*, London: Pluto

Gaskell, G. and Smith, P. (1985) 'Young Blacks' hostility to the police: an investigation into its causes', *New Community*, Vol. 12, No. 1, pp. 66–74

Gatrell, V.A.C. (1990) in Thompson, F.M.L. (ed.) *Cambridge Social History of Britain* 1750–1950, Vol. 3, Cambridge: Cambridge University Press

Gilroy, P. (1982) 'The Myth of Black Criminality', in *Socialist Register*, London: Merlin Press

Hall, S. et al (1979) *Policing the Crisis*, London: Macmillan

Hood, R. (1992) *Race and Sentencing*, Oxford: Clarendon Press

Jefferson, T. and Walker, M. (1992) 'Ethnic minorities in the criminal justice system', *Criminal Law Review*, pp. 83–96

Landau, S.F. and Nathan, G. (1983) 'Selecting delinquents for cautioning in the London metropolitan area', *British Journal of Criminology*, Vol. 23, No. 2, pp. 128–149

Lea, J. and Young, J. (1984) *What Is to Be Done about Law and Order?*, Harmondsworth: Penguin

McConville, M. and Shepherd, D. (1992) *Watching Police, Watching Communities*, London: Routledge

Melossi, D. and Pavarini, M. (1981) *The Prison and the Factory: Origins of the Penitentiary System*, London: Macmillan

Morris, T. (1984) 'Submission to the Commission for Racial Equality', quoted in Lea and Young (1984)

Policy Studies Institute (1983) *Police and People in London*, London: PSI

Pryce, K. (1979) *Endless Pressure*, Harmondsworth: Penguin

Reiner, R. (1994) 'Policing and the police', in Maguire, M. et al (eds) *The Oxford Handbook of Criminology*, Oxford: Oxford University Press

Rothman, D.J. (1971) *The Discovery of the Asylum: Social Order and Disorder in the New Republic*, Boston: Little, Brown

Scarman, Lord (1982) *The Scarman Report*, Harmondsworth: Penguin

Scraton, P. (1985) *The State of the Police*, London: Pluto

Sivanandan, A. (1981) 'From resistance to rebellion', *Race and Class*

Skolnick, J. (1966) *Justice Without Trial*, New York: Wiley

Smith, D.J. (1994) 'Race, crime and criminal justice', in Maguire, M. et al (eds) *The Oxford Handbook of Criminology*, Oxford: Oxford University Press

Smith, D.J. and Gray, J. (1983) *Police and People in London IV: The Police in Action*, London: Policy Studies Institute

Stevens, P. and Willis, C. (1979) *Race, Crimes and Arrests*, London: HMSO

Walker, M.A. (1987) 'Interpreting race and crime statistics', *Journal of the Royal Statistical Society*, A 150, Part 1, pp. 441–459

Willis, C.F. (1983) *The Use, Effectiveness and Impact of Police Stop and Search Powers*, Research and Planning Unit Paper No. 15, London: Home Office

Index